Colors of the Mind

Impalpable bells, transparencies of sound,

Sounding in transparent dwellings of the self,
Impalpable habitations that seem to move
In the movement of the colors of the mind

Wallace Stevens, "An Ordinary Evening in New Haven"

Colors of the Mind

Conjectures on Thinking in Literature

Angus Fletcher

Harvard University Press
Cambridge, Massachusetts
London, England
1991

This book is printed on acid-free paper, and its binding materials
have been chosen for strength and durability.

Library of Congress Cataloging-in-Publication Data

Fletcher, Angus, 1930–
   Colors of the mind : conjectures on thinking in literature / Angus
Fletcher.
     p.   cm.
   Includes index.
   ISBN 0-674-14312-4
   1. Philosophy in literature.   2. Thought and thinking in
literature.   I. Title.
PN49.F59   1991   91-10796
809'.93384—dc20   CIP

To Michelle

Preface

Despite what some theorists wish to say, every book has its beginnings, in Edward Said's sense. The present collection of conjectures began in 1989, when, as a visiting professor, I was invited to address the Department of English at the University of California, Berkeley. There I delivered a lecture, "Iconographies of Thought," subsequently published in *Representations*. A substantial amount of my recent work had been concerned with the relation of thought to word—hence this volume. The field of thought and word is of course much too wide in its philosophic implications for a collection of essays such as the following to illuminate much more than a narrow arc.

Another problem is that of one's own interests being paralleled or anticipated by the work of others. In particular, I regret that I encountered the work of Sharon Cameron belatedly. Otherwise I should have wished to consider carefully her book, *Thinking in Henry James*. In various Jamesian contexts she asks the all-important question: "How could thought have power in the world?" To the philosophically directed *Thinking in Henry James*, I would now further wish to add a complementary text, Ann Banfield's *Unspeakable Sentences*. Here a linguistic approach gives access to the microstructural form of a thinking discourse, since Banfield deals with "the sentence of represented speech and thought." It would be necessary to explore further her grammatical equivalence of speech and thought, as represented "objects." For precisely this collocation of thought and language has been the problematic issue for linguistic philosophy in most of its incarnations, as it has been for the modern novel, with its subtle readings of "inner consciousness" and "outer reality."

I count myself fortunate to have "begun" the ordering of my essays with the Berkeley lecture. For helpful suggestions and for their hospitality I am indebted to colleagues at Berkeley, especially Janet Adelman, Paul Alpers, Julian Boyd, Stephen Greenblatt, Steven Knapp, and Anne Middleton.

Over the years it has been my privilege to teach in the English Department of Herbert Lehman College of the City University of New York. To colleagues, to President Leonard Lief, and to my former chairman Edgar Roberts, I owe special thanks for their support, as to my colleagues and equally to my students at the Graduate School CUNY. The National Endowment for the Humanities aided portions of my work at early stages, by their award of a senior research fellowship in 1979.

Lindsay Waters of the Harvard University Press showed me how the contents of this book might be arranged to produce a discursive sequence. To him and to my editor, Anita Safran, I am most grateful for many tactical suggestions. Two other readers of the text helped in various ways: particularly, Leonard Michaels of the University of California, Berkeley, did his best to impart to me his own remarkable gifts of style, while John Hollander of Yale University furthered and followed the progress of my work, generously sharing his literary wisdom. As always, Harold Bloom of Yale University encouraged my labors in a difficult time. My friends Paul Bray, Cyril Brosnan, Miriam Hansen, Ray Matthews, Mitchell Meltzer, Derek Miller, and Carol Saltus all contributed to the formation of this book, in ways they will recall. At a critical moment my brother, Peter Fletcher, provided much needed technical expertise. Finally, Michelle Scissom, to whom this book is dedicated, worked with me on every part of this book and, quite simply, made it possible.

Acknowledgments

Most of the questions raised in this book were first formulated in public lectures addressed to university audiences at Berkeley, Dartmouth, SUNY Buffalo, Princeton, Emory, Yale, Minnesota, Stanford, and Iowa. Occasions included the meetings of the International Association of Literature and Philosophy, the English Institute, the Aston Magna Foundation, and the 1978 Vico-Venezia Conference. I am grateful to many who initiated or participated in these proceedings, and to the editors of journals and books where I published early versions of some of the chapters, all of which have been reworked for this book.

Excerpts from *The Collected Poems of Wallace Stevens, Opus Posthumous,* and *The Necessary Angel,* by Wallace Stevens, were reprinted by permission of Alfred A. Knopf Inc.

Parts or earlier versions of chapters 1, 8, 9, 11, and 12 appeared as follows:

"Iconographies of Thought," *Representations* 28 (1989): 99–112.

"On the Syncretic Allegory of the New Science," *New Vico Studies* 4 (1986): 25–44.

"'Positive Negation': Threshold, Sequence, and Personification in Coleridge," in *New Perspectives on Coleridge and Wordsworth,* English Institute Essays (New York: Columbia University Press, 1972), pp. 133–164.

"Music, Visconti, Mann, Nietzsche: *Death in Venice,*" *Stanford Italian Review* 6, 1–2 (1986), Published for the Department of French and Italian, Stanford University, by Anma Libri, Saratoga, California.

"The Image of Lost Direction," from *Centre and Labyrinth: Essays in Honour of Northrop Frye,* ed. Eleanor Cook, Chaviva Hosek, Jay Macpherson, Patricia Parker, and Julian Patrick (Toronto: University of Toronto Press, 1983), pp. 329–346.

Contents

Colors of the Mind

Introduction

Thought and its relation to the literary work are the thread upon which most, but not all, of the essays in this book were strung. Originally conceived as reflections upon loosely related, primarily literary topics, the essays are of necessity conjectural. As conjectures, they point to aspects of thinking and suggest some of the different ways that literary language and literary form manage to project or express such thinking. For instance, *The Divine Comedy* is saturated with notions drawn from theology, some of which have a controlling influence upon the form of Dante's epic. The same saturation of ideas occurs with *Paradise Lost,* but now the theology is Protestant rather than Catholic. In both cases, the poem embodies theological notions. One of the poet's tasks is to give this embodiment its most effective literary expression, which means that ideas must come alive as thought.

The essays, taken together, make no pretense of providing a theory of the relation between thought and language. On the other hand, the suggestion more than once arises that for imaginative or discursive literature (such as history), what is called thinking accompanies a corresponding activity of expressive forms. The gnomic sentence and phrase, for example, manage to represent, to express, a degree of mental activity centering upon some cardinal perception or point of belief. Another example is literary transparency or obscurity which centers upon a need to keep the thinking either open or mysterious. Or, the intricate labyrinth is an image of convoluted, disoriented mind. Or, when language is extended to mean other than verbal language, our thinking makes use of the visual icon or the musical theme. My interest has been to ask how such languages (and their framing forms) serve the purpose of a certain thinking activity, or serve to indicate the hazards, the complications, the sufferings, the comedy, the romance of thought.

What thought is may be found in texts of philosophy, whose business it is to think about life and death, mind and body, truth and hypothesis, and to examine the methods by which such "thinking about" is to be ordered. Whether it is Parmenides saying, "To think and to be are the same," or Descartes saying, "I think, therefore, I am," the philosopher is committed to a life of considering things on a level of principle and to uttering these considerations. Formal philosophy has developed a long post-Socratic tradition of questions that raise thought to analytic levels, such as logic exposes. The tradition may ask about being and becoming, about stability and change, about knowledge and belief, about the real and the ideal, about singulars and universals, and indeed about a small army of dichotomies, all of which are seriously presented as problematically thinkable. Not only thinkable, but in need of a thinking consideration, so that philosophy shows a history of what is usually taken to be the highest level of general thinking, the pursuit of thinking for its own sake.

To learn what this classical sense of formal thought may be, one reads Plato, Aristotle, Kant, and Hegel, or Hume and Wittgenstein, or Carnap and Quine, or Habermas and Deleuze—in short, one can peruse accepted philosophic texts. What happens in such texts, be they Davidson on metaphor or Blumenberg on secularity or Bacon on The Four Idols, will begin to sketch a broad picture of the thinker's activity. The philosopher is the thinker, in this sense. Our idea of the thinker is founded on a tie between thought and the philosopher's profession. Yet anyone who seems wise and thoughtful will likely be called a philosopher, if only in jest. In the eighteenth century anyone who brings the attitude of witty, enlightened, skeptical, and progressive thought to bear upon a political, social, or cultural issue will be called a *philosophe.* Thus the notion that thought is what philosophers do includes a thinking attitude, a critical thoughtfulness. Yet narrowed to mean whatever is done by means of logic or broadened to mean whatever is done by focusing a general intelligence, the field of philosophy is only one demonstration of the uses of thought.

There are myriad others, for thought pervades every waking moment of conscious existence, even though such thought may be neither focused, nor logical, nor pure, nor elegant. Mankind cannot make a move without thinking in some fashion. The philosopher may provide the purest case of thinking, if only because his thoughts are disinterested, pursuing the argument, if not "the truth," for its own sake. Logical exercises will also purify the philosopher's discourse. But even philosophy does not have any single, correct model for thinking, since, along with treatises like *The Critique of Pure Reason*, we have Nietzsche's *Thus Spake Zarathustra* or Emerson's *Essays*.

If philosophy understands and exemplifies thinking in various ways, from antiquity to the present, psychology shows an equally varied account of mental processes. Even so we can say that whenever philosophy and psychology examine their own methods, they are thereby examining their own ways of thinking. Such self-examination is exemplary for the student of thought. This student needs to search a text for the manifestations of thought in any area where the mind is able to examine its own methods.

Imaginative literature and the other arts are no less concerned with the life of the mind. In the past, it was conventional to envisage this life as the literary or artistic presentation of ideas, hence criticism could devote itself to the history of ideas. To a degree this made literature a subsidiary of philosophy, from which the ideas had come. Generally these were fully formed problematic concepts, such as the Christian idea of redemption, or the Enlightenment idea of progress, or the post-Darwinian idea of evolution. It is always fruitful to pursue such studies. However, such is not quite the interest of the essays that follow. Rather, they are concerned with thinking as a process, which participates variously in the literary or discursive work.

It will be helpful to have a term for the inquiry into such a participation, or process, of thinking. Parallel to the study of poetics, we may speak of the study of *noetics*, a term arising from the Greek *nous*, mind, or *noiein*, to think. *Noetics* names the field and the precise activity occurring when the poet introduces thought as a discriminable dimension of the form and meaning of the poem. If poetics shows us the ways by which the poet arranges his poem so that it will cohere poetically, as a thing made, then noetics shows us how thoughts, ideas, reflections, memories, judgments, intuitions, and visions are involved in the fundamental process of the making of the poem. Somewhat artificially at times, noetics will extract bits of encapsulated thought from the poetic texture, like raisins from a cake; this is an allegorical procedure. At other times, and they may be the important examples, noetic interpretation shows how thoughts are interwoven so tightly (or so loosely?) into the text that no single items of thought are detachable from the discourse under examination. In this latter case we may say that thought takes on the body and spirit of an author's intention. Suppose a novel in which intention and thought were completely coordinated elements of the narrative. Of such a novel, we might be tempted to say that it is noetically perfect. Novels provide a rich field of noetic activity and management. The tradition of an omniscient narrator permits the novelist to project his thinking about the scene and action of the entire book. Or the novelist severely excises whole areas, which are not then known to the narrator, and this noetic procedure leads to a more elegant, if less comprehensive, version of narrational thought. If a story is told by an idiot, as in Faulkner's *The Sound and the Fury*, the status of thought itself is brought into question, precisely as it shapes or misshapes the narrative. The field of noetics covers all such aspects of the representing process, ranging from realism to Joyce and Woolf, where thought deliquesces into the random fluxions of the stream of consciousness. Noetics in principle covers all of the operations of thought, both detachable (allegorical "ideas") and nondetachable (narrative and thought invisibly interwoven).

Noetics will shed light on texts in which the active *process* of thinking is a dimension of meaning. This might be the case when a story seeks to differentiate between intellectual and emotive responses to experience. The invention of intellectual protagonists in fictions of ideology will also yield an immediate textual play of thought. The same holds for drama, while interesting cases such as G. B. Shaw will represent thought-work *in* the play as well as thought-work *outside* it, made available through lengthy prefaces. One could continue to enumerate the wide variety of ways in which characters are shown thinking, or more broadly, where some aspect of the work yields an intellective content. All such cases would be subjects of study in noetic terms.

One might ask, of course, whether the attempt to express or to embody thought in imaginative works is not slightly perverse. A philosopher like Austin, who spoke of the imaginative as "parasitic" upon normal or serious uses of language, will wish to manipulate thought-patterns only within the idiom of professional philosophizing. A logician like Frege will wish to limit the concept "thought" to propositions or propositional elements which are virtually those of mathematics, and those alone. (It is in a vein of antipoetic thinking that Frege says that we need not give a "psychological" account of the North Sea.) But we need only go back to Descartes to be reminded that philosophy regards its own perspicuous methods of discourse as the only way to handle or to present the serious consequentiality of thought proper. Why then wish a place for thinking in the lyric, narrative, dramatic forms of imaginative prose and verse?

Our answer must depend upon our conception of the reach of thinking. The logocentric model is but one view, and a narrow one, of such a reach. As soon as we turn to the mystery of thought, to the wonder of it, which may constitute a pervasive atmosphere of noetic involvement, we must give the mysterious a major place in works of imagination. Such works can do things that a logically ordered treatise can never do. Fictions can find a place for the experience of vague, unclear thought which may have been engendered by confusion and frustration. Fictions can show how one thinks through an issue or problem, while revealing the conflicts within the mind as the mental struggle proceeds. Fictions can show thoughts slipping away from object-centered clarity, as perhaps some mysterious natural phenomenon meets the protagonist with uncanny force. Fictions can show what seems in life to be the vital *necessity* of incomplete, inconsistent, nonsystematic thinking. All these things, and more, which the philosopher might not wish to consider in the category of thinking, the poet will show not only to be thinking, but thinking of a high order—an order usually registered in metaphor, which is the fastest-thinking linguistic form. Yet for this and similar claims to be true, we need an extended range of what will count as thought and the thinking process.

There is an infinite diversity of work the mind may undertake.

Hence Marvin Minsky will speak of "the society of mind," and will observe how little our advanced knowledge can tell us about the how and why of mental process, because "we don't yet have adequate ways to classify processes," especially the self-modifying processes that occur in the brain. Minsky's example is memories, "which change the ways we'll subsequently think."

Given this sense of processual activity as the central defining property of thought, or rather understanding thought to be mental activity of this self-modifying type, we see how and why the work of art is virtually a life-necessity for the human mind. While literal discourse seeks properly to reduce the complexity of the human and natural condition, a metaphoric discourse is under no such imperative. Metaphor and its natural scene, the story, preserve the processual aspect of experience, exposing an ordered plethora of meanings. Metaphor sustains a flux, a motion, in whatever it expresses, whereas the literal account can only produce a "state-description."

It will be objected that the aesthetic rendering of the processual is mere illusion. One answers that the work of art resembles life and nature, but not in a miming sense. Rather both life and the art work are phenomenological experiences. As more than one author since Cervantes has suggested, the work of art (the so-called illusion) often forces us to see the limited degree to which life can be called "real." In modern Western countries, for example, money is at once real and unreal. It would seem that fictions, like those of Balzac, have greater critical power to expose this tangled web of the real and unreal than could any treatise on the topic of money. Such fictions do not need to be tied to a restrictive, rational account of what is in fact an infinitely varied life-process, the getting and spending of money. The work of art exists, one might say, to illuminate such process-laden domains of human experience.

We are often aware of this illuminating function in literature—one thinks of Turgenev, or Gide, or Beckett, who are strikingly thoughtful. With such authors a critical sense (it may be, an ironic sense) organizes stories and plays so that they reveal the hidden orders of social organization. The same could be said of Jane Austen, whose novels Scott judged to be philosophical in nature. If such cases can be multiplied, it then becomes necessary to ask whether there is work left undone by such thoughtful analysts of society. And of course there is, since the work of art cannot abstract itself.

It may be highly self-reflexive, but that too becomes part of the fiction. The role of philosophy and science—to reduce correctly—remains intact.

To reduce means partly to stabilize, as in describing a *state* of affairs. It also means to regularize, to normalize, to classify, and ultimately to generalize and thence to formulate general laws or principles. Despite the existence of allegory, no work of art does these stabilizing things. Every work of art, even in folk cultures, is an individual, separate production, an example. Given these differences, it is clear that the thinking process enters philosophy and science in one way and literature and the arts in quite another way.

In proceeding toward a clear picture of the literary uses of thought, we would need to ask for the manifestations of thought in literature. Enough has been said to suggest the variety of such manifestations. If they spread out like the branches of a tree, if each thought is, as Whitman would say, a leaf of grass, we must wonder what is the central stem of such leaves and branches. Is it not the power the artist possesses to invent stories and scenes of recognition? Aristotle, in the *Poetics*, claimed that tragic representations climaxed on the scene of recognition (*anagnorisis*). From a noetic point of view the coincidence of climax and recognition is now spread over the text of any work, taken as a whole. Partial recognitions, that is, thoughts, occur throughout any story, on the way to a climactic moment. Thus thought in the work of art may be understood as a species of partial recognition.

Thought as recognition is in part a recollective repetition. Suppose then that characters in a play are shown thinking; their thoughts (if not trivial) will follow each other as elements in the resolution of a puzzle. Aristotle's paradigm, *Oedipus Rex*, indicates that archetypally for Western minds the process of fictive thinking is a kind of mental exploration, which invokes the sayable and sanctioned, the unutterable and forbidden. Step by step Oedipus thinks through a series of partial recognitions of his true identity, until the partials coalesce, finally, into one single all-encompassing *thought*—"I am Oedipus, who slept with his mother and killed his father." This tragic recognition reveals to us, as to Oedipus, facts which had been repressed, whose memory had been blocked. The relation of thought to memory and to caring, which is basic to both the *Oedipus* and to its English analogue, *Hamlet*, is caught by Heidegger's play on the etymological link between *thinking* and *thanking*. "But if we understand memory in the light of the old word *thanc*, the connection between memory and thanks will dawn on us at once. For in giving thanks, the heart in thought recalls where it remains gathered and concentrated, because that is where it belongs. This thinking that recalls in memory is the original thanks." Perhaps it is the most moving and powerful thought which fits the memorious pattern of recognition. Such thought is passionately involved with the present and future, because it rises like an uncanny spirit from a ground of the past, of what has been lived.

Fictions and discourse in general display the infinite variety of thought on which I have insisted. Yet recognition may well be the central modality of thinking, for literary purposes. As in a drama, a recognition occurs only when its partial approximations or approaches have already established an experienced context. Thought of this kind is connected to the full range of human experience and issues from that experience, virtually as its logical result. Recognition is thought in the fullness of life; as such, it seeks to make sense of the enigmatic patterns of a described, narrated, or dramatized existence. From such symbolic involvement with life, thought as recognition derives its chief literary effect—the generation of a higher degree of linguistic and formal intensity than is possible in the casual uses of language known as everyday speech.

Every partial recognition adds to the sum of symbolic energy and activity in a literary work. It is the larger purpose of each *final* recognition to organize a story into a signifying whole, whose gradual shaping is articulated through smaller, partial recognitions; the thoughts, which are thus embedded in the narrative, blaze forth lighting a symbolic region such that their *placement* directly influences and controls the shaping of the narrative form. Hence, in this most powerful of literary thought-structures, we find an equally powerful aesthetic force—the direction of the story *toward* the finality of a larger recognition. And the immediate appeal of the work derives secondarily from the intermediate use of partials within the system of the whole.

Not all fictional literature displays the teleological movement of narrative toward final recognitions. The fabulous uncertainty of Kafka plays off the ironic refusal of recognition; Beckett plays off an arrested or deferred recognition. Thus the notion of imaginative literature as formed of partial and final recognitions that comprise its most powerful thinking holds strictly for a limited number of generic types, such as Greek tragedy. Yet the model seems to have authority over the whole Western tradition, in which we discern the frequency and import of "fables of identity." Even Kafka and Beckett can only react against such a tradition, which remains an irresistible and persistent determinant if only by its negation.

The noetic account of literature, fictive or discursive, needs to reckon with the system of epiphany, and the reader of this book will doubtless wish for a concentrated, theoretically ordered sequence of essays. Instead, the principle of selection has been rather to point conjecturally to a diverse array of thought-situations in literature. I have not always referred to cognition and perception, or such subclasses of the main topic. My hope has been to raise questions concerning the possibility of a critique of thought in literature, as distinct from thematics or the history of ideas. What is needed is the opening of a field of study, noetics, whose emphasis falls upon the *process* of thinking as an aspect of literary (or other) discourse. One might say that lexically "thought" is what Empson calls a "complex word," which means that one might analyze it from different points of view. One might begin with a general assumption, for instance, Frege's statement that a thought is "something for which the question of truth arises," coupled with his view that a sentence expresses a thought. Or one might begin empirically with examples of thinking in literature, such as the use of the dream to frame medieval narratives, or the development of the intellectual hero, say Edouard in Gide's *The Counterfeiters*. Or one might begin with large historical phenomena, such as Bruno Snell described in *The Discovery of the Mind* or E. R. Dodds in *The Greeks and the Irrational*.

If we devise the context for understanding thought in a literary sense, we raise the question of thought from a common, casual level to a higher level, where it is normal to seek the rare and the valuable. Literature, and here the term includes the arts of discursive writing as well, prizes the aptness of expressive means. In this sense, literary thought is, conceptually, an activity of the rarest form, that is, mental activity and its expression or revelation, rather than some unexpressed purely mental process. One way or another, Alexander Pope was correct when he subjected the rarity of wit to the criterion of "what oft was thought, but ne'er so well express'd." Yet one might at once ask whether thought and expression are two facets of a single process, or whether they are two separate processes joined in a complex network of communication.

With strategic choices of this order remaining undecided, it is no surprise that the essays in this book employ such a comprehensive, seemingly imprecise term as thinking. Is not the word "thinking" far too general? Is it an empty catchword, such as freedom or imperialism? These questions are exactly the point: "thinking" is a broad term, but not vacuous. To use it is to accept that in modern philosophy the most critical issues are found to be embodied, defined, and complicated by the forms and functions of natural language. There is no philosophy today of any significance that is not to some degree a linguistic philosophy. The philosopher will attend to the interpretation of a problem by asking how our knowledge of that problem is affected by the specific words in which we define or describe it. The preeminence of the linguistic bias (not always a Saussurean slant) has crossed international borders and furthermore appears in the philosophical treatment of psychoanalysis, social history, and political theory. At times the linguistic bias leads the mystique of language to preempt the sovereign role of thought, declaring in effect that there is no thought; there are only words. I am exaggerating here, as perhaps Octavio Paz was hyperbolic when he wrote that in the modern world the place of God had been taken by language. My exaggeration aims to prevent a loss of the ground gained by the later philosophy of Wittgenstein, whereby thought keeps its central place, precisely because Wittgenstein almost always asks how thought and language interact.

Common usage reinforces the view that we should not jettison the language of thought and thinking. Ordinary usage indicates that we normally and frequently refer to ourselves as thinking, and by implication this usage is contrasting thought with, say, passion or physical action. General notions such as action and passion do not lend themselves to strict semantic boundaries. Nevertheless they serve to demarcate broadly distinctive areas of human experience. Thinking, at least in a Romantic perspective, enters the work of art and much descriptive discourse with a certain amount of stress or even embarrassment. There is often a conflict between the logic of thought and the aesthetic or imaginative ordering of the artwork.

For this reason the role of thinking in literary works provides a particularly sharp index to the nature or boundaries of literature. For example, Stanley Cavell provides a fresh picture of Shakespearean tragedy by analyzing, in *Disowning Knowledge,* the relationship of six major plays to the philosophical problem of skepticism, which might in ordinary language be called the plague of skepticism. Cavell boldly asserts that Shakespeare is dramatistically in control of the central issues raised by the radical skeptic. This critique discerns in drama an unexpectedly high level of implicit thinking. Usually, of course, thinking as analysis and problem-solving belongs to explicitly discursive, nonartistic literature. To discover high levels of cognitive activity in the art work, while initially something of a surprise, finally leaves us more than usually bemused at the intellectual prowess of readers or audiences assumed by works like Shakespeare's plays. Yet this is the nature of such art.

Thinking, the term and the concept, is also required because I wish to assert the primacy of the author. Often in recent criticism we have seen a pretense that no author is doing the thinking; there is only a text. Critics personify the textual as if each text could write itself or as if each text were the automatic product of some magical, corporate, cultural machine known as ideology. Furthermore, these personifications mutate and reproduce; anything at all can be text, or be so called. The net effect of pantextualism has been to weaken the last saving remnant of individual style and wit. It is not always remembered that great works of literature require style and intelligence, which belong to an author. An impersonal critique, claiming the automatic production of texts, tends to enfeeble the reader's awareness that authors may seek to be thoughtful and mindful. To be able to study such relationships requires that we use superordinate terms for the activity of mind, namely "thought" and "thinking." Postmodern critical subtlety cannot supersede such terms. To give but one instance of this requirement, the response of feminists to the Derridean critique of a gendered logocentrism indicates that we need to ask whether men and women indeed do not think, as they write, differently. Women's discourse logically implies women's thought.

My essays explore different aspects of such activity of mind and thought as these in turn *activate* the literary work, while this activity—literary thought—is always rhetorical and poetic in function. A final distinction, which may be more illusory than real, is the difference between the representation of the thoughts of persons an author imagines and the intelligence and mindfulness of the author herself or himself. One aim of a noetic study would be to expose this distinction and the issues it raises.

Recognizing that mind is the source of human power, this book investigates some of the many ways literature expresses and embodies the process of thinking. The method by which the ensuing chapters are thought through is, philosophically speaking, eclectic. The Wittgenstein of the *Philosophical Investigations, On Certainty*, and *Zettel* remains the deepest influence on my own method. I have generally refrained from exegesis of metacritical texts, preferring to consider my own field—texts that are literary in a somewhat extended ordinary sense. Within this various field, and in a frame of mind at least partly Herodotean and Vichian, I have always wished to say "let's start again," returning to the experience of texts we may call primary. There is no discussion of the definition of literature. I simply use the term in a flexible manner, as I use the terms thinking and thought.

Part I. Representing Thought

1. Iconographies of Thought

One purpose philosophy has always allowed itself has been to interrogate its own practices, to ask of what and how it is thinking. Although Aristotle in the *Poetics* speaks briefly of the thought running through a drama—the *dianoia*—this aspect of literature has not often received attention, nor is it likely that it should. For literary works tend to carry their thought indirectly, by showing or expressing the thoughts of some Other, some person whose story is being told, and these expressions appear to preempt the place of thought as a direct philosophic or dianoetic aim of the work. Such refusal of direct expression of thought is the case even when an author fictionalizes a first-person narrator or invents a lyric I. These inventions are taken to be fictive and uncommitted to the utterance of an accountable truth or falsehood. Austin among others, therefore, held literary usages to be what he called "parasitic upon normal use," to be "etiolations of language," which is one philosopher's point of view.

The poet's position is rather different, and by poet I mean the maker of any imaginative literary work. The poet seems happy enough to speak or bespeak any thoughts of the invented persons, be these thoughts true or false or even indifferent to the question of truth or verification. For the poet thought is just one more part or aspect of being alive. We can therefore examine some of the ways that literature has presented thought. Further, we can ask if there is not, here as with other aspects of human experience, an iconographic tradition or at least moments or epochs in historical development whereby literature has sought to place or express the presumed reality of human thinking.

The phrase "iconographies of thought" promises at least one advantage for our exploration: the icon (however loosely understood) seems concrete and fixed, so that it will counterbalance what is obviously the main difficulty of our task, the fact that thought and thinking are always disappearing before our gaze. Our focal topic, thought, is rather like aesthetics, of which a philosopher once said: "It is a subject without an object." For thoughts do seem to be a kind of airy nothing, an empty but powerful relating of a *this* to a *that*. We often identify this relating as "mental activity"; we may speak of it as "part of what goes on in the brain," the conscious part. As to the problematic of the *unconscious*, it is worth recalling that Freud quoted Aristotle to the effect that dreams are the *thoughts* of a person who is asleep. Amidst our uncertainty as to the definition of our field of analysis, we can perhaps accept that although we may not be able to say felicitously exactly what thought is, we can often say what it is *of* or *about*. In turn, we can say that fictions in literature deploy a variety of conventions whereby thought is indicated and tracked in operation.

For example, Anna, the heroine of Jean Rhys's novel, *Voyage in the Dark*, is telling her own story:

> I opened my eyes. I went on crying. She went away from me. I sat up and everything was different. She brought me my handbag. I got out my handkerchief and wiped my face.
> I thought, "It's all over. But is it all over?"
> She said, "That will be all right. In two weeks, three weeks."
> "But it's quite sure?"
> "Yes, quite sure."[1]

Typically for the novel, Rhys evokes an interplay between physical gestures that reveal emotion and the verbal utterance of such emotion, and between both these expressive states and the non-speaking phrase "I thought."

Another case of fictional convention is Henry James in *Daisy Miller*: "Winterbourne reflected for an instant as lucidly as possible: 'we' could only mean Miss Miller and himself. This prospect almost seemed too good to believe; he felt as if he ought to kiss the young

without the thought part, the novel would be only a pretended chronicle.

Opposed to such annalistic forms is the imbricated complexity of fictional form in general. Whereas the great allegorical forms of romantic quest and heroic battle tend to simplify the context of action and tend severely to channel all lines of thought relating to that action, the drift of novelistic form has been to allow protagonists to introduce complexity into their own fictive lives by virtue of explicit doubt and deliberation. Novelistic *dianoia* is a complex summation of the intermingled actions and thoughts of persons who are deliberately chosen by the novelist for the novelty of their coming together under the canopy of some variegated fictive action. The modern novel seems to exist primarily to project human consciousness. Conrad surely develops ideas about colonial greed and terror in "The Heart of Darkness," but he does so by the subtle mechanism of an evoked consciousness, Marlow's awareness and Marlow's blindness. As C. S. Peirce said, "the Immediate runs in a continous stream through our lives." The novel achieves a natural refinement of purpose in authors like Woolf and Beckett. They project a theater of the mind.

Traditional critical parlance would deny to such an art the label of iconography, since the icon suggests the allegorical. But that is exactly the puzzle before us: whether it is not an allegory to say "he thought" or "she wondered." The problem is that it is not clear when and how thought is being adequately presented or represented, in fiction or in any other discourse. What has long been an issue for philosophers is to decide how to understand this word/ thought relation, and deconstruction has shown that the issue is by no means decided.

It seems therefore important that an openly iconic author, take the example of Calvino, will tend to attach the iconography of attendant sensations and perceptions. He invents a character, Mr. Palomar, in order to express the notion of the reflective mind, to impersonate such a mind. As with other fictions, the hero is walking along a beach and we are told "he thinks as he proceeds," or "he knows that in such circumstances . . ." Or we learn that "Mr. Palomar's mind has wandered, he has stopped pulling up weeds. He no longer thinks of the lawn: he thinks of the universe. He is trying to apply to the universe everything he has thought about the lawn."[3]

Such locutions work and have expressive force because they develop the reflective principle, such that to reflect (even as a telescope, a Mount Palomar, reflects) is to evoke the possibility of representing some state of affairs. In what one might call the primitive or early stages of such representations, the reflecting mind begins empirically, like Mr. Palomar, by "reading a wave" at the seashore or scanning a woman's naked bosom. In the later stages of a more articulated thought Palomar moves into meditation—the key chapter is a brief one entitled "On biting the tongue," where we learn that "silence also can be considered a kind of speech." A studied silencing of all the banal expressions of what *passes for* thought allows the mind to enter a domain of meditative emptiness, where affairs are depicted in model or ideal form, where the mind begins to think about its own thinking, or where the activity of thought is to set tasks in an extreme form, such as learning to be dead: "Mr. Palomar decides that from now on he will act as if he were dead, to see how the world gets along without him." This feigned death is a *tabula rasa.*

Calvino's fantastic parable finds a psychic base in the partial revelations of thought itself, as merely partial, as inadequate to all that thought may be. But Calvino belongs to our post-Peircean era in that whatever his Mr. Palomar thinks must also be thought only in that it is inscribed in a set of signs. At the end of this book we read: " 'If time has to end, it can be described, instant by instant,' Mr. Palomar thinks, 'and each instant, when described, expands so that its end can no longer be seen.' He decides that he will set himself to describing every instant of his life, and until he has described them all he will no longer think of being dead. At that moment he dies." Owing to the flexible power of free indirect discourse, we cannot tell for certain what to make of the sentence "At that moment he dies." Is it only what Mr. Palomar thinks, or is it, as before in the book, an assertion of fact written with a verb in the historical present tense?

The point seems to be that the novelist reserves the term "thought" (and its cognates) precisely for naming a limit to our knowledge. Hence the perfect iconographic representation of the elusiveness of thought is to be found in the grammatical form itself, in the free indirect discourse whose indeterminate edges are the ultimate bounds of our limited access to certainty. Such is one aim of this modern or postmodern iconographer.

While Calvino draws upon the resources of recent prose fiction, earlier writers were equally well equipped, though in different fashion, to render the thought process. What might be called the older iconography of thought occurs in English literature, with long centuries of allegorical anticipation, in the Metaphysical poetry of the late sixteenth and early seventeenth centuries. As recent historicist studies have shown, these are times of an accelerated invention of secular selfhood. It would seem necessary, furthermore, that along with this "self-fashioning" there must go a sharpened sense of the mental powers required for such inventions to occur.

The Renaissance term "wit" names the domain in which the inventions of selfhood appear, and hence poets of the Renaissance seek new theaters of wit-work, not least in the theater proper. It is not to be expected that psychological terms such as wit remain stable during the late Renaissance and Baroque periods. With Hobbes and Locke particularly, psychology is taking its first steps into the modern period. The term "wit," as Dr. Johnson observed, is considerably weakened in general force by the time Pope equated it with "what oft was thought, but n'er so well expressed." One key feature of the Renaissance play of thought is its placement, perhaps even what one might call its spatiality. Thought in the Metaphysical poets is attached to a scene of order, often cosmological. For example, in Donne's *Second Anniversarie—The Progress of the Soule*—the poet repeats the word "think" 16 times in the space of 36 lines, about once every two lines. The word is affixed to a controlled contemplation of last things, and after a while the reader has a fairly fixed sense of the term "think." Donne is organizing our idea of thinking in this context of the destiny of the soul, and the result is spatially diagrammatic in the end. The *Second Anniversarie* here sets forth a commanding series of images of the last things, and while (line 121) we are asked to "think these things cheerfully," our main response must be one of relief that the poet has managed to *picture* the mental task at hand. He has introduced method into the thinking process. Of Donne paramountly we may say, as Thomas Carew said in his *Elegy*, that Dr. Donne "ruled the universal monarchy of wit . . . as he *thought* fit," or as Dr. Johnson said of the Metaphysicals in general, that to write in the manner of Donne and the others "one had at least to think."

Donne is celebrated for the inclusiveness of his sensibility, so that his poetry explores the feelings or sensations accompanying thought, as thought struggles or rushes or moves slowly and logically to its conclusions. With such open iconic entertainment of thought and thinking there is bound to be a wide play of wit, especially as wit depends upon quasi-dramatic conversational modes—there is with Donne always a fiction of the intensified listener, the perfected audience. For Donne, too, the cosmos is a vast set design, whose dramatic (that is, soul-making) significance is assumed, mysteriously, to be at least partially intelligible.

The iconic variety of thought during this early modern period is almost as extensive as the many-sided destiny of the soul to be saved by Christian belief and action. In Eliot's phrase, this is a universe of objective correlatives. Hence it seems important that in the mid-seventeenth century, post-Jonsonian, lyric poetry of Andrew Marvell a virtually opposite approach to thought seems to occur. Marvell thinks mathematically, and he tends to choose generic conventions such as "The Definition of Love" or pastoral in order to analyze states of mind into their simplest, most elegant, most mysteriously harmonious forms. With Marvell we may say, as Goethe said of Arabic poetry, that "language is already productive in and of itself, and indeed, in so far as it comes to meet thought, is eloquent." Marvell writes of the passions of the world, especially of loss, but he always moves toward a radical, one might say elemental picturing of such states of affairs. He is able to render the perfect drop of dew existing entire "in its pure and circling thoughts." If he uses the word "plain," he means it in its radical geometric sense, and then, further, with its usual psychological overtones.

Marvell would always establish a place or space for thought—the "easy philosopher" of *Upon Appleton House* muses to himself: "how safe, methinks, and strong behind / These trees have I encamped my mind." Like Milton, whose archfiend can boast "The mind is its own place," Marvell more often than not is inventing an independent or liberated notion of thought. The four pastorals for Damon the Mower permit an exploration of the order of mind itself; the pastoral of mowing goes beyond its immediate link to Death the Reaper (and hence to the most sublime thoughts) and allows the poet to represent a question: Can the mind discern, can it analyze, can it separate out the confusing strands of the cultivated world's excesses? Marvell's mower poems ask how, by thought, one is to meet the frightening distractions of a world "too much with us." Marvell here analyzes excess by projecting images of a natural ascesis, the Mower's aim. In "The Mower against Gardens" the little pink "grew then as double as his mind." Fascinated with the new technology of hybrids (the Tulipmania crash belongs to his lifetime), Marvell can allude to the variegated colors of "The Marvel of Peru" to remind us that whenever mind is at issue, there is an inherent problem of escaping the very self that is analyzing the difference between itself and all other minds. If in most cases pastoral is a stylized reduction or simplification of the way human beings *act*, here pastoral serves a parallel purpose, to reduce and elementally simplify the way human beings *think*. Pastoral shows how thinking sounds.

Sometimes it is scarcely possible to tell what Marvell takes the sounds of language to imply. He plays beyond play. His mortal character, Damon—the conversion of Adam—says: "I am the Mower Damon, known / Through all the meadows I have mown." Where can this circle of life and death, joy and sorrow, end? "Tis death alone that this must do, / For Death, thou are a Mower too," and so ends the poem. The image of mind is at once mystified by pastoral courtesies and specified by geometric usage. For example, the end of the magical "Mower to the Glowworms:"

> Your courteous lights in vain you waste,
> Since Juliana here is come,
> For she my mind hath so displaced
> That I shall never find my home.

Juliana is the chthonic goddess of the mind's placement, as in the turning refrain of the fourth poem in the cycle:

> When Juliana came, and she,
> What I do to the grass, does to my thoughts and me.

In this particular iconography of thought Goethe's principle applies, the language of the refrain is productive in and of itself. That is, the Mower's mind *is* the refrain; his thoughts, like the refrain, are repeated five times in a cycle of merging, as indeed 5 is the mystical

Renaissance number of betrothal and marriage (as in Browne's *Garden of Cyrus*). The mind is, in effect, what its words allow it to be, although here there is a putative action (Juliana's arrival). This action becomes *mentally* active and significant only when it is worded by the poem as a circling, preoccupying reiteration—one might say, obsession. The prime iconicity then resides in the mere rhythm of the poem.

If one could appropriately speak of the rhythm of imagery, then Marvell's deepest explorations of mind partake of such a rhythmic exercise. It suffices to quote the famed stanza of mind from his poem "The Garden":

> Meanwhile the mind, from pleasure less,
> Withdraws into its happiness;
> The mind, that ocean where each kind
> Does straight its own resemblance find;
> Yet it creates, transcending these,
> Far other worlds, and other seas;
> Annihilating all that's made
> To a green thought in a green shade.

On the one hand such a picturing of mind is as close to the ineffable as possible, but on the other a doctrine of creation and of Platonic or Neoplatonic forms gives to the picturing a measure of geometric objectivity. Marvell's work, here as elsewhere, exemplifies the crisis of late Renaissance thinking about thought. The picturing can be given iconic registers, an adequate imagery and syntax. But simultaneously there seems to be an arising awareness of blockage, as if, with all our clarity of image and line, there is still a dark opacity that cannot be crossed, modulating into an illuminating image of mind. What is left, for Marvell, is, oddly, the Wittgensteinian question of color[4] which, as epistemology shows, is no accident.

Generally speaking, the iconography of thought during the sixteenth and seventeenth centuries is allied to the theory of creative and dispositional melancholia. This resource makes it possible for Milton to produce a free-flowing allegory of thought in his diptych, *L'Allegro* and *Il Penseroso*. This psychic lexicon, deriving from theories of melancholia, finds its fullest development in Burton's *Anatomy of Melancholy,* and the massive bulk of his lore might suggest that here is the sufficient context for an account of late Renaissance theories of mind.

There is another aspect to the problem. Social and political historians and commentators have again alerted us to changes occurring in the politics of mind. Significantly—for it amounts to a catastrophe—the libertarian and liberating aspects of the Protestant Reformation and all its political consequences from both sacred and secular literature are all effective, in a major way, in the domain of each individual's own mind. The idea of mind, I am suggesting, is notably politicized. In the crudest terms, the quarrel a Milton might have with Laudian high Anglicanism is a quarrel with an earlier exteriority of cult, which is believed now to need reforming or replacing with a more interiorized, more *penseroso* style of wonder and devotion—in brief, a prophetic sensibility. Changes too subtle and strong to be more than suggested here, changes of attitude too deep in their lasting effects, will be the topic of research as we attempt to trace the mannerist and Baroque extensions of Renaissance iconicities. We note merely that, while Benjamin's study of the German *Trauerspiel* is intensely psychologized in its reading of the role of melancholia during the Baroque period, it is also a constantly political account of European stresses, as the drama of state is shown to project a complex, ruinated allegory of noble mind.

In the background to all such changes of worldview there is, of course, an increasingly sharp sense that mind is inherently an opacity, that mind is at best a mysterious mirror of the world.

The iconography of mind is always and at all times working against its own countercurrent. In a word, this is the obstruction caused by the very nature of the mind itself—its solipsistic wall. As we turn to the larger context in which this iconography must come into being, we cannot avoid this wall. I shall consider some of its aspects and its relation to at least one philosopher, Wittgenstein, and one poet, Shakespeare, to suggest how it is that representing thought will always require ruses and even, one might say, confidence games. The mind's occluded vision of itself may be easiest seen by considering its pictorial representation.

Rodin's Thinker is perhaps the best known Western icon of thought. Without trying to describe this remarkable statue, let me suggest that it emblematizes one main aspect of the French *penser:* its weighing, its pendency, its hangingness, suspension. The left hand, massively powerful, hangs limp over the left kneecap, and the upper body leans forward supported by a complex system of bridging members—right elbow on left thigh, right wrist collapsed backward, providing with the back of the hand a cushion for the thinker's chin, holding up the whole weight of the head, leaving an overall impression a Rabelaisian might call sublime constipation. His mouth is forced shut. Even his glance is pendant; the eyes recede into cavernous shadow—we can only guess that they look down, into some abyss. The statue was created to sit atop Rodin's monumental Gate of Hell, and the Thinker is contemplating the Inferno. The downward glance is conventional in this iconography, as appears from Rodin's other piece, the female, if somewhat androgynous, head entitled Thought.

Such a description of the figure has been couched in language which implies the postures of thought, while biographical material locates a possible object of the Thinker's contemplation. Nevertheless, the fact remains that we do not know what the Thinker is exactly thinking. Nor do we know exactly what Rembrandt's philosopher in his study is thinking, though details of the painting suggest it might have something to do with Plato's cave; nor do we know what Dürer's Melancolia is thinking, in his great engraving. If iconic signals are to provide an answer, in the case of Melancolia, given all the hermetic bric-a-brac surrounding her, she might well be pondering a dozen different academic or practical subjects.

Suppose we begin with pictures, and suppose we admit there is at once a question, because pictures do not in the usual sense utter words or speak ordinary language. But suppose we begin with the iconic representation of men, women, and children thinking, as opposed let us say to bathing or strolling. Are such persons allowed (believed?) to think as well as bathe and stroll? As long as we start from the agent of thought—the thinker—we seem to have a predetermined noetic vagueness. Bad swimmers may be thinking harder, for instance, than good ones. But then good swimmers may be solving math problems as they cross the Hellespont. The point is: who would know, judging from outward appearances? The barrier, the occlusion seems strong.

For that reason and in that light, it appears that the revelation of a thinking process requires special communicative instruments—and it seems critical to note that we are using the example of visual representation, as by a painting or statue. Owing to the mind-barrier, thinkers (and artists) of thought have evolved conventions of a more or less allegorical sort to convey the content of the thinker's thought. Among various emblematic accessories in Dürer's engraving of Melancolia there is a dog, lying asleep, presumably dreaming. The iconic link to the goddess of speculative mentation, to Melancolia, is that the dog is naturally good at tracking a scent, or so Piero Valeriano's learned commentary teaches us to interpret this canine emblem.

Typically, this emblematic dog fills out one corner of the iconography of the thinking of Melancolia, the flairing, scenting, intuiting aspect of her thought. What could not be iconically seen within her, can be suggested externally, by metonymy. If St. Jerome in his study is not alone, if there is a skull on his table-top, we are led at once to the iconography of the *memento mori*. Can we be sure he is meditating upon death? Perhaps he is thinking of the angels. The opacity of his external appearance is only partially remedied by the appended iconography of secondary things. Furthermore, there might be iconological subtleties, blocking access to any knowledge of his thoughts—an angel hovering in the background might or might not be "in his mind," and only the iconological tradition would give us a clue to the better reading of the picture. In any case there seems to be difficulty in trying to make pictures of thought.

Wittgenstein held in the *Tractatus* that "we make pictures of facts," but we can hardly picture thought itself with much success. yet nothing is more evident than the fact that thought in some form does get expressed, or at least appears to be active in some way. Moving away from the *Tractatus*, Wittgenstein said to Russell he did not know *what* the constituents of thought were, but he knew that thought must have constituents corresponding to the words of language. On other occasions, he found thought to be expressed in the idiomatic choice of words.

Wittgenstein resembles a believer in the Sapir-Whorf hypothesis,[5] particularly when he is asking such questions as should we not have a separate word for "a thought expressed in a sentence," another for "the thought which I may later 'clothe in words,' " another for "wordless thinking as one works." He opined that, if a lion could talk, we could not understand him. He asked if indeed thinking is a mental activity (*Tätigkeit*) or indeed an activity of any sort? In *The Blue Book* he wrote, "We are tempted to think that the action of language consists of two parts: an inorganic part, the handling of signs, and an organic part, which we may call understanding these signs, meaning them, interpreting them, thinking. These latter activities seem to take place in a queer kind of medium, the mind: and the mechanisms of the mind, the nature of which, it seems, we don't quite understand, can bring about effects which no material mechanism could."[6]

For the later Wittgenstein, language-games and indeed language in general do not simply reflect or project "forms of life." The question of the life or deadness of language is more elusive; rather, the language-games are *involved* in the forms of life. Paragraph 143 of the *Zettel* reads: "in all cases what one means by 'thought' is what is alive [*lebende*] in the sentence. That without which it is dead, a mere sequence of sounds or written shapes." Elsewhere the philosopher meditates on the phenomenology of this life in language:

> Compare the phenomenon of thinking with the phenomenon of burning. May not burning, flame, seem mysterious to us? And why flame more than furniture [*der Tisch*]?—And how do you clear up the mystery [riddle/*Rätsel*]?
>
> And how is the riddle of thinking to be solved? Like that of flame?
>
> Isn't flame mysterious because it is impalpable? All right—but why does that make it mysterious? Why should something impalpable be more mysterious than something palpable? Unless it's because we *want* to catch hold of it.[7]

This riddle-conscious set of questions about the phenomenon of thinking is connected to Wittgenstein's cardinal awareness that art is a special case—as he put it, "The way music speaks. Do not forget that a poem, even though it is composed in the language of information [*Mitteilung*], is not used in the language-game of giving information" (*Zettel*, #160). Further he said, "A poet's words go through and through us. And that's connected causally with the use that they have in our life. And it is also connected with the way in which, conformably to this use, we let our thoughts roam up and down [*schweifen*] in the familiar surroundings of the words" (*Zettel*, #155). In effect, poetry and fiction and plays—where language is not ordinary—get their piercing power from their contextual affiliation with the most ordinary uses our words have "in our life."

The preceding sense of the literary use of language, in relation to thought, is strongly conditioned by Wittgenstein's later belief that "what lies at the bottom of language is 'our *acting*,' not something's 'striking us as true'." In the very late collection of paragraphs, *On Certainty*, he states: "Giving grounds, justifying the evidence, comes to an end;—but the end is not certain propositions striking us immediately as true, a kind of *seeing* on our part; but it is our *acting* which lies at the bottom of the language-game" (#204). Action here includes making, especially making situations change. The level of action can be radically simple, to the point of apparent inanity. The philosopher asks: "Why don't I satisfy myself that I still have two feet, when I want to get up from a chair? There is no why. I simply don't. *That is how I act*" (*On Certainty*, #148).

The most remarkable scene of action to be found in the later Wittgensteinian canon is his description of Shakespeare, who is important to him because the plays stand for the most miraculous expression of the power to evoke what Stanley Cavell calls "the human form of life." Wittgenstein ties this power to thought itself.

Wittgenstein presents a Shakespeare in whom the iconography of thought is so highly developed that we can hardly call it an iconography. This Shakespeare seems to be privy to the most inward, hidden thought-signs. Somehow this Shakespeare conveys the life of thought itself, as if he knew the exact wording for every thought. "I do not believe," says the philosopher, "that Shakespeare can be set alongside any other poet." Such judgments, so phrased, abound in the annals of bardolatry. But here the judgment has a quite unprecedented source, the question: "Was he perhaps a *creator of language* [*Sprachschöpfer*] rather than a poet [*als ein Dichter*]?"

Allied to this claim is the statement that nobody could speak of "Shakespeare's great heart," though one might speak so about Beethoven. Instead, as Wittgenstein put it in the collection known as *Culture and Value*, for Shakespeare's creative identity "the supple hand that created new natural linguistic forms . . . would seem to me nearer the mark." I myself would prefer to call the poet not an intertextual, but rather an interlingual master. The "new natural linguistic forms" are the very outlines of thought, as if the thinking game were parcelled out along with a continuously self-generating language-game of some superordinate kind. This Shakespeare has access to the "inside" of the iconography of thought because he is able to create language. Thus a wider range of metaphors for the process of thought is opened to him, whether or not such a process is expressed in any given speech; the point is, it could be if the author so desired. Nothing seems to bar Shakespeare from the metaphors that express the activity of the speaker's mind.

"Creator of language" and "the supple hand that created new natural linguistic forms" are markedly metaphoric phrasings. Yet they do convey some reason for our sense that Shakespeare is more than, or different from, the creator of "characters." Whoever speaks in the plays will be revealing those tiny particles of thought that usually can find no utterable place or space of expression. The poet treats expressive speech as if it were articulated through a seeming infinity of small verbal gestures, like a face of mercurial expressivity, an actor's face. (As Tolstoy said, Shakespeare was an actor, and an intelligent man.) Such a link of deep expressivity and linguistic invention marks, at the same high degree, perhaps only one other English author with whom Shakespeare is often compared, namely Charles Dickens. With the novelist as with the playwright, we get an impression that the author is racing around inside the minds of his characters, who "find words" where ordinary mortals lack them.

The philosophic attitude that gives to Wittgenstein his unusually radical Shakespearean affinity is related to the problem of private minds and private languages. If Rodin's Thinker recalls to us that other minds are largely private to themselves, the case of language and expression recalls that even words have private senses. Wittgenstein had analyzed this problem into its extreme statements, so that, as the *Investigations* observes, a private language is one in which the individual words "are to refer to what can only be known to the person speaking; to his immediate private sensations . . . [hence] another person cannot understand the language."

Shakespearean diction hovers always on the edge of paralanguage, of "oh's" and "ah's," of ruptures, pauses, verbal fugues. This art culminates in his manipulation of the dramatic soliloquy—an artform that flourishes precisely when self-hood and self-speaking come to be cardinal issues for early modern culture. Strikingly, the soliloquy uses iconic markers in order to frame the speaker's thought process and its approximation to an immediate expression. In this art there can only be approximation, approach towards, touching upon the privacy of thought. Hamlet says to himself (that is, to us, his most indulgent auditors) "let me not think on't . . ." in a soliloquy—and we know precisely that he *is* thinking about the "frailty" of woman. The soliloquy, of course, has its theatrical marks; its iconicity of thought includes the withdrawal of other interlocutors from contact with the soliloquizing speaker, so that we know, allegorically, that this is to a degree a private speech. Yet soliloquy is always verging in the plays on an invasion of all modes of dialogue, as if these were plays in which large numbers of people talk back and forth to each other, taking turns at speaking in soliloquy. This is as if such persons were all out there on stage, attacking the philosopher's question: can there be a private language, and if not, why not?—since that in an absolute sense is all we have. But a calm view of the plays and the poems would seem finally to indicate a more mixed view of things: language is always, in this view, semiprivate, and thought is only to be expressed in approximate purity of representation.

In Shakespeare's *Sonnets*, for example, thought is identified metaphorically as wounded ("gored"), nimble, killing, jealous, buried, and so on. Thought here is not allowed to be purified or essentialized, but rather is linked with terms of feelings, sensation, perception, doubt, dreaming, questioning, hoping, wondering, and above all estimating and valuing—as if the whole array of expressions were intended to gloss the sentence, "there's nothing either good or bad, but thinking makes it so." This follows from a deeper insight: "what's aught, but as 'tis valued," or in Heideggerian terms, what is thought is what is thanked. Above all, thought is here conceived to be an activity of mind, the activity giving us access to a world "out there." Sonnet 44 uses the icon of mental travel:

> If the dull substance of my flesh were thought,
> Injurious distance would not stop my way;
> For then, despite of space, I would be brought,
> From limits far remote, where thou dost stay . . .

Shakespeare's "if" announces the conditional clause that besets all meditations with and upon thought, for, as the Sonnet later exclaims:

> nimble thought can jump both sea and land
> As soon as think the place where he would be.
>
> But, ah, thought kills me that I am not thought,
> To leap large lengths of miles when thou art gone . . .

To wish to know thought absolutely, to be able to say it, to utter its *form* is finally impossible, because there is an inescapable corporeality in its agency, since all our thoughts issue—so far as we are human—from the encasement of our dull bodily substance. This is the limiting condition that virtually forces an iconography upon the writer. There cannot then be a stated thought, purely and as such; there can only be images and various icons of thoughts, that is, there can only be iconographies of thought.

Large areas of differing iconographic procedures have emerged from the preceding remarks. The novelist simply says "she thought," and supports such discursive announcements with a wealth of somatic and other conditioning indices to the likelihood of thought actually (that is, fictionally) occurring. Any metaphysical poet and painter, whose concern is a more fundamental, more essentialist view of the mind, will in most cases employ allegorical emblems of thought, such as the dog in Dürer's *Melancolia*, or Marvell's "ocean," as standing for the immensity of mind, for its procreativity. The novelist invests the thinking process with a natural aura, while the metaphysician, in poetry or philosophy, invests mind with an opposite character, with mystery. Between these two poles there seems to lie an infinitely varied play of rhetorical devices whereby authors have attempted to render thought as phenomenon, thought as idea.

Always the specter of solipsism haunts the field of these iconographies. In such a context the case of Wittgenstein is cardinal, because he latterly allowed to thought a high degree of animism. He would ask, for instance, what if "the chair is thinking to itself . . . Where? in one of its parts? Or outside its body; in the air around it?" (*Philosophical Investigations*, #361). Such queries are attempts on the philosopher's part to open up the same topics that Shakespeare opened up in the inset rustic drama, staged by Bottom and his friends, in *Midsummer Night's Dream*. If in such theater Wall and Moonshine can "speak," then a deeper than usual exploration of thought is occurring, an exploration Wittgenstein associated with a play of Shakespearean language-games so rich that he could only call it the "creation of language." Shakespeare was of course *not* creating words, though his vocabulary is significantly one of the largest of any major author writing in English (or perhaps any other tongue).

For Wittgenstein's insight to have weight, it must imply something different, something within his own philosophic purview. Perhaps "the creator of language" means, rather, that Shakespeare *plays the language-game of creating language.* In that activity his works would come closer than most to revealing what Peirce called the "thought-signs" of the thinking mind, and hence would possess that quality of animation that so strongly identifies both the poems and the plays. Certainly, if thought is as infinitely restless as it appears to be, especially in a historical period so restless as was Shakespeare's, the rendering of thought would seem to require the invention of an unusually large number of language-games. Since thought is always to some extent *other,* these language-games will necessarily partake of an indirect iconographic—that is, allegorical or metaphoric—procedure of naming.

Having reached the limit case of Shakespeare playing the language-game of creating language, we can ask how such an author is better able than others to express the life of the mind. Language here is understood to mean a natural language capable of seemingly unlimited development through devices of poetry, primarily of metaphoric extension. The game then is to have characters speak with numerous and variously different means of access to the shifting contents of mind, covering a multiplicity of thought-trains. For example, the idea of relieving pain might be expressed in terms of the lessening of pressure, of an increased sense of bodily wholeness, of flight from a dungeon and the dark, of breathing easily and without impediment, or finally of careless and idle appeasement of some hunger. To "create language," on this basis, is to extend the normal limit of a natural language such as English of the late sixteenth and early seventeenth centuries.

Such a creative extension of linguistic resources implies a broader and deeper access to what I am calling thought. Thought is understood then to include a wider variety of mental acts than may be considered allowable by the philosopher. It includes perceptions, cognitions of all sorts, judgments, ruminations, analysis, synthesis, highly figurated representations of inner states, as when a poet personifies a passion. Such mental acts, along with others, would not be allowed as thought by some philosophers. Hannah Arendt, for example, would distinguish thinking from judging, which follows from Kantian principles.[8]

If there is, as we have seen, a solipsistic wall separating every person from every other person's thoughts, thought always preserves a certain otherness and opacity, despite its representation through poetic devices. This situation brings about the preeminence of metaphor, as the most fluent and daring device of finding words in which to express thoughts. To the extent that an author like Shakespeare speaks with streams and cataracts of poetic figures, the assumption seems to arise that thought is whatever can be put into language, *somehow*. If an author has only a simple and impoverished language, he will express a relatively narrow range of thoughts, while the converse is also true. My approach will be to suggest, if only conjecturally, some of the range of literary and artistic representations of thought. The field of such representations is immense; only a small number of relevant examples will here be given to the reader. Yet such a limited sampling is enough to indicate that we do well to follow the philosopher's footsteps in tracing the lines of mental activity that confer interest upon imaginative works.

2. Two Frames in the Iconography of Thinking: The Satanic and the Quixotic

The province of narrative seems to be the mixed domain of story-telling, emotive expression, and the ordering of ideas and thoughts centering upon story and expression. So far as thought itself is concerned, when an idea or concept is perfectly fixed, like an item that can be labeled, this will be the allegorical mode in action. The thought of constancy will be rendered by some personifying device that shows itself always perfectly constant, and may be named Constancy, or, in a romance, a young woman named Constance.

More interesting are the cases where we witness a character in the process of thinking. Here we discover a particularly strong strain in the English Renaissance literature that we may loosely call Faustian, after Marlowe's invention of Faust in dialogue with Mephistophilis. Since this type of character and its dramatic congener, Hamlet, is processually driven to endless thinking, the key interest for the critic will be to show that even here the poet must find an iconography by which to stabilize the process and its flux. In this light, the character of Satan, as Milton develops it, is perhaps the most striking case of an iconography of thought coming forth within the process of thinking itself.

Thought as Suffering

Book IV of *Paradise Regained* focuses the agon of Satan and Jesus on a temptation to control a whole tradition of the powers of thought. For Milton, as for the Tempter, these powers inhere in the broad span of classical learning, whose content includes the widest ranges of art and philosophy. Satan glozingly proffers all this honey of poetry, logic, and eloquence, reaching back to the oracular wisdom of Socrates. The Savior may choose to "revolve" all these sources of power—the mental equivalent of an empire—either in the desert or "as thou lik'st, at home." This thinker, so empowered, would revolve the noblest models of intellect the West had known and, closer to Milton's poem, the Renaissance had brought to renewed availability and prominence.

As before and later in the poem whenever it reaches a climax, Jesus rejects the tempting object. He clearly understands its legitimate appeal, but rejects any attempt to displace the central text for wisdom and Miltonic truth, the Holy Bible. For only in the latter is humility fully enshrined, not least in visionary books of prophecy. By contrast, Greek and Roman learning and culture are tied to rhetoric, here called "oratory," but also to be taken in the broadest sense of persuasion-as-power. Jesus has to reject the exclusive dependence upon any intellect that relies on rhetorical manipulation. Hence his diction in *Paradise Regained* is often radically sparse, amounting at times to brutal simplicity. For he is countering a Satanic equation, the equivalence of temptation and rhetorical force. The Tempter wishes to "sell" his interlocutor. A converse is here also true, that rhetoric almost necessarily enforces a temptation of some kind. The brief epic thence is to a degree reduced in grandeur of style, because Milton wishes here to analyze the rhetoricity of temptation in general.

When Jesus turns away from the seductions of a self-sufficient classical lore, he is turning away from what is tempting about that lore, its potential for rhetorical duplicity. Instead, Jesus will appeal to the sublime simplicity of Biblical revelation and law.

Such is the context of the remarkable epic moment. As he begins his arguments for the appeal of classical lore, Satan, whose fallen career represents in highest degree the perils of thinking in a certain way, wishes at once to flatter and manipulate his opponent. To Jesus he says:

> Therefore let pass, as they are transitory,
> The Kingdoms of this World; I shall no more

Advise thee, gain them as thou canst, or not.
And thou thy self seem'st otherwise inclin'd
Then to a worldly Crown, *addicted more*
To contemplation and profound dispute . . .

                                    (IV, 209–214)

This, Satan observes, has to be the case, for even as a young boy
Jesus went into the Temple—the place of con-templation—

Among the gravest Rabbins disputant
On points and questions fitting Moses chair,
Teaching, not taught . . .

                                    (IV, 218–219)

This is the wondrous child who prefigures the man who virtually
must be bound to thought, "addicted to contemplation," that is,
addicted to a certain kind of thought.

To deal, first of all, with Satan's second allegation about Jesus,
that he is addicted to dispute, we may note only that throughout
Paradise Regained Jesus refuses to dispute with his enemy; instead,
he affirms what he knows from inside the circle of his own knowledge, his self-containing Biblical knowledge, namely his own role
and future as the One heralded by John the Baptist, as the Savior.
But he does not dispute, since he knows that he is facing a falsely
motivated disputant, as distinct from any of the Rabbis who were
honestly looking for truth.

More important, however, is the primary allegation, that Jesus is
addicted to contemplation. Two things about this allegation lead us
to see what role thinking plays in the doomed career, the fall, of
Satan. Satan is here both misconstruing and projecting. He fails to
grasp the fact that if contemplation means meditating on spiritual
things, quietly studying, calmly and attentively and freely viewing
an object in a stillness and openness of regard, then it is impossible
to be addicted to it. To obsessive thought one is or may be addicted,
but not to contemplation, the thought occurring in the freeing sacred space of the temple.

The Satan of *Paradise Lost* had said that the mind is "its own
place," and hence could make in and of itself either a hell or a
heaven. But the true contemplative is not pursuing a solitary definition of the place of mind. Even in the desert Jesus is not pursuing
that isolation, for he goes to find his true voice, that is, the voice

of the One who would speak with his Father or who would learn to encounter his enemy, the Tempter. Contemplation cannot be addictively pursued, for it precludes an alienation from the Temple, the place of con-templation.

That in the second level of meaning Satan's allegation is at odds with itself is no less revealing. One asks, Why is it that he ascribes to Jesus what is true of himself? The crudest answer may be that Satan wishes to rid himself of a torment, a contradictory torment as we have just seen, by ascribing it to his opposite, an Other. We can then ask how thought and contemplation are held prisoner in Satan's mind. That he identifies the mind as "its own place" gives us the clue. For Satan is throughout shown to be fixated on "place," whether it be the place of Paradise, or the status-giving place of the other angels, fallen or blessed, or the status of Adam and Eve. To be free would be to be free of his insane "location" of mind. It would be more Christlike to say the mind is God's place; that is, everywhere and nowhere.

Throughout both Miltonic epics the state of being fallen, or of falling, is hence identified as a kind of thinking the place of mind. This iconography of thought depends upon this identification, for only through it can the processes of thought become the tortured playground Satanic obsessions inhabit. For it is the paradox of fallen thought, as represented in *Paradise Lost*, that the angels of Pandemonium—the angels now transformed to their demonic parodies—indeed have "thoughts more elevate," but these devils are *thereby* "in wandring mazes lost," since "false Philosophie" is charming them through rhetorical sorcery for a mere moment's re-lief of their pain. That pain is the consequence of their high think-ing. In fact they cannot escape their "troubled thoughts," as Satan cannot escape his "thoughts inflam'd of highest design," his plan to wreck the human world.

Within sight of Eden and its noble pair, especially at first perhaps of Adam, who is formed "for contemplation and valour," Satan thinks of himself as wondering. One might assume this to be a benign state. But it is not. "O Hell! what doe mine eyes with grief behold, / Into our room of bliss thus high advanc't, / Creatures of other mould . . ." Thoughts of them can only pursue, hunt, track, at all times track without rest. Consistently Satan's mind is de-picted as a place of most cruel unrest, because by a psychic reversal place here has become all mind—that explains how Satan can carry Hell with him no matter how far from the cosmic "place of hell" he ventures. He can correctly say "Which way I flie is Hell" precisely because "my self am Hell," which here means because I am nothing but mind, and that mind always tortured by having no rest. Place should be resting-place. But if it is hoped that the mind will be its own place, its own carved solitude, then the possibility of rest may be forever lost.

This hellish inversion of contemplative wonder has doubtless no ultimate explanation. It is given in the myth of the war in heaven and of the subsequent fall of man. It is given in the context of Edenic thought, which is aligned with songs of praise and grateful prayer, that is, with an awareness of what lies *outside* the mind—"So pray'd they innocent, and to thir thoughts / Firm peace recoverd soon and wonted calm" (*Paradise Lost*, V, 209–210). Peaceful thought is then mostly praising and praying. It is not analyzing. Peace in thought seems to be an emptying, and Milton represents the opposite case by calling Satan "inly wracked," as if his mind were a torture chamber from which he finds no exit, and in which always "a multitude of thoughts at once / Awaken'd in me swarm" (*Paradise Regained*, I, 196–197). The swarm is without any harmonic principles, unlike the Virgin Mary's "composed" thoughts. The room of Satan's mind is a jungle.

The room, the space, the "place" of Satan's mind thus provide an iconic model for the thought of ruined mind. So fixed is the isolating drive to maintain this separate place that every physical travel of the fallen Archangel merely serves to carve a deeper incision between Satan's solitary howl of despairing ambition and a possible exit into light. Such an exit is not possible for him, and iconically we may say it is impossible because he cannot really speak to any Other. He cannot reciprocate an Other's speech.

In the late English Renaissance, then, after the flowering of soliloquy in the drama, after the "pleasing analysis" of mental states in *The Faerie Queene*, after the excursions of the Metaphysicals into the dialogues of self and soul—after all these and in the midst of a vast weather system of tractarian probing of religious doctrines and attitudes, Milton contrives a character, his Satan, to represent with iconically reductive force the whole effect of thought driven always to justify itself, rather than to justify some larger divine order.

To provide the thought of divine justice would be to require, at the very least, a dialogic hero, a hero in dialogue with the Other. To be caught within his own space of mind is doubly tragic—perhaps Hamlet was thus trapped, with suicidal thoughts coursing through his mind, but Hamlet would free himself in a final, because secular, act of revenge upon self and other. Satan cannot speak through the wall of a divine will; his silence is inevitably complete. He is never to be free to speak outside his own echo chamber, the more so since the louder he cries, the more eloquent grows his rhetoric.

Satan becomes the archetype for the purest sort of iconicity—a double icon. He is fixed by the deepest paradox of incessant mental activity producing incessant communicative failure; and this fixation causes his reduction to the most massive iconic monumentality, an effect as "tall" as his stature when he rises from the Burning Lake of Hell. Everywhere Satan imagines iconic fixity in the world he sees, and everywhere his imagination falls back upon himself, turning him into the composite summation of all the swarming thoughts and hapless problems and solutions his restless mind keeps proposing. There is no exit here because it is the perfect prison, since the mind can incessantly propose only false exits to the entrapped thinker. Milton has created the largest and most heroic image of the hero as suffering thinker, or, to personify, of thinking as suffering. For unlike Hamlet, who dies in a wild melodrama of dueling, the defeated antagonist of Jesus can only watch his opponent go quietly home to his Mother's house. There could be no more tragic isolation.

The effect of such isolation is not, however, tragic in the usual sense of a personal tragedy—the tragedy of a "whole" person. Rather this is the tragedy of mind, that mind which is "its own place." To a considerable degree Satan personifies this mentality, always more powerfully when he goes into action against mankind.

Throughout his career Milton remained interested in and deeply impassioned by all aspects of thought, not least in its Satanic bent toward isolation and negation. He wrote of the speed of thought, of its lightness, of its tendency to error, of its ordering through logic, of its relation to language and public utterance, of its culminating redemption through prophetic insight. Such matters come into focus early with the diptych of picturesque poems, L'Allegro and Il Penseroso. These two works exemplify Milton's evocation of musical and pictorial forms through poetic composition. They employ the picturesque in order to naturalize the emblematic. With such uses of picture the artist presents and limns a landscape that looks real, but only because it is pictureable, in short only as a deliberately framed and artificed unreality. A picturesque rendering of a system of ideas merely pretends to be a natural mimesis. One is tricked by the picturesque into not noticing that one is being enabled to think along certain ideal, iconic, emblematic lines. *Il Penseroso* shows the basic iconology for Milton's thought, in that it provides us with the benign fundamental form of contemplation, the work of the melancholy seer, the very opposite of the power-driven Satanic adventurer. Oddly, there is a manner of almost conversational ease in *Il Penseroso* and its twin poem. This results from the easy shifting of personifications and a generally metamorphic atmosphere, both of which contribute to our growing, evolving sense that benign melancholia marks the very nature of contemplative freedom—the very opposite of Satan's stressful mental struggles to escape himself and his own mental orbit.

A digression is in order to talk about the benign form of isolated mentality which corresponds inversely to its negative, Satanic form of isolation. The woven sense of *Il Penseroso* will defeat any broad generalizations about the poem. However, we can say that at once Milton distinguishes thought from daydreams, the tenants of an "idle brain." The opening lengthy invocation to Melancholy makes her "sober, steadfast, and demure." She walks like a "pensive nun" in the night.

> Come, but keep thy wonted gait,
> And looks commercing with the skies,
> Thy rapt soul sitting in thine eyes:
> There held in holy passion still,
> Forget thyself to marble, till
> With a sad leaden downward cast,
> Thou fix them on the earth as fast.

The psychic and the physical accompaniment to this motion of the mind, from sky to earth, are personified: Peace, Quiet, Spare Fast (divine "diet"), "retired Leisure," and finally the Cherub Contemplation (see Dürer).

With the appearance of the nightingale a sudden metamorphosis occurs—the poet assumes the role of Melancholy. He goes walking abroad, "to behold the wandering moon,/Like one that had been led astray/Through the heaven's wide pathless way." Now, it is the moon that has lost her way; but the thinker's mind no less begins to be identified with the external vessels of thought, the moon included. Throughout the remainder of this poem there is a constant intercourse between mind and nature, or, as Heidegger puts it in *What is Called Thinking?* the thinker's "nature"—his "surround"—is "thought-provoking." He allows different scenes to be fully around him, and they "call" to his mind. One reason this invocation to thought is powerful is that Milton conveys its mentality by interweaving ancient myths—these, we know, are made up by the mind speaking; thought encompasses stories "where more is meant than meets the ear."

The thinker walks through the night, and when morning comes Milton in a few lines calls up the story of Tithonus, Aurora, and the son of Aeolus. This "Attic boy" is Cephalus, the brain, that which wakes up. Aurora herself wakes the world to an almost painful sensitivity of perception. Thus:

> [She comes] Not tricked and frounced as she was wont,
>   With the Attic boy to hunt,
> But kerchiefed in a comely cloud,
> While rocking winds are piping loud,
> Or ushered with a shower still,
> When the gust hath blown his fill,
> Ending on the rustling leaves,
> With minute drops from off the eaves.

The thinker's perceptual refreshment needs to be more actively protected, however, and as the sun climbs in the sky the poet retreats to "arched walks of twilight groves," lies down next to a murmuring stream, retreats from "day's garish eye." He undergoes a new sort of falling asleep; sleep for him is "dewey-feathered."

> And [he prays Melancholy] let some strange mysterious dream
> Wave at his wings in airy stream,
> Of lively portraiture displayed,
> Softly on my eyelids laid.
> And as I wake, sweet music breathe
> Above, about, or underneath,

> Sent by some spirit to mortals good,
> Or the unseen genius of the wood.

By this point in the poem time, chronological and historical time, has evanesced. The thinker grows old in the course of twenty-one lines, and the poem ends in a prayer that, schooled in ecstatic dissolution, his words will at last become "spells" and his "old experience" will "attain / To something like prophetic strain." Then, with a sudden return to the picturesque, Milton one last time recalls the magic words of Christopher Marlowe:

> These pleasures Melancholy give,
> And I with thee will choose to live.

The picture frame has detached the vision from things; the poem floats away, its iconic detachment virtually perfect.

If *Il Penseroso* exemplifies the lyric play and final closure of an insistently prophetic iconography, the picture of the prophetic strain, and if in vastly expanded ways *Paradise Regained* and *Paradise Lost* carry the iconography of Satan's mind into a picture of place, we say readily that Milton in all these cases has constructed poetry to yield what one might call portraits of thought. In Satan's case the iconicity is doubled, as I have suggested. His thinking is obsessive from beginning to end, but that obsession is torturously reinforced by virtue of the fact that Satan has come to believe that his thought is solely "its own place." The mind has become for him a monstrous figure of speech from whose spiraling self-involvement and solipsism there is no escape, because he has concretized or reified the flux of mental life in terms of a room walled everywhere with mirrors. His mind cannot stand outside of its place, because it has conceived itself to be merely place, whose mirrors serve only to increase the sense of hopeless distance and separation from the world. Satan is bound on a wheel of false self-representation.

Thought in Action

Milton's noetic procedures in *Paradise Lost* and *Paradise Regained* establish the extreme situation for the tragedy of mind. We can look elsewhere for the opposite, comedic extreme, as exemplified in Cervantes. *The Adventures of Don Quixote* is not the only example of the countercurrent to Faustian excess in the long history of the novel. However, outside of the drama, it remains the significant contrast to Milton. The conversations between Don Quixote and Sancho Panza give rise to these differences for the whole subsequent tradition of the novel and contrast the Satanic iconography of suffering thought with a model of thought in action. The novel allows such scope for action in its emotive shaping that, for example, Joyce can effectively have Stephen Daedalus speak of his own "mind when wearied of its search," or of "his mind, in the vesture of a doubting monk." These Joycean personifications belong partly to the lyric metamorphic world of Milton's diptych and partly to realistic fiction, to its direct statement of thought-processes. Milton, so much earlier in time, had perceived the flux of mind to be capable of iconic rendering, through slight modifications and bendings of the device of personification. In a certain sense, the work of Cervantes had already begun to undo the medieval romantic notion that the mind can be expressed through personification.[1]

The first great novel comes into view as *Don Quixote* breaks down the mirrors of the rooms of mind, at which point the mind as merely its own place ceases all pretension to be the governing model for the central role of thinking in human affairs. Quixote is especially concerned with mirrors and doubles, while his story may be read, in the large, as his encounter with the magic enchantments of every sort of mirror effect. He is able to pass all his friends and foes alike through the looking-glass, and can bring them back from that upside-down land at a moment's notice—or rather, at any moment when his thoughts take an odd realistic turn. As we know, these realistic turns away from enchantment occur partly because of the pressure of real events, knocks and falls, buffets and buckings. They also occur because Sancho Panza abets the reality principle. If Quixote thinks from the sky down, Sancho thinks from the ground up.

Where Quixote and Sancho meet is in a certain kind of animation, the spiritedness of their conversations. As they talk, and often debate vigorously, they enlarge the field of each other's thoughts. No thought on either side goes unchecked or uncritiqued. By mainly courteous disagreement, most courteous when most sharply in conflict, they gradually establish an area of free play, where thoughts are set free for us the readers to ponder. Whereas Satan would control us and his victims by the power of his conclusions, these two mortals in essence give up all final control, even though each strives heartily to maintain mastery for the brief time of "saying his say."[2] Thought here, then, is not entrapped in its own potential for iconic imprisonment. If anything, the conversations between Knight and Squire spiral outward.

Remarkably, such conversations spin out in the light of common day from twin starting points that show an equal degree of obsession on both sides. The Don's obsessive drive to reinstate the institutions of chivalry, including its magic, its enchantments and disenchantments—all its charms, in short—still counts as one of the great monuments of compulsion. Equally, Sancho's desire to possess worldly comfort and power is every bit as extreme in its opposite earthbound fashion. The final result of the conversations is that to a degree each unwinds the coil of the other's spiral, so that effectively in Part II Don Quixote becomes almost secondary, almost squirelike, in relation to Sancho's dream of becoming Governor of an island. Each partner brings the other into a more subtle and more trustingly tangible relation to the real world of a very real Spain, a Spain Cervantes depicts with such precision that it becomes a magic landscape with universal appeal to readers of all nations.

Kafka suggested in one of his parables, "The Truth about Sancho Panza," that Quixote was Sancho's demon (*seinen Teufel*), a devil first rising from Sancho's omnivorous readings of old romances and then exorcised when, as a demon now named Don Quixote, he adventures freely forth in the maddest, albeit quite harmless, ways. Sancho delights in these exploits, and as a free man follows them happily to the end of his days. Kafka holds us suspended; we cannot tell how real or unreal this pursuit is. But it happens.

What is happening is the liberation from a single-pathed monomania, a liberation occurring because the action of each Quixotic adventure carries with it its own commentary. Always a two-sided commentary, shared in equal partnership by the two equal-unequal friends, each conversation expands upon the possible meanings any adventure may have. No adventure is permitted to get stuck in a single-sided path of interpretation.

Thought emerges in the conversational space established between the two men. Thought is never iconically reduced, although it may be dealing with potential obsessions, such as a belief that windmills are enemy giants. The conversation undoes Quixote's illusion to a degree, but never fully and definitively. Hence there is always a residue of idealism left free on the Knight's side, while a similar process allows a residue of sense and creatural wisdom to remain when Sancho has been rebuked for his lack of vision. These residues are the traces of the thought and thinking that Cervantes has brought to life, has set free from any iconic entrapment such as Satan's ruminations led him to, blocking any twin-sided, dialogical escape. The freedom from a blocking iconicity is even greater, indeed, when Quixote and Sancho exchange roles, the former speaking for earthy realism, the latter speaking for dubious yet useful proverbial wisdom. Finally, there is no role in the dialogue that cannot be assumed by either party. Thought is set free to come into their world, as they speak.

The situation of the pair is unusual enough—they come to the reader as participants in what may be the most powerful love story in all literature. Their dialogue is endlessly interactive, and yet no less forgiving and at the same time oddly abrasive, depending on the situation. "Sleep yourself," says the Don, "for you were born to sleep. Or do what you will. I will do what suits my profession best." "Don't be annoyed, good master," replies Sancho. "I didn't mean to make you angry." Or: "I don't know what to think," replied Sancho, "not being so well read as your worship in the errant writings. But, all the same, I'd be prepared to swear that these apparitions here around us are not altogether Catholic." "Catholic! Holy Father!" replied Don Quixote. "How should they be Catholic, if they are all demons . . ." The Don has been caged, but his faith in his own enchantment is complete as a metaphysical conceit, and he is now able sagely to explain his beleaguered situation as a complex result of the craft of various demons—who in fact are ordinary humans, but are transformed in Quixote's vision of things. The wonder is that Sancho both accepts and does not accept the vision of perpetual enchantment. He is aware that any obsession coming from powerful books must have a legitimate magic, in which he is only minimally an adept. The love between the two men arises from Sancho's knowing these limits, both his own and his master's.

Similarly, Don Quixote opens himself to appreciating his squire, with the result that on both sides a special element enters the process by which their conversations generate thought and lively cognition. For the counterchecking of the one by the other pulls the discussion away from any fixed iconic emblems by which the thought of either might become obsessive and isolated from reality. Their situations now enter time and the field of a historical moment, a moment wherein all iconicity is subject to the critique of temporal change. As Ortega y Gasset put it—the same Ortega who first showed the binary, interactive cooperation of Knight and Squire, in his *Meditations on Quixote*—"every concept claiming to represent human reality carries a date inside or, which is the same, every concept referring to specifically human life is a function of historical time."[3] From this requirement of historical embeddedness follows the second Ortegan requirement, an *unfixing* of concepts and images. "Whoever aspires to understand man—that eternal tramp, a thing essentially *on the road*—must throw overboard all immobile concepts and learn to think in ever-shifting terms."

Such is the radically new effect of the Quixotic narrative: what I am calling *conversation* liberates mobile concepts and prevents the great pair from becoming victims of the immobility of the solipsistic icon, which so traps Satan, the monomaniacal thinker who has dug his own hole and cannot climb out.

Finally Cervantes sets the thought-space entirely free of literal dependence upon the fixity of the authoritative "signed" letter: with the onset of Part II and the appearance of a false continuation of Part I, the whole saga of Don Quixote is relativized to an exquisite degree. It is no longer positively possible to say that any circumstances of the *Life* count as genuine, since only their arrangement is what is genuine. Avellaneda's spurious continuation serves one main purpose for us the readers: it forces us to think through what Quixote has all along been thinking through, the truth of his existence as a knight errant. This sort of thinking the novel is perfectly suited to advance, because this literary form, as Edward Said remarked, "shows a desire (almost the principal action of many novels) to turn the text back, if not directly into speech, then at least into circumstantial, as opposed to meditative, duration."[4] The text of the novel is a real event, whose circumstance is its deep textuality, so that, as with the *Quixote*, it can be doubled by an Avellaneda, who then becomes a character in the infolding of the doubled text. Through the foliation of such textual play, the Quixotic genre acquires a feel and facticity of historical momentousness. Mobile concepts take over from the fixed icons of the most ancient myths and legends, from a story such as the loss of Paradise.

If we ask how the contrast between Milton and Cervantes is possible, it is not sufficient to mention their difference of genre as a simple explanation. Rather, the final differentiation has to do with time and their chosen genres. Milton's epic looks back, and in Satan's case it looks back to an original fall from which there could be no logical escape: he could not be the first son, hence he would be damned as second. His fate is sealed by logic and is timeless. Quixote, by contrast, lives in a present Spain and his fate is sealed by his own metaphysical imagination. This fantastic valor leads him to adopt a secondary fate, that of Sancho Panza, which is always circling in a planetary motion around the Don's primary obsession, always deflecting it downward to a real world and away from the private mind of a Satanic monomania. The more fantastic the adventures, the closer to the actual the Don moves—he would attack the lions in Part II, but they are so tired of this game of being show animals that they turn their backsides on him, and go to sleep. Such is the reality of bearding the lion.

It is in this play of two variant imaginations, Quixote's and Sancho's, that thinking can begin as a process. In this space thinking escapes fixation. In this space it is always testing the unreal limits of logic and rational system (whose archetype here is chivalry or the governorship of an island).

The contrast between Milton and Cervantes, broadly and roughly drawn, is a contrast between the presentation of the idea of two iconic frames of reference. Milton invents a Satan who cannot exist in conversation, but only as a powerful rhetorical manipulator. He ends in dialogue with himself, that is, finally, with no one outside the place of his own mind. Quixote knows no such entrapment; his reading of books opens him to a reading of all humanity, so that he becomes what Unamuno called "a sublime madman," great because the root of the madness was, as Unamuno says, "the inextinguishable longing to survive, a source of the most extravagant follies as well as of the most heroic acts."[5] Such madness puts Quixote in touch with himself and his book-turned mind, with his displaced sense of the actual circumstances of his adventuring life, and above all with Sancho, the Sancho who has the wisdom to seek whatever enjoyment and faith is possible in this world. In this connection to actual life, to Sancho's life, to his own idealized phantasmagoria of life, Quixote sets up the conditions for a representation of the full range of a mind, a double mind, that can be fully alive to all the possibilities of thinking. Long as the story of the great pair is, the mental scene changes like Shakespeare's theatrical setting, unexpectedly from moment to moment, the "swift scene" flying "in motion of celerity as swift as thought."

At this juncture one can hardly help asking what is the most developed instance of a verbal art where there is a merging of myth and its timeless forms, on the one side, and the novel with its mobile historical forms on the other. Where is the combination of the two? Or, putting it another way, what is the twentieth-century destiny of the twin streams of poetic art, the Miltonic and the Cervantean? If there could be a merging, where would it lie? Surely, in some kind of history; but also, in some kind of radically reductive *mythos*, such as Satan's. A final rehearsal of the differences may reveal what is not quite unexpected.

The story of Satan's mind and its own place provides an iconography and a legend of the fixed symbol, the obsessively fixated terms by which thinking is bound to the wheel of its self-involvement. This yields allegory, in sum. The mind is compartmentalized space, a one-place that fractures always into other, repeating one-places. Unlike this process, the "mind" of the novel has many places, its symbols are mobile. As the archetypal parable of the Bakhtinian heteroglossia, the novel provides what was missing from the radical mythos—humor.

The Play of Humor

Let us now jump ahead to our own epoch. Freud appears and frames the ancient question of humor in a theoretical context. He is one descendant of a marriage of the two modes of narration. For a developed theory of symbol and its relation to all levels of mind, including the unconscious, there must be some merging or combining of these hypothetical Miltonic and Cervantean strains. Freud and his followers early developed the lexicon of fixed Freudian symbols, but such a repertory would provide only the crudest psychology were it not crosscut by an increasingly subtle theory of the mobility of symbols. Ortega's man-on-the-road is the creature of this mobility; his pilgrimage is one of endless dis-placement, the very process by which fantasy, wit, and the dream-work proceed to undo the fixed allegorical system. The novel in effect establishes movements of displacement, condensation, negation, undoing, and so on, in order to prevent any simplistic but complicated allegorical structure from becoming the preferred image of the mind's complete workings. Above all the novel allows for the free play of wit, which may well be subversive because it critiques fanaticism. Furthermore, the Cervantean novel allows for the play of humor and forgiveness in the presentation of what will be allowed to count as thought, to count as thinking.

Humor is a particular response to the upsets and setbacks of history. In his 1927 article "Humor," Freud suggested that humor comes into play when the superego abandons its harshly censorious role and instead takes a forgiving view of one's errors of behavior. For the Cervantean world of Quixote and his partner there is a double system of humor. The Don can laugh forgivingly at the simplicity of Sancho and his philosophy of comfort; but then, in turn, Sancho can censor, but forgive, the extremities of fantasy that people the Don's world with too many ideal objects and aspirations. Censor and forgiver combine in one person, on both sides of the pairing. Thus the "conversation" is enriched and is enabled to break away from the narrowness of any fixating repertory of mental symbols—from the Freudian symbols of the Quixotic world of chivalry and Panza's world of creatural reality. Where there can be little comedy in Milton, there is comedy everywhere here. In the combination of Miltonic and Cervantean elements, broadly dispersed through Freudian discourse, we find that myth and novelistic narration align themselves in a new, more modern combination in the Freudian iconography of thought and mental dynamics. Humor allows a completely free play to symbolic images of the endlessly varied vicissitudes of the instincts, their diversions, their conversions, their punning and allusive metamorphoses—in short, the language of fantasy and dream.

By the beginning of the seventeenth century there was a need for Quixotic conversation, as in the twentieth there has been a need for Freudian discourse. Humor plays a major role in the liberation of word play as the key to the involutions of the psyche. Our ever-increasing sense that language dominates thought is not necessarily the last word. However, what does emerge from the above consideration is some idea that there had once been a time when language, thought, and action were more unified than we find them to be in the Quixote. As Lukacs, Bakhtin, and other students of the novel have noted, Quixote's quest and Sancho's counterquest allow fiction to separate the hero from what Bakhtin calls a new world defined by its "immensely growing real material contact," a new world of technological development. But as the hero is distinguished and separated from this world, he is joined in struggle with it. A disunity of mind and action ensues, a disunity whose opposite we must seek in early classic epic. For in the *Odyssey* and *Iliad* thought and action interconnect more fully and easily. There is struggle, but with Odysseus the struggle is merely to find scenes where his mind can flourish as the immediate spring of action. The play of the epic is the demonstration that thought instantly begets the possibility of action. It is this openness between thought and action that eventually disappears, so that Milton's antihero, Satan, finds himself in a realm of purely isolated thought, where there is no opening to action. Hence the latest of the great epics reverses the assumption of the earliest, namely that action breeds and interacts directly with thought. It is the somewhat earlier *Quixote* (though it too belongs to the seventeenth century) that analyzes the role of action and thought in the chivalric romances, those whirling narratives that mark a decline of original epic clarity. And finally Quixote and Sancho ask the most puzzling modern question: Is there any sure guarantee that thought and action will ever again harmonize, after the advent of technological enhancements of individual human powers? Thereafter, it would appear, thought stands in need of psychoanalysis. Thought awaits the coming of that scientific movement, a movement powerfully dependent upon all the post-Quixotic transformations of the novel in all its forms.

3. The Distractions of Wit in the English Renaissance

In a negative sense, distraction means roughly the opposite of mental concentration. The distracted mind cannot concentrate on some given task long enough for it to be accomplished. In a way, distraction is not hard to describe. Either the task breaks down into too many disparate problems, or external pressures bear upon the mind working—the promises of reward or success are too insistent, or too much speed is demanded by our employers—so that we want to finish the job prematurely, or some other itch trips a mental process whereby we lose power to attend steadily to our object. Distraction is a familiar phenomenon to anyone living in a modern city. Siegfried Kracauer observed that going to movie palaces in the 1920s was part of a "cult of distraction" (*Zerstreuung*), particularly for women, in European cities. In 1948 Auden won a Pulitzer Prize for his *Age of Anxiety*, which named the modern mode of a distracting "fear without an object." Harold Bloom has emphasized the role of anxiety in the transmission of literary culture. In both life and literature there is every reason to suppose that distraction remains, now as before, very much with us.

As a psychological term the English word "distraction" dates from the late sixteenth century. Though rather late in its noun-form, the word has rich latinate overtones that come through from its earlier common use as both verb and adjective. The old fourteenth-century adjectival form is the word "distract," with its modification "distraught," which we can find in Gower's *Confessio*

Amantis (1393) and which we still use. The semantic scope of the term "distraction" is wide, ranging from the gentle French usage, *se distraire*, to be relaxed, amused, and set at ease, through a middle ground where it suggests the divided attention of the mind, to a dark and fearful connotation of dismemberment. The first definition given in the Oxford English Dictionary for the archaic adjective "distract" reads thus: "Torn or drawn asunder, divided, separated; scattered; torn to pieces," and the exemplary usage comes from John of Trevisa, in 1398. (Incidentally, Trevisa was expelled from Oxford in 1379 for "unworthiness.") Obviously, one can be pulled to pieces mentally as well as physically, either gently, or under the normal pressures of life, or savagely.

Between the two extremes distraction expresses a variety of meanings. In 1380 Wyclif uses the verb to imply a deviation from a right line of conduct: "We shulden be war to kepe hem [the Christian rules of life] soundeli, for bodili thingis distracteth men to kepe hem right." The Apostle Paul, in First Corinthians, as translated in the King James Bible, urges the true believer to "attend upon the Lord without distraction." We still have this common understanding of the term, and it contrasts with the power of attending directly and wholeheartedly to solving the problem at hand. One disturbing tendency of the mind is to slip from its determined focus. No fact of nature or life is more certain than that distraction is always just around the bend in the river.

Focusing on the distractions of wit in the Renaissance is useful since we need to account for one of the most powerful traits of English literature in that period—the capacity to live with a wayward mind and its ambiguous means of showing itself. The distraught, troubled mind ("troubled mind" occurs in *The Steel Glass* of the Elizabethan George Gascoigne) appears sometimes bemused, sometimes confused and perplexed, divided and rent, even deranged, but whatever its manifestation it is not hard to find in English Renaissance literature. Yet this distractedness does not prevent poets from somehow maintaining a supreme ease and power in their work.

Let us approach the topic from two points of view: the intellectual and linguistic conditions of authorship and the internal formal properties of aesthetic objects, in this case various kinds of poetic work.

As the City of London—the English scene of wit-work—expanded in power and influence, it became the training ground for a new war of nerves. London, as a contemporary said, was "the third university." Its businesses developed that special anxiety we associate with the monetary language of profit and investment and competition, the refined art of undercutting and outproducing the other fellow in the same line of commerce. Monopolies sprouted. With this busy-ness went a collateral method of driving men mad, the law, with its endless litigation. Donne, in *Satire 2*, cursed "the vast reach of the huge statute laws," and their "words, words,

> which would tear
> The tender labyrinth of a soft maid's ear,
> More, more, than ten Sclavonians scolding, more
> Than when winds in our ruined abbeys roar. (58–60)

The law has the inherent power to complicate disputes and multiply distinctions. It would be hard to estimate the degree to which common parlance is enriched, or transformed, by legal practices, but, in any event, the changes were effected by what Donne called "words, words."

Lawyers were singularly well educated at that time. Yet they were only one group sharing in a larger movement toward wider and more useful, less scholastic, education. They were, in a way, simply the most organized of the University Wits. As a tribe the University Wits went to Oxford or Cambridge, studied a bit, or a lot, and then at the appointed time came to London, to make their fortunes. Those afflicted by the *cacoethes scribendi* would try hard to publish a saleable work, or sell it one way or another. If a literary type happened by luck to meet up with the lawyers, as he could hardly fail to do, his task would take on new and fantastically complicated form. The lawyer helped to create a fresh market for verbal legerdemain, for witty intricacy. It has been argued, for example, that *Troilus and Cressida* is "difficult" to the point of inscrutability, because it was written for the Inns of Court men. Linguistic matters in such a context could not help becoming complex, and such complexity arises out of the burden of the law, which is to create arguments and, in a sense, foment divisions. Because it is the law, the form of its activities takes the shape of an exceedingly complicated language-game, the game of legal dispute. Common law, Sir Edward Coke's sacred domain, depends upon "record," that is, it is case law and builds on a language of special wordings, the wordings of previous cases. Law required verbal virtuosity and technical learnedness.

It is noteworthy how many of the plays, both comic and tragic as well as historical, find the armature of plots in some legal argument. Plays like *The Alchemist* and *Volpone* positively display their legalistic foundations, but the law is active in a majority of plays of this period, of whatever kind. This reflects upon the high degree to which the protection of property and person was subject to the superordinate language-game known as "going to law." This language-game, by definition, is based on the just purpose of reparation, but in practice litigation puts the society precisely under the strain of what I have been calling distraction. Law cases are fought in the adversarial mode.

In general, the adversarial behavior of Donne's "litigious men" finds a favorable climate in a period of increasing individualistic competition which, in turn, can be seen as a struggle to acquire better control over "the language." Ben Jonson, who accused Shakespeare of failing to wield the blue pencil, irresistibly fell into more than one page of logorrhea. Maintaining decorum, he did, however, impart his excesses to his most excessive characters, such as Sir Epicure Mammon.

The new masters of the quibble appear fully distracted by their own learning. Only a few, Marlowe the most metaphysical, Nashe the wittiest and most ironical, could manage to control their insanely inkhorn savvy. When it was all over, Robert Burton looked back with dismal humor, every bit as wild in the eye as any of his predecessors, and summed up an almost bygone age of university wit, knitting together one of the maddest and most perfectly paranoid, obsessively organized, etceterative assaults on the feeble human powers of concentration ever attempted, the *Anatomy of Melancholy.*

It seems important that a great city played the major role in the urgent drama of a new literary form, the free-formed prose works of the period. The University Wits were verbal technocrats armed to the teeth with intellectual weaponry. They set out to carve, or should we say blow, their way to fame and if possible fortune. There before their gluttonous eyes sat London, the big apple. To tire of London, as Dr. Johnson was to say, would be to tire of life. London's hunger for talent and brilliance, coupled with a similar appetite at the royal and aristocratic court, was no doubt balanced by the writer's hunger for civic and courtly applause and reward. The natural target was the theater, where fame and fortune met.

To the call of this brutally competitive, restless life, the poets responded in various ways. Marlowe became involved with the secret police, but before that miserable saga was over he somehow managed to encompass the whole domain of University Wit in a series of epoch-making dramas—his wit, like Milton's, described its own universe. Shakespeare accepted conditions as they were and by dint of his talents and his forensic combativeness thrived as actor, writer, and producer. Jonson, who really knew the city, became the compulsive master-builder, the complete city-poet.

Playwrights were perhaps the most necessarily distraught of all as they struggled to meet deadlines and to keep up with the troubled times in their choice of dramatic theme. Notably, the pressure of deadlines was so great that multiple-author collaboration was the only way a theater company could keep up with the demand for new plays. For "plays," what a ludicrous irony! Theater people could testify to the painful, last-minute confusion of three or even four authors stitching together a play from bits and pieces of old scripts that had been stuffed away in the theater files, no doubt crumpled, smudged, and hardly legible. The script written, the play had still to be produced to please that most relentless of all human institutions, the audience.

Poetic invention kept pace with the need for new forms of popular appeal. To harness his imperial thoughts and to give them speed and power in expression, Marlowe invented his "mighty line," which Chapman, Tourneur, and others carried still further into the free realms of hyperbole. Perhaps it was in reaction against the Marlovian method of tremendous verbal speed that Webster, Middleton, and Marston attempted a terse, austere poetic mode. Yet Webster's most powerful scenes include the violent madhouse of *The Duchess of Malfi*. *The Malcontent*, with an induction by Webster which talks of ear-cropping, presents the archetypal distracted man, Malevole, of whom we learn that "the elements struggle within him; his own soul is at variance within herself; his speech is halter-worthy at all hours" (I, ii, 34–37). *Hamlet* is the greater study of this inner variance. A hectic, contagious overgrowth of good and bad conscious afflicts other characters in *Hamlet* besides the hero: both Claudius and the Queen are increasingly distraught, as is Ophelia, while the comedy, or black humor, of distraction weighs heavily in the portrait of Polonius, whose very rhythms at times are distracted. For example, "Tis true, tis pity . . . and pity tis, tis true." Even the galant Osric cannot put his bonnet to its right use. Such creations indicate that the melancholy mind, alienated from reality even to the point of schizoid madness, is an absolutely central Shakespearean theme.

Turning to the nondramatic forms of literature, we find that these might seek support in the institutions of patronage, that is, in the ambivalent system. Patronage could mean strategic abasement and flattery, as in *Timon of Athens*. Dr. Johnson's letter to Lord Chesterfield is not the first expression of the poet's deep separation from his patron. Rather it rings the death-knell of the old order, whose ambivalence darkens almost every letter of dedication in the Renaissance period. These letters of dedication express the strain the poet felt when he had to write *his* poem, yet at the same time please his scarcely accessible patron. Scholars have shown both sides of the picture: intellectual repose of the "great house" tradition on the one side, and anxiety deterrent to the free play of poetic imagination on the other. The pressure would be to support the aristocratic establishment. A certain distraction, or a measure of intellectual strain, would seem to be betrayed by the excessively encomiast tone of the letters, or of dedicatory poems. Perhaps then, as now, the relation of poet to patron was a complex one, and it remains hard to assess just how great a degree of distractedness accompanied the acquisition of a strong patron.

A much larger context for stresses in poetic thought during the Renaissance period was the recurrence of overt, or suppressed, civil strife, including the use of political informers. Some poets, such as Marlowe, had a clear link with secret spy activities. Others, among them George Gascoigne and Philip Sidney in the Elizabethan period and Richard Lovelace and John Suckling in the Stuart period, went off soldiering in the wars. They engaged in a persistent, Europe-wide civil strife, which finally, as in the English Civil War, came home to be fought on native soil. The refrain of a Gascoigne or a Lovelace is that permanent affection is not possible for the soldier-servant, whose seriocomic displacements are classically set forth in Nashe's *Unfortunate Traveller*. The debate over the primacy of the two professions, arms and letters, is indeed Quixotic. When the English Civil War finally broke upon "a splintering world of contending absolutes" (Danby's phrase), the country at large was driven to distraction. Andrew Marvell caught the full pathos of this internecine conflict, which showed "a cause too good to have been fought for." The Civil War was a massive break-up, wrought upon a whole people, whose final recourse was to accept (perhaps fortunately) the single guidance of one mind, Cromwell. Even Cromwell avowed that no man could be certain what to think, when general uncertainty was the main fact of life.

The tensions of war, declared and undeclared, had for the Renaissance an even more fearful analogue in the recurrence of the plague. This scourge is, I think, the ultimate instance of the powers of distraction. F. P. Wilson reminds us that "Elizabethan London was seldom quite free of the plague. The four years from 1597 to 1600 were commonly supposed to have been 'clear,' yet 48 plague-deaths were recorded in 1597, 18 in 1598, 16 in 1599, and 4 in 1600."[1] Quiet times. Then in 1603 (the year of Elizabeth's death and James the First's accession) the bubonic plague struck with a forgotten fury: between August and September of that year no fewer than 1,700 people died of the plague every week in London. As cold weather came the ravage lessened, and by October deaths fell below a thousand a week. Thus the black death stalked London's narrow streets by day and by night. What is modern is that the losses of life were *recorded*, in weekly "plague bills." When plague struck again in 1625 (the year of Charles the First's accession), Wilson estimated from such records that of London's population of more than 300,000, "at least one sixth . . . had perished."

Literary life was directly affected by the plague, like other urban activities. Shakespeare took time off from theater work, and for a patron wrote his two narrative poems, which were published in 1593 and 1594. What else did he do? We can only guess. Nashe wrote *Summer's Last Will and Testament*, a dramatic threnody on the death of the comic spirit, as "brightness falls from the air." Thomas Dekker and others practiced a new branch of journalism, the plague-pamphlets. When Donne published his *Anatomy of the World* in 1611, he was able to conceive the whole metaphysical picture of the sundered universe under the emblematic guise of a plaguelike cosmic sickness of the world. What we cannot tell, from these and other examples, is whether the plague itself, or some *idea* of the plague, came first in these visions of the decay of the world. Was the apocalypse real, or was it a mode of self-fulfilling prophecy? It seems clear that the plague year is an experience of ultimate, total distraction, in the original sense of the word. If man is torn apart, the social fabric rent, philosophy put all in doubt, sects allowed to dissect each other, communions left to blow about on the dust heap of wornout religions, this absolute assault upon the body politic finds its physical analogue and ominous harbinger in the actual bubonic plague. The plague was real, and it was terrifying, because inexplicable. (It may be an accident, but if so surely a significant one, that Boccaccio had framed his "modern" work, *The Decameron*, as the yield of a strategic retreat from the plague.)

If, then, we had to summarize the various aspects of "the distracted globe" of Renaissance letters, we should have to say that during that period authors lived with the fear of all things coming apart and the hyperexcited hope that no such thing would happen. For the pain of such dissolution there were few effective anesthetics, physical or spiritual. There were few real anodynes and little mental therapy, although the placebo of an earlier Catholic "cure of souls" still worked beneath the surface of English religious life.

What made it possible for authors to endure their own distraction without totally falling to pieces? We have to assume that Renaissance man knew an opposing wholeness of his body with an unimaginable intensity. Pain made him fully aware of health, of wholeness and ease, of pleasure when it came. On a corporate scale the same assumption must also pertain. The Tudor body politic suffered from all sorts of divisive pressures, both internal and external. Yet it remained during a brief and extraordinary period of English life a *body*, an organism which could seek its own health, as well as wealth. London, the center and capital city of the realm, was, as European capitals went, inordinately populous and large, given the size and population of the country. But London was then, as now, a fairly livable city. It permitted a community of arts and letters such as had not existed since the Athens of the fifth century. Clubs were not yet coffee houses, let alone private, alienating gatherings of exclusive men. There was, we have to believe, a greater closeness and communal warmth than during prior or subsequent periods. At the same time overcrowding began. Coaches congested the city's inadequate thoroughfares. Housing was either miserably dense, or too expensive. Sewerage and garbage disposal problems remind one of today's urban crises. Yet there was the possibility of a communal celebration of life.

Coleridge suggests how such a sense of community found its way into literature. He claimed that the best writers discovered what he called "method," by which he meant an approach to life quite opposed to the rigid application of Cartesian system. He used the term Method to mean "an intellectual or mental initiative" whereby "things the most remote and diverse in time, place, and outward circumstance, are brought into mental contiguity and succession, the more striking as the less expected." This might be a rewrite of Dr. Johnson's "metaphysical wit," but Coleridge's favorite example was Shakespeare (though he greatly admired Donne). This Shakespeare finds a way of living with distractions, rather than suppressing them through the tyranny of artificial rules. The more open he is to life's troubles and diversions, the more he achieves his natural decorum. Like Donne, Shakespeare keeps changing metaphors in midstream. Yet in the lyric poem, as in the high-speed montage of *Antony and Cleopatra* or the weird condensations in *Macbeth*, the poet avoids aesthetic disarray. Economy of line, in short, comes not from the stubborn blockage of the forces of distraction. It comes from exploiting these forces in what later poets were to understand as "organic" forms. As I. A. Richards once remarked, referring to cybernetics, "Two channels are better than one." This is the Renaissance view of the way round and through distraction. As we shall see, literary forms were invented and perfected that would permit the poet to go through distraction, rather than pretend that it did not exist.

Perhaps the most striking Renaissance literary device for handling distraction by means of semiotic *laissez-faire* is the essay. Montaigne effectively invents, and Bacon adapts, this free form, and both authors are thus enabled to control the opposed pulls of focus and diffusion. Bacon limits Montaigne's studied indirection, but both authors make no attempt to suppress distraction. Rather they are able to *express* its exuberance, Montaigne at length (increasingly as he moved into Book 3 of his *Essays*), Bacon always in the most economical and brief compass. Of Bacon's method of "partition" Brian Vickers observes: "He avoided its potential weakness—

rigidity, mechanical symmetry—exploited and even improved on its known virtues both in practice and theory, constantly embodying its form and function in organic imagery."[2] The essay raises most of the key questions regarding the literary history of the divided, wayward mind. Montaigne put it well when he said: "If I could make decisions, I would not write essays."

If we turn to the most powerfully condensed poetry of the age, that of Donne and his "strong line" contemporaries, we find an intensity which is matched by a complementary acceptance of fragmentation. These metaphysical poets (most of them qualify as University Wits) betray a revealing inclination toward a poetic of bits and pieces, which is surefooted in satire and invective. Today one can hardly *begin* to follow the thread of a Donne satire, so strenuous and detailed will be its projection of the fragments of a pressured civic life. Ben Jonson writes metaphysical verse, with neoclassic elegance, but also writes metaphysical farce, which presses into oneness more material than a play can easily afford to hold. Jonson's plays aggress against their own superflux of ideas and images, and for that reason remain difficult to perform, even to read. The lesser satires of Hall and Marston formally resemble the plague-bill lists, recounting the separate deaths of human spirit that accompany the emergence of new, competitive ways of London life.

It was becoming clear to writers that as the city grew more crowded, its internal dangers of infection increased; even outside the medical sphere its cultural conflicts were heightened by urban congestion. Satire was best fitted to encounter this congestion. Satire returned to expansive Juvenalian and Menippean forms, most memorably with Burton, whose *Anatomy of Melancholy* splayed out a delirious "civil wilderness" of competing allusions all over the interminable street-map of its encyclopedic body. The *satura*, since Juvenal at least, had always been able to contain the multitude of conflicting attitudes any great city requires its citizens to perceive. Complementary to the *satura* of satire is the equally important, equally maddening twist of the metaphysical conceit which, while projecting an appearance of logical sequence, disperses its thought through devices we might imagine derived from the new science of map-making. Here the term "projection" is a technical term. By means of a topographic projection the "flat map," as Donne called his own body, tortures the sphere, to make it projectively flat. (As cosmographers have known since the Renaissance, one can accurately project either the size of the sphere or the shape of the topographic area upon the sphere, but one cannot accurately project both size and shape at once.) Now, while the conceits of the Metaphysicals may have to be logical distortions, they nonetheless permit the projective mapping of ideas and emotions. The Metaphysicals could think about the unthinkable.

The most unthinkable of all subjects is God, and it is not surprising that the metaphysical functions of prose are most elaborately developed in the sermons of the time. Here the standard technique of divisions upon a text leads both Donne and Andrewes, in their expansive and restrictive ways, respectively, to refine the most extreme of all distracted arts—the allusion. Allusions carry the mind from one context to another, more remote one. Because allusions are intertextual, they permit a return of mind as well as an excursion. The mind goes out from the New Testament source to the Old Testament analogue, and then comes back again to the New. In a way this means a transtextual movement as well: from the present (inhering in the New Law) to the past (inhering in the Old). Andrewes in particular seems to have been fascinated by the mental speed required by such textual interplay. For him Biblical allusions are like "the steps of their faith . . . coming such a journey, at such a time, with such speed" (Sermon of Dec. 25, 1622). This journeying is not a detached exercise of pedantry. It roots the listener in the present moment of the sermon and its time and place—I have been quoting from the famed Journey of the Magi sermon, for Christmas Day, 1622. No doubt congregations slept and wandered off into daydream as these clouds of allusions floated by (Donne has a great description of the itch to get away from prayer),[3] but a majority of listeners must have tried to follow the thread of a potentially distracting discourse.

Pastoral poetry, when optimistic, found ways of countering distress by containing it in nostalgic visions of a better life. Comedy and its green and festive world flourished in plays like *Twelfth Night*. Dekker wrote *The Shoemaker's Holiday*, for city folk. Greater pressures gave rise to the new dramatic art of tragi-comedy. But, throughout the period, it was pastoral, most abstractly, that sought to escape the incessant blundering, pain, and competition of city and court life, by recourse to controlled nostalgia. Certain modern scholars have suggested that pastoral had always had its "hard" tradition, and I should agree, but my feeling is that *both* hard and soft pastoral try to handle the world that is too much with us. Typically for its period, *The Shepheardes Calender* balances hard and soft pastoral, as if both types had to be pressed into a complementary relationship. Spenser would make the subject of a whole book on poetic distraction, being our most perfectly wayward poet; yet it seems important that he moves away from the *Ruins of Time*, his early obsession, to the experience of time, his later achievement, as his great work proceeds towards its bittersweet fadeout in Book Six of the *Faerie Queene* and the enigma of the *Mutability Cantos*. Pastoral and satire weave intricate melodies through the counterpoint of his epical, syncretist, labyrinthine search for a settled, settling end.

> When I bethinke me on that speech whyleare,
> Of Mutability, and well it way:
> Me seemes, that though she all unworthy were
> Of the Heav'ns Rule; yet very sooth to say
> In all things else she beares the greatest sway.
> Which makes me loath this state of life so tickle,
> And love of things so vaine to cast away;
> Whose flowring pride, so fading and so fickle,
> Short Time shall soon cut down with his consuming sickle.

> Then gin I thinke on that which Nature sayd,
> Of that same time when no more Change shall be,
> But stedfast rest of all things firmely stayd
> Upon the pillours of Eternity,
> That is contrayr to Mutabilitie:
> For, all that moveth, doth in Change delight:
> But thence-forth all shall rest eternally
> With Him that is the God of Sabbaoth hight:
> Of that great Sabbaoth God, graunt me that Sabaoths sight.

Spencer writes in high, conventionalized style, drawing on the archetypal genres of Western literature, looking back to Homer, Virgil, Ovid, and the Bible. At the opposite end of the scale similar attempts to contain the distracting detail are equally apparent. Take the pamphlet. Normally an Elizabethan pamphlet would be a small, unbound treatise on a topic of burning current interest—the perfect form for what Rollins and Baker once called "angry, scurrilous and tedious controversy." When Thomas Nashe and Robert Greene attacked Gabriel Harvey, because Richard Harvey (Gabriel's younger brother) had attacked Greene, all in the course of the pseudonymous Martin Marprelate's attacks on the Anglican Church, pamphleteering scurrility broke out in a late Elizabethan storm. The controversy is well known to Elizabethan scholars. My interest is only in one of its characteristics: its authorial combatants were university men, and they peppered their prose with all the learned pedantry that only inspired, slightly mad mandarins could muster for a war of words. Gabriel Harvey was the master pedant, Thomas Nashe the Nimrod of this clash. Nashe tried to use a perfectly balanced Arabian scimitar, Harvey a massive claymore. Yet even Nashe could not resist a paragraph without an allusion (probably false) to Tiberius Caesar. He defended his own vices by taking the offensive. We have, for example, his lists of neologisms coined (he claimed) by Harvey. He intends it to be an epitome of the wildness of university wit.

The list records a considerable number of words that are alive today, which suggests that the once-extravagant inventions of the University Wits were destined to become the commonplaces of certain modes of modern discourse.

> Conscious mind; canicular tales; egregious an argument (whenas "egregious" is never used in English but in the extreme ill part); ingenuity; jovial mind; valorous authors; inkhorn adventures; inkhorn pads; putative opinions; putative artists; energetical persuasions; rascality; materiality; artificiality; fantasticality; divine entelechy; loud mentery; deceitful perfidy; addicted to theory; the world's great incendiary; sirenized furies; sovereignty immense; abundant cautels; cautelous and adventrous; cordial liquor; Catilinaries and Philippics; perfunctory discourses; David's sweetness Olympic; the Idea high and deep abyss of excellence; the only unicorn of the muses; the Aretinish mountain of huge exaggerations; the gratious law of amnesty; amicable terms; amicable end; effectuate; addouce his melody; Magi; polymechany; extensively employed; precious trainment; novelets; notoriety; negotiation; mechanician.

Nashe adds: "Nor are these all, for every third line hath some of this overracked absonism." Maybe Gabriel Harvey did rack his brains (the expression deserves note), but whether he did or not, it is clear that he, like his attacker and like other great University

Wits, including the greatest of them all, Marlowe, simply "knew too much."

Of all those authors who knew too much, Shakespeare is the most interesting with regard to the management of wayward thought. Among the sources quoted in the OED under our heading, his typical usage is the one most powerfully concentrated on its extremest grimness: for him distraction almost always means madness, nothing more nor less. In *2 Henry IV* he speaks of "a poor mad soul . . . poverty hath distracted her." Elsewhere (the *Lover's Complaint*), the soul is "to every place, and no where fixt, / The mind and sight distractedly commixt." Sonnet 119 speaks of "the distraction of this madding fever." The madness may be only temporary, as in *Antony and Cleopatra:* "Give him no breath, but now make Boote of his distraction" (IV, i, 9). In *Julius Caesar*, the lady "fell distract, And, her attendants absent, swallowed fire" (IV, iii, 155). In *Midsummer Night's Dream* and *The Tempest* we find milder manifestations of a "distracted fear" and Ariel's "distractions" wrought upon the villains. In *Timon* and *Hamlet* distraction always means madness, and in the latter play we get the line "While memory holds a seat in this distracted globe" (I, v, 97). Shakespeare's use of *distraction* is not as deep as his use of *dog* or *drown*, but it is articulate, and it leans to the grim end of the spectrum.

Shakespeare is fascinating because he seems to do things so easily. In his essay on *The Tempest* Henry James depicted Shakespeare the improviser, playing, as evening falls, "for his own ear, his own hand, his own innermost sense, and for the bliss and capacity of his instrument." This romantic vignette of the poet improvising is critical, for it recalls the *extempore* aspect of Shakespearean art, whose extreme haste of production required that for him, as for his contemporaries, style must become, in James's phrase, "the very home of his mind."

The extempore is the momentous, spontaneous method on which the resistance, or successful response, to distractedness depends during this great period of our literature. We cannot otherwise explain how so much of English Renaissance literature achieves a concentration scarcely equalled in the poetry of Pope. Certainly Dryden could not equal it, though he was well aware of it. It seems that the Tudor and Stuart poets controlled mutability by fully accepting it. They understood the passingness of things, yet never lost the desire to form that moving constancy into aesthetic shapes.

Recently it has become clear that one approach to this complementary art is through the concept of the threshold, or liminality, an idea most fully developed in the anthropology of Arnold van Gennep and Victor Turner. Shakespeare's contemporaries studied the liminal conditions of living and perception. Their fixations were stages of controlled passage.[4] The movement of living had to be a crossing, through phases of never-ending initiations.

It would be wrong to move towards the end of this account of distraction and its liminal resolutions without mentioning the most remarkable of all wayward minds in English literary history, John Milton. I have sometimes tried to argue that the Miltonic conception of the Fall is itself a rethinking of inherited fixations, that is, that with him the verticalities of the Fall are translated into a visionary geometry of horizontalities, into a lateral fall. Whatever the case, Milton sends his mind out upon discovery, and develops, partly from necessity, a method for discovering a corresponding poetic line. We know he dictated his largest poem; we do not always notice that thereby he was forced to improvise its wonderfully varied paragraphs. Normally it would be good strategy to show that, along with continuous allusiveness, *digression* in all its varieties is the technique by which literature had always handled distraction when it impinged upon the larger forms, such as epic. Shorter forms too may be thus digressive, *Lycidas* for example. In such a context digression marks a semiotic turbulence at a moment of mental overload. *Paradise Lost* is the more important case. From what we might call a cybernetic point of view, a view much involved with the true reading of Spenser's second Book as well, *Paradise Lost* is an epic written (or dictated) to contain the distractions, not of a university wit merely (which Milton was), but of a universal wit, restless beyond belief. If the University Wits, especially Marlowe, knew too much, then Milton knew even more. Only his strange calm of mind found ways of constraining the terror of the plethoric—not by butting head-on against it, but by yielding to it. Well could Milton write of Satan, "Horror and doubt distract his troubled thoughts." Well could Milton create the epic of the ultimate liminal passage, from eternal paradisal life to the mortal life that we know. He represents in the highest degree the Renaissance capacity to live with the fact of ceaseless passage. He writes a poetry of troubled mind that, by yielding to distraction, enables the poet to concentrate his thoughts. Somewhat in the manner of the High Romantics, the Renaissance poet anticipated naive phenomenology. From this native ground issued a revel of new forms: the dramatic soliloquy, the syncretic epic, the alchemical farce, the essay, the "rhapsody of rags," the lyric monody, the metaphysical conceit.

The history of distraction does not end, as it had not begun, with the Renaissance. Yet finally even distraction had to take a firm grip on itself, to say: No, No more of this, let wit be controlled by will. Augustan restraint set new bounds, but, as we might expect, to no avail. The comedy of manners, the novel, gave gossip a fine literary and dramatic outlet and, not much later in literary history, authors like Swift and Sterne renewed the old, distracted art. The wayward mind could hardly have died an ignominious death, under the Neoclassic lash. It had lived, not wisely, but too well, in the Golden Age. Perhaps Sterne was thinking back, as much to that time as to anything else, when he said, "Digressions, incontestably, are the sunshine." Swift again took the darker Shakespearean view of distraction as madness, but it was still possible for the genial Sterne to look on the lighter side. In the earlier period the tradition had spanned both light and dark, and the need for us to think further about this dimension of literature is apparent from the fact that, at least in the Renaissance, distraction could be comic as well as tragic. When, with Milton but even more critically with the lyric poet turned satirist, Andrew Marvell, the English literary Renaissance effectively came to an end, it seems essential to notice that one key figure is The Mower, Marvell's wondrous pruner of all excessive divagations of the garden-maze, Marvell's fairly grim reaper of all the luscious distractions of the "green Seraglio."

4. Standing, Waiting, and Traveling Light: Milton and the Drama of Information

Milton in his sonnet on his own blindness compares himself with the angels who carry celestial messages to and fro in the universe. The sonnet concerns itself with the creative gift and process. If we ask what is the nature of the angelic message, our inquiry soon reduces to a humanist question: what is man's relation to knowledge and information?

The humanist idea of man as a worthy being depends cardinally on the belief that man can become informed. Many students of Milton have held that particularly when the poet fights for this belief, in tract as well as poem, he marks a high ground in the history of humanism. With this view I have no quarrel. I think, however, that we have to ask what this belief in the informative implies for a poet who wishes to narrate a great epic story. What would the drama of information be, if Milton sought to present or re-present it for us? In the light of these questions Sonnet 19 seems revealing.

> When I consider how my light is spent,
>   Ere half my days, in this dark world and wide,
>   And that one talent which is death to hide
>   Lodged with me useless, though my soul more bent
> To serve therewith my Maker, and present
>   My true account, lest he returning chide,
>   "Doth God exact day-labor, light denied?"
>   I fondly ask. But Patience, to prevent

That murmur, soon replies: "God doth not need
    Either man's work or his own gifts; who best
    Bear his mild yoke, they serve him best. His state
Is kingly: thousands at his bidding speed,
    And post o'er land and ocean without rest;
    They also serve who only stand and wait." [1652?]

A contrast in the poem is posited between the myriad angels who "post o'er land and ocean without rest" and all those who "only stand and wait." At first, such a contrast looks like praise for the angels. Yet the theology of the poem requires that man and angel are at one in a crucial way; they equally may serve under God. In serving, both man and angel are equal—the service being the defining attribute of any creature's right relation to the Creator. It follows, then, that the fate of standing and waiting, of being still, of being poised in a prolonged readiness are not cause for despair. Rather such patience saves man because he who stands, waiting, is ready to become an angel, or at least to become angel-like. He is ready to carry a message. (Perhaps this idea is to be reinforced by a secondary sense of "wait"; it also means "to sing.") In principle a message, like the gospel, is what makes the messenger. God moves all, but below this level of the whole cosmos the angels are equally prime movers. Were this not so, *Paradise Lost* would not have the "metaphoric structure" which Jackson Cope so elegantly described, and on which Thomas M. Greene's *Descent from Heaven* is such a useful iconological commentary. As Greene says, "*Paradise Lost* is the only epic to incorporate the celestial descent into a larger, and indeed a comprehensive pattern of imagery, a pattern which includes the poem's major events—the falls of Satan and of Adam. Milton interweaves these events into a fabric of multitudinous references to height and depth, rising and falling, which appear on virtually every page and bind every incident of the narrative into closer unity."[1] Viewed as a narrative of many messages, then, *Paradise Lost* employs a galaxy of images and the agency of angelic travelers to *place* the falls of Satan and Adam. Motion in this poem is primally the motion of the angels. In like manner standing becomes significant in *Paradise Lost* because that is what Satan and Adam fail to do. They fall, in vertigo. Falling is apparently the wrong kind of motion, because it is uninformed. For Milton, significant motion is full of information, whereas pernicious motion lacks self-governance and leads therefore to a bad death.

Having said this, the critic, remembering the idea of the Fall itself with its redemptive felicity, must go on to ask if Milton does not "need" death, for his great argument. The answer must be, yes. But the answer should, I think, be examined only *after* we have talked more about the Miltonic view of what information is. Is all information good, for example? What about doctrine, or false rhetoric? What about the uncertain state of scientific knowledge, in Milton's or any other age? Such questions have been asked again and again about Milton, and it may be helpful to insist that he characteristically links the problem of knowledge with the problem of the angelic, and man's relation with the angelic.

Noticing such a connection, we may clarify the narrative procedure of a poem so strange as *Paradise Lost,* or, if we wished, the dramatic procedures of a presentation so strange as the masque we call *Comus.*

Universal History and Personal Doubt

In principle any argument about the narrative of *Paradise Lost* should begin with an admission of the obvious. In a sense what is most obvious about the poem is its size (Dr. Johnson: "no man ever wished it longer"). Yet this magnitude has struck different chords in different readers, and we may isolate three characteristic critical ways of thinking about it. These three ways have old beginnings, but they are readily patent in three of the Miltonists who have been, to me, interesting commentators on Milton's form. I believe that it would be correct to say that broadly the three attitudes are "poetic," "stylistic," and "rhetorical" in their focal emphasis.

(1) *Paradise Lost* as a poetic structure. The way taken here was first laid out by Aristotle's *Poetics,* whose most notable modern descendant is Northrop Frye. In *The Return of Eden* Frye begins his account of *Paradise Lost* by quoting the Latin commendatory poem of Samuel Barrow, in which as the poem says, when you read this epic, what are you reading if not the "story of all things"? Frye sums the view: "The epic, as Renaissance critics understood it, is a narrative poem of heroic action, but a special kind of narrative. It also has an encyclopaedic quality in it, distilling the essence of all

the religious, philosophical, political, even scientific learning of its time, and, if completely successful, the definitive poem for its age. The epic in this sense is not a poem by a poet, but that poet's poem: he can never complete a second epic unless he is the equal of Homer, and hence the moment at which the epic poet chooses his subject is the crisis of his life."[2] This view of epic makes it a containing form of vast proportions, which must make use, as J. B. Broadbent reminds us, of an "omnific word" as well as a "mortal voice." Encyclopedic epic aims at a cosmic representation of things and events. In *Paradise Lost* this cosmic scope appears on two planes: first, we learn of an immense natural and supernatural universe, replete with God, His Son, the angels (standing and falling), Adam and Eve, and all the creations of our world; second, this universe projects for us an inner form of divinely ordered structure— the Divine Plan of Providence—which is the metaphysical counterpoint of the physical universe.

To take only the most important result of such a broad view, while the action of *Paradise Lost* may be cyclical (as Frye believes), this cyclicality is Christianized, so that the poem envisions a final escape from the endless repetitions normal to classical containment-myths. There will be "an end of days," which the poem envisions. The enormity of this vision may be grasped when we recall that, in Roland Frye's phrases, "the total shattering of all evil must come before man can enter on the life everlasting."

The reader of Milton finds that when such critics as Northrop and Roland Frye take this large view of the poem, they are confronted with the cosmic structure which at the least must be called "providential" in its scope. It seems perfectly normal for such structures to be rendered in criticism by what amounts to shorthand, by diagrams of man's fate and man's world of fate. The diagrammatic is the norm for instant representation of the infinitely large, the unbelievably complex. The beauty of an orientation toward Miltonic *poetics* is that we easily can speak thereby about what is *in* the poem. We can readily say, the story of all things is in the poem.

(2) *Paradise Lost* as a poetic subject. This perspective is attuned to what I believe to be ultimately a stylistic approach. My example *par excellence* is C. S. Lewis, not always considered a stylistic critic. Lewis often suppresses his pleasure in stylistic differences, which only in his sixteenth-century *History* did he let loose to run most

freely and fantastically. His *Preface to Paradise Lost,* however, stands on the notion that there is a cardinal difference between primary and secondary epic, and this difference comes from a shift in fundamental style of poetic thought.

Curiously, an origin of this attitude is to be found in Dr. Johnson's *Life* of Milton, where the emphasis falls on the projection of the Miltonic mind. What fascinates Johnson is the way Milton chose a subject on which too much could not be said—which sounds like an interest in the poetic structure of *Paradise Lost.* Yet a closer reading of Johnson betrays his proto-Romantic interest in what the vast structure permits to Milton. It allows him to project a gigantic demiurgic mentality at work in the display of its own powers. Johnson is amazed at what we would call the "creativity" of the poem, and this is what surges up in the distinction Lewis was later to make between primary and secondary epic.

My own reduction of the two modes would be that, following Lewis, primary epic narrates the fortunes of an individual, while, in the strict sense of the word, secondary epic narrates the great subject (for example, the fate of the Arthurian court, or the Fall of Jerusalem, or the Fall of Man). On this basis neither the *Odyssey,* with its quest for home and heroic knowledge, nor the *Iliad,* with its battle for heroic identity, qualifies as secondary epic. What is distinctively useful in the view is that, as Lewis says,

> Primary Epic neither had, nor could have, a great subject in the later sense. That kind of greatness arises only when some event can be held to effect a profound and more or less permanent change in the history of the world, as the founding of Rome did, or still more, the fall of man. Before any event can have that significance, history must have some degree of pattern, some design. The mere endless up and down, the constant aimless alternations of glory and misery, which make up the terrible phenomenon called a Heroic Age, admit to no such design. No one event is really very much more important than another . . . Nothing "stays put," nothing has significance beyond the moment.[3]

This lack of meaning is supplanted in Milton by the providential theory of history evolved through centuries of Christian speculation, with Augustine as its chief architect in *The City of God.*

Two things strike the reader when confronted with Lewis's distinction. First, the historical shock of the arrival of an epic "subject." Second, the resulting need felt by Lewis to explain what he calls the "style of secondary epic." For it follows that if secondary epic expatiates, when primary did not, then secondary demands an expatiatory style, a method of cosmic reticulation and expression. For a truly great subject looks two ways, inward into the minutest detail of history, outward to the vastest design. Milton's brief epigraph on "The Verse" reminds us how technically subtle yet powerful is his answer to this need for variously "drawing out" the sense "from one verse into another," so that the unity of the subject, in all its dimensions of interior finesse and exterior planning, will be preserved within the poem.

Milton finds his great subject in the field of universal history. In this sense poetic object and poetic subject seem to converge, having been emphatically separated by the two critical stances. History is a complicated business because, on the one hand, it is in a sense all we have (as Frye says, "We face the past"), but on the other, it is all we have lost. Furthermore, there is a question as to what orders of thought are implied by the very idea of history. Lewis's stylistic concerns lead to a variant of Frye's formula: *Paradise Lost* is not just the story (the narrative?) of all things; it is even more the *history* of all things. In what measure that statement is true should perhaps remain a point of debate.

(3) *Paradise Lost* as a rhetorical process. The third view of the poem to be considered is Stanley Fish's now classic treatment, *Surprised by Sin*, but it also appears to a lesser degree, recognized by Fish in various allusions, in Joseph Summer's *The Muse's Method* and in his York Tercentenary Lecture, "The Embarrassments of *Paradise Lost*." Fish quotes Summers: "Milton anticipated . . . the technique of the 'guilty reader' . . . The readers as well as the characters have been involved in the evil and have been forced to recognize and to judge their involvement."[4] Others have adopted somewhat similar views, but perhaps we should say that the one critic who has gone the whole way with Fish's commitment to rhetoric in Milton is that apostate angel himself, William Empson, whose attack upon the Almighty in *Milton's God* is not made for the fun of it (despite Empson's obvious glee), but really for the sake of the experience of the poem, which involves questioning and doubt.

Fish has explored the reader's experience of *Paradise Lost* and has included in this experience the knowledge of many fine points of doctrine. This exploration leads to analysis of innumerable local details of Miltonic speech and narrative. We discover strange turns in the poem's logic. We discover its sudden discontinuities of line. We discover ourselves in the course of this discovery of Milton.

Stanley Fish conceptually shifts the ground of the earlier critical positions. Where it was possible to discuss the structuralism of a poetic approach and the stylistics of Lewis's approach in terms of "object" and "subject," now we have to discuss the poem in terms of "objectivity" and "subjectivity." That is, in Fish the objects of a poetic structure and the subjects of a poetic style are driven into a violent collision, to produce an essential conflict of effect. This conflict yields the question: should we as readers of *Paradise Lost* stress its content or its form, to which the rhetorician's answer is, and must be, let us overstress both, exaggerating the place of doctrine and the place of a personal *reader's response*, and thereby escape into a middle ground—an "experience" of the poem with all it might entail. Reading the poem becomes an ordeal, and the participial involvement of the reader becomes increasingly valid to the degree that he submits to the processing which the poem forces him to undergo. Thus Fish is far and away the most modern of the three critics I take to be exemplary. Notice how, in his admirably clear opening theses, Fish directs the argument of *Surprised by Sin* toward a quasi-dramatic, or at least scenic, presentation of the reader's mental activity, especially in the form of doubt.

Fish begins his book, "I would like to suggest something about *Paradise Lost* that is not new except for the literalness with which the point will be made: (1) the poem's center of reference is its reader who is also its subject; (2) Milton's purpose is to educate the reader to an awareness of his position and responsibilities as a fallen man, and to a sense of the distance which separates him from the innocence once his"—and here perhaps a rupture is in order, since Fish's points 1 and 2 clearly owe something to critics like Lewis (no. 1) and Frye (no. 2). But Fish proceeds to his third and most important point, deriving it from the first two, or carrying it along with them: "(3) Milton's method is to re-create in the mind of the reader (which is, finally, the poem's scene) the drama of the Fall, to make him fall again exactly as Adam did and with Adam's troubled clarity, that is to say, 'not deceived'." Fish then notes that points 1 and 2 will be well enough received, but point 3 has not been "accepted in the way that I intend it." This third intention leads to the main burden of *Surprised by Sin*. Fish employs a full-scale rhetorical treatment of Miltonic narrative and its manipulating (in the present participle) of the reader's response.

What counts in this strong yet subtle approach to the surface of the poem is precisely its tenacity. By emphasizing rhetorical process and our experience of it, Fish has enabled us to revel in one kind of Miltonic fullness, his scene and rhetoric of scene, whereby he manipulates his reader's thoughts in a dance of ideas which he leads and in which we join hands.

The three critical paths I have been sketching achieve, in different ways, an equally tough yet equally varied responsiveness to the magnitude of information Milton requires us to tolerate. We discover this mass of data equally, whether we come at the poem as a poetic object, a poetic subject, or a rhetorical process. What abides is the mass of data, and what I wish to recall is simply that it is a mass of information, whose aim is to inform, or if you wish, to educate. All three critical stances remind us that Milton not only wrote "Of Education"; he also lived his own education and shared that life with his reader, believing, as he did, that "a good book is the precious life-blood of a master spirit . . . the breath of reason itself . . . an immortality rather than a life." To read *Areopagitica* is like reading Derrida's *La Dissémination* three hundred years *avant la lettre*. Milton does not cast forth any single seed nor cull the fruit of any single tree; he casts forth whole bags of seed, and speaks of repressive licensing as a "massacre." It is the massing of human activities and thoughts that interests him.

Models for Holding Data

Two ways of thinking about the control of massed activity present themselves to us, as to the poet. First, he develops a static model for containing his materials. Numerous commentaries on the Miltonic method have been put forward, many of them dealing, quite rightly, with his "universe" in *Paradise Lost*. Milton appears to hold ambiguous views of the firmness of his cosmic structure, though it derives roughly from a traditional poetic use of the Ptolemaic "syntax." Ptolemaic sphericities are poetically powerful because of themselves they, vaultlike, may contain a grand action. Second, as we shall see, Milton plays with the contradictions and ironies of any chosen course of action, so that he induces various doubts about his comic, that is, happily containing universe. He allows dissymmetry and flux to bend its perfect circles. These warpings have given rise to much ingenious and rightly querulous criticism. Yet every critic still wants a big structure in which to place *Paradise Lost*, in spite of the inherent confusions of Milton's devious practice.

My own static frame is simple. I like to think of *Paradise Lost* as a poem in which almost nothing happens. Unlike Aristotle's ideal epic, *Paradise Lost* does not give us the mimesis of an action. It imitates the processing of information. This mimesis includes the drama of disinformation, with the Fall. In Aristotelian terms, *praxis* becomes either *noesis* or *dianoia*. Yet, in some obvious sense, things must happen in this as in other epics. I answer, the happening is a learning. Here I am agreeing with my three model Miltonists. My framework question then is, *where* does this learning happen?

A useful analogy may be drawn from architecture. *Paradise Lost* then takes on the formal properties of a large baroque palace or temple, with two flanking wings joined by narrow corridors to a massive central hall. A diagram may be efficient and helpful. This diagram is not intended for competition in the Grand Prix de Rome,

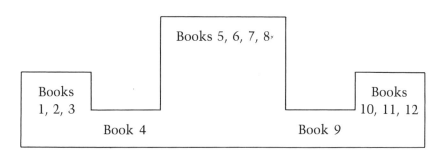

and those who like architecture and the baroque must forgive its notable lack of grace and proportion. Even so, it may indicate the static frame of architectonic containment that holds the background and foreground actions of the poem, as Northrop Frye describes its main bulk. The two wings and central section hold a distanced report of either vastly remote action, as in the opening Books, or a notably reported *historia* of materials both close and far, in relation to the world of the enclosed garden. Books 4 and 9 provide the main scenes of foregrounded action, as indeed they must, since they display the immediate conditions of the Fall. There are overlappings between Books and between architectonic sections— as there would be in a baroque palace, where certain good pieces of furniture are too much for one room and spill out into the adjacent spaces. Yet something like a baroque, balanced structure is apparent for the whole poem. By the same token, the baroque flowers into dissymmetry, as we know from the spiral forms of Bernini and Borromini. These twists belong to the unbalancing of a deeply classical, underneath-it-all balanced style and format.

The importance of models such as these (and, it must be reiterated, architecture is only the simplest structural model), is that on the level of a *static* containment of its "story of all things," *Paradise Lost* requires skeletal, *under*lying structure.

Much recent criticism, however, prefers, quite reasonably, an opposite aspect of the poem, its dynamic. If *Paradise Lost* is a cosmic picture-show, housed in a baroque palace, how then are the pictures to be seen and the music heard? Who passes through the long galleries? Who settles in the chambers? Who crosses the lawn outside the French windows? Our answer, however we elaborate it, might be: the mental traveler.

Dynamics of Miltonic Information

Most close readings of *Paradise Lost,* particularly those inspired by a concern for the linguistic, poetic, theological, philosophical and historical origins of its text, have been *de facto* contributing to the analysis of its informative aspect. These researches have tried to find out the details or the general principles by which Milton attempts to communicate or manipulate a mass of data. The researcher wants to see how he would transmit, store and process information. In cybernetics, the science of servomechanisms and their methods of control, we learn that information exists primarily as message and comes significantly into being whenever it is transmitted, or transduced. (The interest of such a theory for a student of metaphor like Richards is at once manifest, while the limits of its use are discussed in Geoffrey Hartman's book *The Fate of Reading.*) Without trying to be technical in cybernetic terms, it seems a useful metaphor to discover that poets like Virgil and Milton, looking back to the *Odyssey*, long ago realized that every message needs to be "piloted" past various kinds of noise, redundancy, and interruptive barrier.

This love of pilotage, this cybernetic quest, had also appeared in Spenser, particularly in Book II of *The Faerie Queene*, a pre-text of manifest importance for Milton's thoughts about the poetic career. Furthermore, when we transfer the field of message-carrying from the pagan to the Hebraic-Christian field of iconography, a "higher" mode asserts itself. Now the passing of messages becomes an art of celestial navigation, an enrichment not lost on the great national poet of a maritime people who had, in the sixteenth and seventeenth centuries, at last reached genuine maritime power, with genuine navigational accomplishments.

The reader of *Paradise Lost*, however, travels in space, rather than at sea. Long ago, he might have noted Queen Elizabeth the First's claim: "The use of the sea *and the air* is free and common to all," or were he a scientist and *au courant* with astronomic discoveries, would have assumed with Kepler (see his *Discussion with Galileo's Sidereal Messenger*) that it would not be long before men gained the power to fly directly to the moon, thus obviating the need for examining its surface through the telescope. Space, in short, is the physical ocean of this new cybernetic field of transmitting information.

If the Miltonic age saw the expansion of potential as well as actual domains where information could be transmitted, it also marked the beginnings of a sense that information could be a basic human resource: "stores of information represent a new kind of transactable commodity, ranking in future human importance alongside material and energy resources."[5] That Milton's father was a scrivener who also loaned money has always seemed to me the most notable biographic fact about the poet's origins, after the fact that his father was, like the son, an accomplished musician. In the Milton household informational transactions, real and imaginative, musical and monetary, were a conspicuous early influence on the poet's thought.

Most readers have been astonished not so much by the amount of Milton's learning, as by its inner dynamism, its life along the way. One metaphoric in *Paradise Lost* suggests a reason for this liveliness of knowledge, the analogy Milton always draws between knowledge and whatever nutriment can be assimilated by the human species. Thus knowledge becomes "intellectual food," making the universe of *Paradise Lost* subject to the laws of good diet and prudent consumption of nature's goods. Doctrinally, as the poem and as *The Reason of Church Government* suggest, this metaphoric equivalence of food and knowledge stems from the Johannine vision of the consumable Book, which Milton recalled as "that mysterious book of revelation which the great evangelist was bid to eat, as it had been some eye-brightening electuary of knowledge and foresight." The true minister of the incarnate word was enjoined, in David Paraeus' words, "earnestly to devour or eat up the doctrine of salvation divinely written and received of Christ, that is, diligently to read, understand, and meditate, and as it were to turn it into their very moisture and blood." According to such a myth, the Christian and ministerial poet—the author of *Lycidas*, let us say—assimilates his intellectual food in order to persist with health in his spiritual quest, which demands its own "precious life-blood." Thus the Word is the ultimate resource for the dynamism of Miltonic knowledge.

The angels, who are the carriers or couriers of this life-giving knowledge, bring its spiritual sustenance to mankind.

The Governance of Song

Halfway through Raphael's edenic lecture series, at the beginning of Book VII, the poet appeals to Urania for inspiration. His specific request is clear: "Still govern thou my song, / Urania, and fit audience find, though few." Urania, the Heavenly Muse, is to be the governor, or pilot, the *cybernetes*, of the epic voice, particularly in a purgative role, since she can drive away the Dionysian confusions of "Bacchus and his revelers" (VII, 33). The Invocation has been taken rather narrowly, to indicate the poet's turn toward cosmic information, "how and wherefore this world was first created." True, the Divine act of Creation demands a Heavenly Muse for its recounting. But the appeal has also a general force, since *all* of *Paradise Lost* depends upon the Myth of the Creation (as indeed its noblest descendant, Haydn's *Creation*, suggests to us).

My thesis must be that Milton, when thinking largest, thinks in terms of a universe that is created as an informed, counterchaotic organism. Appealing to Urania, he prays for a guidance of all the information that in-forms this Timaean "body." Urania, in short, is to govern the movements of the messages carried by the angels. What needs government, cybernetic control, is the daemonic transmission of all the myriad messages that make up the controlling, Apollonian message of the universe. This universe is alive with thought.

Adam and Eve

These "first parents" live in a context of angelic influences flowing all about them, sometimes lightly, sometimes with great stress. Their destiny is to encounter the angelic, or, more generally, the daemonic. For Milton this means that they must encounter knowledge and survive the encounter, since knowledge is first learned as information, and information—the content of messages—comes to us via the messengers of light: for this reason Raphael is specifically called the "divine interpreter" (VII, 72). Adam and Eve's error comes from not being able to interpret or translate such messages. Satan comes to them bearing a new and dangerously ambiguous message, which they cannot read aright. The crises of the poem, therefore, consist almost entirely of aborted interpretation. The Fall is a failure to decode correctly a message of seemingly clear but actually confused meaning. It follows that the narrative of the epic is designed to give as much space as possible to reading, as little as possible to mere acting. Whatever we think action is, it cannot here resemble that of the *Iliad*, where "Hector first aimed his spear at Ajax, who was turned full towards him, nor did he miss his aim. The spear struck him where two bands passed over his chest—the band of his shield and that of his silver-studded sword—and these protected his body." Nor can it be like the *Odyssey*, where "as he spoke day began to break, and Menelaus, who had already risen, leaving Helen in bed, came towards them. When Telemachus saw him he put on his shirt as fast as he could, threw a great cloak over his shoulders, and went out to greet them" (XV, 56). Butler's prose translation increases the sense of physical activity, but it is not unfair to either Homeric poem. By contrast, the Miltonic narrative has to keep the reader from wanting such noble and natural physicality. Even the exquisite "nature" of Adam and Eve in the Garden has to allude continuously to something beyond it, that makes it significant. They cannot even lie down at evening together, without our thinking that this means something. Whatever it means is to be understood as the evangelic function of an informational purpose.

Bad Data—The Fallen Angel

It is too easy today to depreciate the grandeur of Satan. Yet Milton sets him up for such a surprising fall, and instructs us that Satan is preeminently the purveyor of wrong information. He is the original confidence man. Perhaps this aspect of Satanic rhetoric in *Paradise Lost* has been done to death. Even so, I should observe that the famous cluster of similitudes accompanying his rise from the Burning Lake constitutes an almost perfect deconstruction (Fish might call it a "self-consumption") of the narrative line.[6] Before advancing far with the description of Satan's appearance, Milton deliberately spirals out into a more than double digression into simile-beyond-simile, as if to tell us: "You think this giant is getting somewhere; I can't even keep track of my notes." Satan's presence is such that he himself, or the poet creating his presence, tends to force *digressio* or sidetracking of the narrative away from whatever naturally ought to be occurring. If a man rises from the water, we have some interest in what is happening; Satan's rise provokes thoughts only of what it portends—because he is in the portending, advertising business. His mere presence inflates the rhetoric of any passage in which he participates. He is a bad, the worst, angel, and he perverts simple narrative description accordingly. On the other hand, this perversion leads to enormous reader-response, because rhetoric has one foot in the real world, but another in the world of fantasy and projection.

Good Data—the Immortals

Learning is associated in Milton with speed, which amounts to an absolute limit on the speed of travel in space, the speed of light. As scientists tell us, the things they learn to describe with mathematic precision are, as phenomena, things already well known to ordinary, percipient humans. Thus the inverse square law of gravitational attraction was in some strange way known to the author of the

Inferno. Few men have understood light as well as Milton. Few have labored so hard to understand it.

Yet as poet he is a phenomenologist and uses light for his own reasons. He knows that in the Old Testament the cherubim and seraphim are ablaze with light. They are the heavenly powers of that first, elemental being we discover in Book III of *Paradise Lost.* Their concreated luminance derives from their association with God, who first appears to us (III, 55 ff.) sitting enthroned on high, looking at us with one eye, "his eye," the "eye of God." A more primal poet would have simply said, God is an eye. He would have meant, God is the Sun. Milton draws maximum force from this primordial pun and empowers his entire poem with its omnivalent meanings. Christ, similarly, exists perfectly because he is a "radiant image" of his father. If we prematurely psychologize this and other similar relationships, we shall fail to see that they make metaphysical sense, and bring to the heavenly scene a necessary logical perfection. If God is All, then the very best thing to be, to be nearest him, is "the radiant image of his glory." Milton may not have succeeded, but he worked to make the heavenly scenes of ultimate discourse as clear and logically coherent, as Euclidean as possible. Hence in *Paradise Lost* all order derives from the idea that God is light. He lives in absolute enlightenment. But that argument lies outside my interest, which is to notice, among other things, that God's doings are relatively not as important in the poem as the doings of his angels, fallen and unfallen, along with the doings of man. In the poem, we may say, God's absolute light is a self-evident truth. Yet somewhere "underneath" this truth there exist other dependent truths and realities. The angels and man occupy this secondary place.

When Milton thinks of information, he thinks, as I have said, of angelic powers of transmission. He early began to ruminate on this subject, in his two delightful undergraduate poems on Hobson, the celebrated University Carrier. These poems are a useful key to the Miltonic theory of angels and messages. We need only note two phenomenological points. First, Milton tells us that Hobson thrives on the "weight" of his messages; the heavier they get, the more lightly burdened he feels. Second, we learn that Hobson died, according to the conceit, because he was prevented from overdoing his weekly rounds between Cambridge and London. "Too long vacation hastened on his term." Hobson (whose "choice" incredibly prefigures the absurdity of the Fall) was as regular in his motions "betwixt Cambridge and *The Bull*" as a planet in its orbital movement:

> But had his doings lasted as they were,
> He had been an immortal carrier.

These short poems resemble other early Milton works, such as the *In quintum Novembris*, in their prefiguring function for his "long choosing" career. They are extraordinary, however, in that they completely humanize the role of the messenger. Hobson is the mailman, who carries undergraduate requests for money to parents in London, who brings tuck-boxes back to college from town, who communicates between the dim monastic cold of Cambridge and the life-giving warmth of London town. And he is the archetype of the angel in the Miltonic pantheon: he is the messenger.

Hobson "died for heaviness that his cart went light," and the paradox persists, less flippant, in all later Miltonic treatments of the carrier of information. The incredible swiftness of the angels is due to their lightness, and their lightness is due, paradoxically, to the immense weight of significance of what they carry, pure information, pure light and enlightenment. Thus it is that in *The Reason of Church Government* Milton says of knowledge that it is "the best and lightsomest possession of the mind . . . no burden." So that it may not be "a load to any part of the body, it did not with a heavy advantage overlay upon the spirit." Again and again Milton speaks of the "weight" of knowledge, he speaks of "aggravating the burden" of knowing, and so on. When his noble England rouses itself, Samson-like, and free, that rising is a lifting movement.

Thus along with the most complete sense of the weight of knowledge, as it may be painfully acquired, Milton has the most exquisite sense of its lightness, when it is known. His angels are the daemonic agencies of this lightness, and he is always showing us their power to sustain and transport knowledge from place to place. Thus, for example, the Archangel Michael pauses at the start of Book XII:

> As one who in his journey bates at noon,
> Though bent on speed, so here the Archangel paused . . .

"Bent on speed"—the mark of the celestial messenger. Uriel possesses a garment of pure surrounding velocity, "his habit fit for speed succinct," while typically the guardian angels Ithuriel and Zephon move with "winged speed." Uriel's arrival in his mission to the Archangel Gabriel is a justly celebrated rendering of the speed of light as it compares with slower traveling entities:

> Thither came Uriel, gliding through the even
> On a sunbeam, swift as a shooting star
> In autumn thwarts the night, when vapors fired
> Impress the air, and shows the mariner
> From what point of his compass to beware
> Impetuous winds. (IV, 555–560)

One of the cosmic ironies Milton depends on is the kind of apparently opposite slowness of his Abdiel, who, instead of shooting away like a star from the rebel angels, after he has refused to join them, simply passes slowly forth from their company. Satan has just advised him to carry the tidings of rebellion to the Annointed King: "Fly, ere evil intercept thy flight." But Abdiel passes slowly forth, almost as if standing still. If the angelic powers of thought are infinitely fast, the angelic capacity for truth must be capable of sustaining itself steadily and slowly.

It would be tedious to insist further on the Miltonic equivalence between the speeds of light and thought, and their association with angelic movements. We need only note that the angels are the messengers that bring to Adam and Eve most of what they ever know, and consequently are the immediate causes of whatever they do and learn. Satan brings them an evil message; encodes their eternal life with the fantasies of death and narcissism. The Guardian Angels try, with known result, to counter and prepare for this bad data. In the poem's final architectonic wing Michael "repairs the ruins" of a lightsomeness which had, before the Fall, been man's condition. In a word, the "book" of *Paradise Lost* belongs almost totally to the angels, good and bad. And what gives them power over man is their manipulation of messages.

The Tuscan Artist

Any investigation into the angelic messages that make *Paradise Lost* what it is, must include a glancing reference to the enigmatic messenger of the poem, Galileo, the "Tuscan Artist." With Columbus, he is the only contemporary person other than Milton himself to be named or directly alluded to in *Paradise Lost.* On some theories of epic he thereby at once becomes the "hero" of the poem. I think he is not its hero, but, in an astronomical phrase, moves in some planetary motion relative to whoever may be the hero. For Galileo is clearly heroic to Milton, as *Areopagitica* implies. When he appears in Book I, in the famous shield simile, we are unable to see exactly what point of view the poet wishes us to adopt toward his telescope and its discoveries. Similarly, in Book III (588–89) we cannot quite tell what we are to think about the sunspots the astronomer sees through his "glazed optic tube." There is an odd "perhaps" in these lines.

What indeed may be thought of Galileo? I think the answer lies in the final, and according to Kepler the most stunning information reported in the *Sidereal Messenger,* as it has come to be known: namely, the existence of Jupiter's moons, or, as they came to be called, owing to the vagaries of Renaissance patronage, the Medicean Stars. These moons were interesting to astronomy for various reasons. Most critical of all, their motions implied something that men like Bruno, and, from a different angle, Kepler and Galileo had for some time suspected or believed to be the case, namely that the universe was not a system of ultimate fixity, but of ultimate relativity. Earth had always had *its* moon, the Copernican sun had enjoyed *its* earth and planets; this seemed the end of the line as far as relativism went. The discovery of the Medicean Stars now led to the strong conviction that the lights of the universe, the motivic suns of its whole constellated form, were all subject to a freedom never before conceived: they were all seemingly held in an infinitely relativistic system of bonds, as these tiny moons of Jupiter were held to *it.* In his letter to Galileo (*Discussion with the Sidereal Messenger*), Kepler suggests that every main body in the universe can now be believed to have some other body belonging to it. No absolute solitude or quite separate community of stars is any longer conceivable. All is henceforth relative, and particularly motion is basically relative. This breaking of the circle is one more stage in a long process of breakdown of the ancient theory of universal order.

The intellectual pressure that brings about such a breakdown may simply be called New Information. The fundamental form this new data takes is a clearer interpretation of light, its properties, its effects in the phenomenal world. Optics, telescopy, and the analysis of light-emitting sources and light-receiving bodies may rank as the "highest" of seventeenth-century scientific concerns. They are also the concerns closest to the Divine Science of theology. The greatest changes in physical science, to be associated mainly with men like Kepler, Tycho Brahe, Galileo, and Newton, make for the greatest changes in theological context. This interaction is familiar to us.

When Milton calls Galileo "the Tuscan artist," he draws our attention to the Galilean technology, the use of the telescope to observe anew. Galileo is not solely a theorist; he is noted for his use of an artifact.[7] This suggests that an identification of calling draws the poet and the Tuscan astronomer together. They are both makers of instruments.

Yet it may be more important that Galileo makes a certain "Miltonic" use of his instrument, the telescope. That is, Galileo is the hero as researcher. He represents the new mode of free inquiry into the knowable order of the natural world. For a Galileo adventures are not those of crossroads and inns, but of stars and planets and their pathways. In turn this adventuring, which depends upon heightened observation, leads to an increasingly mental definition of heroic quest.

At the same time inquiring mind turns inward, spiraling back into the study of human history. Too often we forget that Herodotus' term *historia* does not mean our "story." It means "research." His history of the Persian Wars, as his book is often called, came forth into the world as his "researches." Equally they might have come under the title "travels." Herodotus travels about the known world, and into some of its far reaches, to gather legends, facts, rumors, and other bits of information. As researcher, he is our classic Heraclitean, Ionian relativist (if we discount the author of the inset tales in the *Odyssey*). He tells us that he feels duty-bound to report everything he is told, but that he need not believe it all. This is the researcher's peculiar mode of instrumental doubt, and it is a doubt which *Paradise Lost* intricately shares. For *Paradise Lost* historicizes its worldview and its myth, leaving us with the primary sensation of having undergone a rigorous exposure to a grandiose research project in the Humanities. Because Milton impregnates his research with systematic doubt, he is also able to project an *understanding* of the universe, that is, an image of universal order which is as much a subject as it is an object.

It is tempting to believe we need a third category, of "tertiary epic." In this mode of epic the hero is the undeterred observer and analyst. Such a class of epic is then not quite the Miltonic class—it is Wordsworthian, or perhaps Blakean.

Milton shows us Adam and Eve wending their way to the edge of Eden. Wordsworth imagines what man must be, as hero, after he has left the Garden.

Poetic Health: A Tentative Conclusion

If in *Paradise Lost* Milton presented and represented research into a cosmic plenum of information, the action of the poem then resides mainly in a processing of various data, and we should always keep this view of the poem in mind. To say that *Paradise Lost* has more information than action is, perhaps, so obvious that we may be forgiven if we do not always ask what follows from this. Certainly it implies a change of emphasis from the objective to the subjective, and probably from the merely poetic to the additionally rhetorical. But it implies something more: the invention of a new stillness in narrative art. For if the battles and voyages of the ancient heroes are exemplary in their world, the stillness of the nighttime astronomer, looking out into the sky above Fiesole, is exemplary for the modern world. Pride for the ancient was fundamentally physical pride, pride in the body (as Paul always said); it could also be spiritual and intellectual pride, the kind of detective vanity we discover in Greek Oedipus, or the religious complaisance of Hebrew Job. Now pride finds new locations, since the mathematical intelligence links up with physics, to create, or at least control, new worlds.

Pride achieves its absolute limit in the power of human interpretation. Man the understander has now to fight against man the rapid-fire interpreter. Health is more than ever a balancing act. While Milton is visibly inspired by the example of Galileo, whom he had met—old, blind, and under house arrest—he is able to engraft this inspiration with another, that of the evangelical Word itself. He would, I think, have accepted the Word as the final informing power. His would be the formulation we find in the great cosmologist-theologian Cudworth, who said: "The great Mysterie of the Gospel, it doth not lie onely in *Christ without us*, (though we must know also that [meaning "what"] he hath done for us) but the very Pith and Kernel of it, consists in *Christ inwardly formed in our hearts.*" This is a theory of sanity. Cudworth continues, "Nothing is truly Ours, but what lives in our Spirits. *Salvation* itself cannot *save us,* as long as it is onely without us; no more then *Health* can cure us, and make us sound, when it is not within us, but somewhere at distance from us; no more then *Arts and Sciences,* whilst they lie onely in Books and Papers without us; can make us learned" (*Quintessence of the Gospel,* sermon of March 31, 1647).

It is then clear why we have to say that *Paradise Lost* is the first epic to build its body entirely with the sinews of information: it is the first epic which self-consciously travels, as lightsome as possible, to the boundaries of the informing quest, and it makes this trajectory of light in order, dramatically, to show the whole body of a concerted thought. It demonstrates a continuous, almost medical care for the health of that whole body. The poem indeed seeks a paradise within, by bringing inwards all that is without, much as Cudworth described his intellectual system of the universe. Through this infolding and exfoliating "systasis" (Huntley's word) *Paradise Lost* becomes the most percipient and perceptually oriented epic created up to the time of its composition. The poet's trajectory of light furthermore reaches out and up to a fully conscious mode of augury, which in his nineteenth sonnet he called "consideration." To consider "how one's light is spent" is to measure the truth of things and the weight of the phenomena through a star-ridden, sidereal message-reading. In the most literal sense *Paradise Lost* fully accepts the influences implied by ancient theories of the harmony of the heavenly bodies, theories which also include discords in the celestial order.

Somewhat ironically, this poem of information has its own proper spheres of activity. Action here is intellectual movement—the conflict, the wandering, the homecoming, and the resolution of ideas bound on a dialectic wheel of fire. Among readings of the Miltonic trajectory, Geoffrey Hartman's short essay, "Self, Time and History," almost perfectly catches this mental travel in "one of the really magical moments in literature, not uninspired by theater and masque"—the ending of the first Book of *Paradise Lost* (761 ff.). Suddenly the giant fallen forms of the Pandemonians are metamorphosed into a fairy ring which the returning laborer "sees / Or dreams he sees" in the moonlight. Thus Hartman describes the Miltonic *diegesis:* "Formally considered, this sequence is an elaborate digression from the apparent line of action; it creates in the narrative not only a moment of rich, conspicuous, even irrelevant foregrounding of the poetical texture but also a ghostly, dimensional shift from action to observation, one which slows the narrative flow even as it quickens the reader's mind by the sounded wealth of allusions."[8] Hartman calls this moment "a strange turn, or troping, or deviousness"—it is all of these—and, Miltonically, describes such shifts of thought as "curiously weightless."

A deliberate ballistic procedure orders the text of *Paradise Lost,* whereby allusions are fired into literary/historical space. However transumptively, Milton always roots his imagery in a knowable, natural world. Thus, I think, it is inherently plausible that, as Christine Brooke-Rose has argued, Milton should richly exploit the "genitive link" type of metaphor; such linkages ("If music be the food of love" would be a Shakespearean instance) are logically mediatory—there is always a third, "angelic" term through which "we can guess the proper term if it is not stated."[9] Milton remains the poet of the Creation. The sidereal messenger generates, as he transmits, information.

Satan and his fellows generate false data. The Archangels Raphael and Michael generate true data. Adam and Eve generate questions. God, through the Son, generates the possibility of approaching with infinite, Zeno-like pains, an infinitely receding galaxy of answers. If we accept this informational ordeal, Milton seems to say, we shall somehow live the life of the angels, who, unlike Franz Kafka's desperate couriers, do question the messages they bear.

It is by analyzing the question-bearing aspect of the enunciatory in *Paradise Lost* that we shall be able to place the idea of death sustained by the poem. For *Paradise Lost* is neither tragic nor comic, nor, in the ordinary sense, romantic. The poem, at its climax, when Adam and Eve fall, is liminal, suspended "in evil hour," while Eve in particular "knew not eating Death" (IX, 792). Both she and her uxorious mate share in a trespass—the most astonishing of threshold-passages—so terrible that twice Earth trembles, "from her entrails." The Fall, I believe, is a suspension. Milton knows that death is not an event, but a mere passing over, from here to there.

Part II. Representative Thinking

5. Allegorical Secrecy, Gnomic Obscurity

One way literature projects its knowledge and thought is through what Blake called "allegory addressed to the intellectual powers." On the highest levels of generality such allegory is able to present visions of cosmic order which, however distinct their imagery, will always display a measure of mystery. It is this latter characteristic, the mysterious, that marks the allegorical mode when most powerfully employed. Allegory exploits obscurity, complex rather than simple, and makes various language-games out of the need to decode and illuminate the various facets of the obscure. One especially suggestive form of the obscure is the gnomic utterance. Gnomics are, in my view, quintessentially obscure. Yet they have an illuminating function, particularly when an author is dealing with extreme conditions of existence, such as ecstasy, pain, sensory deprivation, bewilderment. Although these are extreme states, they still cry out for expression. They are, as Wittgenstein would say, "forms of life." The importance of Wittgenstein in this setting is manifest: he makes a place in philosophy for explicating extreme uncertainty *and* ties this attempt to his notion of language-game.

The Symbolic Facade

In literature, perhaps the most obvious carrier of thought is likely to be an allegory of some kind. The ancient Greeks denoted an intellective, cognitive purpose when they called allegory *hyponoia,* or underthought. Allegories could carry meanings hidden beneath the superficial sense of the text. The question that concerns me is: does the thinking process, expressed in an allegory, invoke the concept of literary secrecy, or literary silence?

The combinatory play of written thoughts in an allegory, both composed *into* and read *out of* the text, could be such that it produces a questioning of a silence. Pierre Macherey (*Theory of Literary Production*) quotes Nietzsche to illustrate the relation between the spoken and the unspoken: "Insidious questions: When we are confronted with any manifestation which someone has permitted us to see, we may ask: what is it meant to conceal? What is it meant to draw our attention from? What prejudice does it seek to raise? and, again, how far does the subtlety of the dissimulation go? and in what respect is the man mistaken?" (*Dawn of Day*, sec. 523). In his discussion of the spoken and the unspoken, Macherey observes that certain meanings and ideas may simply be missing from a given text. The critic's task is to find a method of "measuring silences," that is, of determining whatever a given text actively dissimulates or keeps *hidden*. For example, the critic may need to discover how a text is "diverting attention" from its *hyponoetic* underthought.

If allegories evoke hidden meanings, projected by dissimulating language-games, they then acquire the status of an unusual kind of open secret. In the Christian tradition, the allegorist may use symbols whose meaning is well known, but these are treated in the text as if they were secretly significant, that is, part of a larger mystery. Or perhaps particular reserve and reticence are maintained toward particular sacred arcana. If the reader explicates such obscure symbols, these symbols enter the reading as obscured and clarified, as secret and open. Even when known, such symbols tend to preserve a measure of the original obscurity. The open secret thus protects and preserves a symbolic facade.

Kafka's *The Castle* shows the hero, Joseph K, attempting to penetrate such a symbolic facade. Ironically, both revelation and concealment of the truth here issue from the same source, an oblique and parabolic presentation of the law and its authority. As with other modern allegories, Kafka's *The Castle* is self-reflexive in that the reader is forced to experience the same doubts as Joseph K. The law remains as enigmatic to us as it does to the hero. He and we also are called upon to sharpen our intellectual engagement with the story at large. Commonsense, literal approaches to such sublime works will be quite inadequate to the decipherment required.

It was his sense of the enhanced position of the noetic and intellectual dimension of allegory that led William Blake to put forward his celebrated definition: "Allegory address'd to the Intellectual powers, while it is altogether hidden from the Corporeal Understanding, is My Definition of the Most Sublime Poetry; it is also somewhat in the same manner defin'd by Plato" (Letter to Thomas Butts, July 6, 1803).

Modern critical theory would equally intellectualize the workings of allegory. Paul de Man, for example, would have argued that time, and the passage of time, and an awareness of losses occurring in time are the constitutive causes of the allegorical secret. Time is the maker of the secret, the occluder of meaning. According to de Man, temporality includes the ideas of timelessness, the Symbol, and the eternal return, and such temporality is opposed to the authentic time of allegory (as distinct from the Romantic Symbol). Time is an enhanced dimension of allegory because all allegories allude to earlier signs and symbols, that is, allegories use symbolic conventions, which are necessarily inherited from past uses. Furthermore, allegories are based on narrative forms, which means that they exploit time-frames of earlier and later within their own telling or narration.

The temporal structure is, in de Man's words, "characteristic of what we have called allegories of unreadability. Such an allegory is metafigural: it is an allegory of a figure (for example, metaphor), which relapses into the figure it deconstructs."[1] A text figures forth an ideal "allegory of unreadability," often by pitting an earlier readability of an early part of a text against a later unreadability. For example, de Man states that Rousseau's *Julie* exemplifies that "the readability of the first part is obscured by a more radical indeterminacy that projects its shadow backwards and forwards over the entire text. Deconstructions of figural texts engender lucid narratives which produce, in their turn, and as it were within their own texture, a darkness more redoubtable than the error they dispel."[2] In order to entertain such a complex view of allegory, Paul de Man has to posit extraordinary analytic powers of mind. Allegory, here, is projecting a highly involuted process of thought, and such thought in turn is very much the point of the engagement with allegory.

It may or may not be important that recent revelations of de Man's wartime writing indicate that he either permitted, or chose, to keep secret the fact and nature of some of that thinking and writing. If we personalize the question of intention here, we cannot but conclude that de Man's strategy in proving the allegory of *unreadability* was meant to provide a defense that during his life he never had occasion to use. Biographical issues, on de Man's own account of the "temporal destiny," should in theory be relevant to his account of allegory.

Psychoanalysis may be seen to view allegory in a somewhat similar relation to temporality. Insisting on the link between allegory and compulsion, psychoanalysis would also note the associated link between allegory and the process of mourning, suggested by Freud's "Mourning and Melancholia." If mourning is a structured response of letting go of the lost cherished object or person, and insofar as allegory is the expression of "high melancholia" (as in Dürer's print), then allegory is, also, just such a structured letting go. Allegory releases the lost object in such a way that the object is continually recuperated into the present. This in turn suggests that "behind" the lost object there is some secret significance which the allegory never openly acknowledges. Or, the allegory preserves the secrecy in some fashion so that the process of mourning will never end.

Walter Benjamin develops the connection between allegory and mourning throughout the latter part of his *Trauerspiel* book. The thought of mourning is a reflection on the past, in the sense of a rethinking. Benjamin first established the temporality of the mode by noting that baroque allegory displays a passionate awareness of "man's subjection to nature," meaning death, and "if nature has always been subject to the power of death, it is also true that it has always been allegorical."[3] Allegories are responses to an impossible demand, which later (p. 188) Benjamin calls the self-contradictory demand of "dispersal" and "collectedness." Allegory is always in conflict with itself, as it attempts to "mourn" for some lost central governing moment which can never be entirely collected, but cannot (in allegory) be fully given over to oblivion. It begins to appear that, as Kermode set forth in *The Genesis of Secrecy*, the allegorical releasing of interpretive activity requires that narratives build functional secrecies into their narrational forms. Allegory implies secretive thinking.

The secretive aspect of allegory effectively elicits a mental attitude or predisposition to look for secrets and to value them. Sissela Bok, in her *Secrets*, reminds us that "Although they are not always present in every secret or in every practice of secrecy, the concepts of sacredness, intimacy, privacy, silence, prohibition, furtiveness and deception influence the way we think about secrecy."[4]

The framework for thinking about secrecy might best be provided by Walter Benjamin's remark in *Central Park*, which refers to Baudelaire: "That which is touched by the allegorical intention is torn from the context of life's interconnections: it is simultaneously shattered and conserved. Allegory attaches itself to the rubble [*Trümmer*]. It offers the image of transfixed unrest."[5] We may say that it is the final residual core of secrecy that produces the tensions of Benjamin's "transfixed unrest." Because of the secret, all major allegory remains opaque to interpretation at some level of significant depth, a level containing the hidden thought, the obscure.

The question arises: what, then, shall we make of the presence of secrets in nonallegorical works? For example, *Heart of Darkness* is just as much a realistic story as it is an allegorical fable; some would call it mythic, others visionary, while the student of colonial discourse will emphasize Conrad's awareness of harsh realities. Conrad's tale delimits the obscure territory of some terrible secret, what is meant by "the heart of darkness." We need to be flexible; with the rise of realism in fiction and drama, allegory becomes more than ever a mere *dimension* in literature. For example, Kafka's works are often allegorical, but there are residues of realistic purposes throughout the text. In the background to such altered conditions of allegory and allegorizing, there is the vital fact of the decline of theological authority, with a consequent movement away from the strictly allegorical genres known to the Middle Ages and the Renaissance.

From these considerations it follows that we can shift the secret away from its fundamental positioning in the allegorical mode to a partial, contributory function in literature of all kinds. There seems to be no reason why a realistic fiction, for instance a psychological novella such as Dostoevsky's *Notes from Underground*, should not convey a secret of some kind at the heart of the narrative. While an allegory, therefore, derives from a secret center, not every secret is allegorical in its expression.

The term "allegory" has to be used here in a dimensional way so that the effects of allegorical composition may be allowed a place in literary works which are, in essence, nonallegorical. By treating allegory as a dimension of linguistic usage, as a partial language-game, we are set free to notice the presence of secret knowledge throughout literature in general. Freedom in the discernment of secrecy would apply even to such thinking and writing as journalism, criticism, and philosophy itself. For example, Sissela Bok quotes *The Universal Dictionary of Trade and Commerce* (London, 1757), which describes the preservation of industrial secrecy in the manufacture of porcelain: "In order to preserve this art as much as possible a secret, the fabric [factory] at Meissen, which is near Dresden, is rendered impenetrable to any but those who are immediately employed about the work; and the secret of mixing and preparing the materials is known to very few of them. They are all confined as prisoners, and subject to be arrested if they go without the walls; and consequently a chapel, and everything necessary is provided within."[6] This paragraph might just as well be a fable of Kafka, Cioran, or Borges, yet in terms of genre must be labeled journalism.

The secret can occur in any kind of literature, and we can now say that secrecy releases the hermeneutic response. The secret provides a clue and the reader senses the presence of this clue and deciphers its meaning. It appears that some form of secrecy, even reaching to the ineffable, will give to literature the power to raise the question: what does this mean, what does it *really* mean? Whenever we ask such a question, we acknowledge that a given text uses obscurity as one of its methods of meaning whatever it means.

Complex and Simple Obscurity

A text centered on a secret will itself be obscure, and this will be the case whether the secret is more or less manifest in its outline or deeply hidden at the level of a latent content. The embedding of secrecy in a text marks the degree to which it will have an oblique intention and leads us to consider the nature of literary obscurity. Obscurity conveniently falls into two classes, which I call the complex and the simple. These two classes of literary effect bring about the result that some works are considered more difficult than others.

A claim might be made that allegory, in a traditional sense, encodes its narrative or vision in a language of complex obscurity; whereas symbolism, in a High Romantic sense, arises from the use of simple obscurity, but these claims would require extensive demonstration. In the interim, it will be more profitable to explore the distinction between complex and simple obscurity as such.

George Steiner's essay "On Difficulty" discriminates four classes of difficulty in literature, three of which are complex and one simple.[7] His three complex sources are *contingent, modal,* and *tactical.* With the first of these, the problem is what Steiner calls "homework," the job of looking up and deciphering all the lexical and semantic obscurities, such as the fact that Mallarmé's "ptyx" is a conch. With the second, "the order of difficulty is not removed by clarification of word and phrase. It functions centrally." This *modal* difficulty arises when, despite our having looked up all the contingent obscurities, the text remains opaque and will remain so until the reader masters the worldview of that text. Steiner instances the modal obscurity of a strange Cavalier lyric by Richard Lovelace. The third, or *tactical,* class of difficulty arises when, with various motives possibly at work, the author deliberately chooses to obscure certain meanings, as in the Aesopian tradition of allegory.

All three classes of difficulty seem to yield complex obscurities. They are complex because the text has increased the number of ideas, words, images, and relationships that the utterance puts forward. This multiplicity of questions increases to the point that the reader (of *Finnegans Wake,* for example) can only with difficulty process the informational overload. Such is the nature of complex obscurity.

Simple obscurity is more interesting and results from an input that is usually minimalist, as when Shakespeare describes blood flowing into the ocean as "making the green one red." Clearly such phrasing from *Macbeth* belongs to a different order of difficulty, the ontological.

Steiner recaps his taxonomy as follows:

Contingent difficulties aim to be looked up; modal difficulties challenge the inevitable parochialism of honest empathy; tactical difficulties endeavor to deepen our apprehension by dislocating and goading to a new life the supine energies of word and grammar. Each of these three classes of difficulty is a part of the contract of ultimate or preponderant intelligibility between poet and reader, between text and meaning. There is a fourth order of difficulty which occurs where this contract is itself wholly or in part broken . . . . *Ontological* difficulties confront us with blank questions about the nature of human speech, about the status of significance, about the necessity and purpose of the construct which we have, with more or less rough and ready consensus, come to perceive as a poem.[8]

Steiner instances "certain elements of Rimbaud, the poetics of Mallarmé, the esoteric programme of Stefan George," and other such modernist proceedings. Paul Celan's poem "Largo" is a test case for ontological difficulty. "An action of semantic privacy" leads us to question the text on a deeper level. "We ask: for whom then, is the poet writing, let alone publishing?" Ontological difficulty obscures the text at a foundational level.

Allegorical secrecy may be encoded as any of the first three of Steiner's four types of difficulty, and the total effect thereof will inevitably be complex. Steiner's first three types of difficulty and hence of complex obscurity will yield a clear picture to any persistent, penetrating examination, although, as we have said, a residue of mystery will remain in Blakean allegory. They are in principle decipherable or, in Paul de Man's term, "readable." The cryptic meaning can be read out of the text. We may be tempted, indeed we seem forced, to employ the term "allegory" for the uses of complex obscurity, while we reserve the term "symbol" for uses of simple obscurity. Certainly the so-called "difficult ornament" of standard allegory is in principle decodable. I have already suggested that even when clarified, the allegorical code will remain a partial enigma. This residue appears to be the symbolistic culmination of the most powerful allegory, an end-state, which in Medieval exegesis is called *anagogy*. For it is only when we encounter simple obscurity and ontological difficulty that an almost impenetrable barrier confronts the interpreting mind. What, for example, is the reader to make of the word "green" in the following couplet from Andrew Marvell?

> Annihilating all that's made
> To a green thought in a green shade.

The color-term here is obscure and difficult on an ontological plane, as is so often true with similar apparently simple phrases in Marvell.

Thinking about Marvell's oddly lucid obscurity, we discern in his poetry the vague outlines of a hidden system of thought. We are called to seek out an occluded system or method of binding lyrical expressiveness into a private, constrained, and highly controlled manner of poetic arrangement. Clearly Marvell is managing an obscurity that simply slides past the casual attention of the untrained reader. It appears that color-terms such as the "green" of "The Garden" and perhaps also spatial terms such as a pun on "plane/plain" may not in themselves have an absolutely clear and distinct meaning, but serve nonetheless to order larger combinations of ideas within a given poem. Marvell is in touch with an elemental level of thought, which he expresses in elemental phrases or phrasal units. These singular phrases are at once islands in a larger discourse, linked with each other, as with others of similar meaning, across some hidden system of coordinates, perhaps geometry or the theory of color perception. This buried system may be hidden from the reader at first glance, but the singular appearance of some key term will stand out from the text like an island in a mysterious ocean.

Under these conditions obscurity comes to be a releasing mechanism that generates literary puzzlement, which in turn elicits an enquiring cognitive response. The mind begins to engage in various pieces of detective work, and the resulting clarification of meaning, if it comes, brings relief to the initially puzzled mind. Whenever a literary style shifts from the level of lexical homework to the radical enigmas of simple obscurity, the mind must necessarily follow this shift with increased vigilance and imaginative daring. The text interacts with the mind-set of the reader.

When simple obscurity pervades a text, such a text will have a style that conforms to its oblique purposes. A style is required that will support ontological questioning. No single element of style can be made responsible for the whole range of such a task. On the other hand the mere use of a color-term would appear to engage the reader in an enigma of solipsism, since every reader's sense of a particular color will be unique to that individual—and yet, of course, we use color-terms with a belief in their power to communicate. The poet of ontological difficulty will be bound to search his lexicon for such terms as Marvell's "green."

The Gnomic Utterance

A class of elements, *gnomics*, will serve to designate the fundamental units of discourse whenever there is ontological difficulty and simple obscurity. My usage extends the standard meaning of gnomics. The dictionary informs us that a gnomic utterance is a short, pithy statement of general truth or fundamental principle. Examples are the proverb, the apothegm, the aphorism, the maxim. Standard usage speaks of the sententious sixth-century poets such as Solon and Theognis as the "gnomic poets." My usage of the gnomic as a mysterious, enigmatic, and pithy phrase or sentence depends upon the secret aspect of knowledge. The term "gnomic" derives from the Greek verb for knowing, that is, a species of thinking, and it relates to the mysterious term "gnostic." Rather than coin a new word for this thinking process, I prefer to develop the traditional idea of a gnomic element in literature.

In no special order, consider the following examples of gnomic utterances:

- *Keats:* Beauty is truth, and truth beauty.
- *Whitman:* The sea whispered me.
- *Wittgenstein:* Roughly speaking, objects are colorless.
- *Greville:* Absence is pain.
- The opening line of *Hamlet:* Who's there?
- *Heraclitus:* The wise [meaning wisdom] is one thing, to be acquainted with true judgment, how all things are steered through all.
- The self-identification of the dull-witted constable in *Love's Labours Lost:* "I am Anthony Dull."
- The first line of a sonnet of *John Clare:* "I feel I am, I only know I am . . ."
- The last line of that same sonnet: "But now I only know I am— that's all."
- A sentence in Borges's story, *The Zahir:* "At length, weariness deposited me at a corner."
- *Thoreau,* in *Walden:* "I was determined to know beans."

- The last words of the Lord, to Jonah: "And should I not spare Nineveh, that great city, wherein are more than sixscore thousand persons that cannot discern between their right hand and their left hand; and also much cattle?"

Note that the gnomic need not be an indicative sentence nor need it be a statement of some mysterious or enigmatic identity, such as "God is love" or "Absence is pain." These may indeed be gnomic, but their gnomicity resides in some virtually mysterious function or use or play, which something about their verbal construction permits them to work upon us as readers or listeners. "Mysterious function" is an oxymoron, so that I would make a point of the "function." Gnomicity is an actual function of some kind, despite its resistance to any attempt at a positive definition.

If we believe that the gnomic involves mysterious or enigmatic utterances of some aspect of the knowable, we must then identify the gnomic with ontological obscurity. For this reason the purpose of gnomics needs to be distinguished from that of the mere maxim or humorous aphorism. For all of these other sententious forms, let the *Maxims* of La Rochefoucauld serve as paradigm. The *Maxims* are many-faceted, but they all, unlike true gnomics, are instantly decodable in terms of their author's psychological principle of *amour propre*, a driving, irresistible, machinelike spring of human action. For instance: "The refusal of praise is only the wish to be praised twice" (no. 149). Or else, the *Maxims* of a more general kind are decodable in their own immediate terms: "The world oftener rewards the appearance of merit than merit itself" (no. 166).

To the extent that paradoxes are equally decodable, according to some analytic procedure, they too fail of being gnomic. So-called deep paradoxes, such as The Liar, might on this principle of nondecodability be called gnomics. If decodability is the issue, then every true gnome (another classical name for gnomic utterance) will be opaque in some ultimate sense, hence nondecodable. In this light a paradox approaches the status of a gnome when it reaches nondecodability, or, in deconstructive parlance, when it reaches the gap or aporia of finally undecidable meaning.

The heterogeneous list of gnomes given above sufficiently indicates an underlying strangeness in all the examples cited. This strangeness is easier to exemplify than to define. The gnomic always suggests some problem of expression, as if each gnomic utterance partook of the language-game of questioning the limits of language. When the "Ode on a Grecian Urn" ends with the question about truth and beauty, which is written in the form of an assertion, more perhaps is being asked of language than it can deliver. But if we allow to Keats's line a gnomic status, then we shall enjoy some security in knowing that the line is attempting to approach a limit as it moves our thoughts toward an ultimate question. The same sort of allowance must be applied to other gnomic writers, such as Wallace Stevens or John Ashbery. Stevens embraces the fragmentary where one might least expect it, which makes him an important exponent of the gnomic, especially in his later poems. Ashbery exhibits a curiously impersonal blankness in his sometimes comic use of the sententious. Lines of influence might be traced, as the gnomicity of Stevens and Ashbery finds its precursor in poems of Whitman and John Clare.

The path of the gnomic stretches backward in time to Heraclitus, if not to much earlier moments in the Book of Genesis. It may involve the poetry of every age, even the neoclassic era of the seventeenth and eighteenth centuries. If it touches authors like Heraclitus or the ancient Greek gnomic poets, it also touches a modern author like the quirky Thoreau or the coruscating rhetorician, Emerson. The range of gnomic text and context is wide indeed. Prose narrative will serve as well as poetry or drama to exemplify the process in action: let us take "The Open Boat" of Stephen Crane.

Stephen Crane as Gnomic Author

Like Hemingway, Crane was for part of his writing career a journalist. He had actually experienced in person the events narrated in "The Open Boat." In "Stephen Crane's Own Story," written for the newspapers, he told what happened to the ship *Commodore* as it foundered on January 2, 1897, what it was doing on that particular voyage, and what happened before the ten-foot dinghy of the second, fictionalized story ("after the fact") cut itself loose from the rafts on which other survivors hoped to reach land.

Without recounting the story, we note that it is divided into seven short chapters; it tells the phases of the small boat's painful return to land; it tells us of the four men in the boat and sketches for each a character. As has often been noted, some or all of its dialogue, sparse in the extreme, anticipates Hemingway's speech-patterning. Before Hemingway became the master of this particular species of gnomicity, Crane had found the voice and voices of utter desertion. They both excel in telling the story of the extreme situation. With Crane less analytically than with Hemingway, the narrative style and its spare dialogue are laconic not merely because men and women under extreme duress have not got much to say. Crane manages to set the emptiness of dialogue and scene in a telling framework of thought, a gnomic frame, a Heraclitan frame.

One might thematize the Heraclitan aspect in this story by focusing on the ways it shows men *against* the sea, so that the correspondent finally imagines maybe it would be "a comfortable arrangement" to drown—a "cessation of hostilities accompanied by a large measure of relief." For Crane warfare is a kind of primal strife of the elements, and of man as element, so that whatever applies to "The Open Boat" will apply *a fortiori* to *The Red Badge of Courage*.

It is the extremity of the elemental strife that counts in the short story. Crane needs and produces a perspective by incongruity (Kenneth Burke's phrase), and periodically lets into his story a note of weirdly discordant land-based experience. For example: "Many a man ought to have a bathtub larger than the boat which here rode upon the sea." Now *that* is bizarre, as a thought! The discord can occur more tonally, by a personifying allusion to some common human behavior: "A singular disadvantage of the sea lies in the fact that, after successfully surmounting one wave, you discover that there is another behind it just as important and just as nervously anxious to do something effective in the way of swamping boats." Here the mockery of the landsman's jargon smells of what Constance Rourke called "American humor." Another example: "By the very last star of truth, it is easier to steal eggs from under a hen than it was to change seats in the dinghy." This weird domestication occurs again in one of the story's most remarkable perspectival incongruities:

When it occurs to a man that nature does not regard him as important, and that she feels she would not maim the universe by disposing of him, he at first wishes to throw bricks at the temple, and he hates deeply the fact that there are no bricks and no temples. Any visible expression of nature would surely be pelleted with his jeers.

One could argue that such sidelong phrasings are humorous, and this by contrast heightens the terror and the weariness of the narrated experience. They also mark the isolation from mankind at large that besets the four men. This isolation in turn is all the more intense because it is shared. "It would be difficult," Chapter 3 begins in a typically conditional mood, "to describe the subtle brotherhood of men that was here established on the seas. No one said that it was so. No one mentioned it. But it dwelt in the boat, and each man felt it warmed him. They were a captain, an oiler, a cook, and a correspondent, and they were friends—friends in a more curiously iron-bound degree than may be common." If this is a new aspect of dwelling, in a different system of "iron-bound degrees" (punning on "decrees"), we are never allowed to imagine it as closing upon the actual land where friendship, *societas*, most commonly is made and bonded into some actuality. Instead, "These two lights were the furniture of the world." What is left over from experiencing this incongruous displacement of society is that there is always something like humor, working to bond the men in an unexampled state—brotherhood that "dwelt in the boat." Humor, as Freud wrote in his late essay, is the one case where the ruthless superego is kindly, allowing a permitted return to childhood. Humor, unlike wit, is noble and triumphs even over death. In gallows humor it is a kind of mysterious wit, a sacred wit. Here, humor erupts when the all-too-human cook addresses the oiler, who is the hero of the story: " 'Billie,' he murmured dreamfully, 'what kind of pie do you like best?' "

Crane conveys every possible *human* aspect of these men's physical, natural, and not-human isolation from all the reassuring things that dry land means. Whatever these effects show in detail, the story line itself proposes the promise of land, which is then withdrawn as wind, wave, and shore-surf make a first approach impossible, and the boat is forced out to sea again. This story itself is like a bad joke played on the sailors and the correspondent. For the latter the mere telling of the story is itself a secondary story line. Thus the whole story as a sequence of events and nonevents gets to be humorized.

Crane shows that small kindnesses and weary gentleness and momentary expressions of courageous humor are the heroic response to the extreme situation.

Up to this point our reading of the story might still not suggest a particularly gnomic interpretation. The narrative so described merely provides a probable setting for some larger gnomic purpose. You could get humor, fellowship, the sense of mortal isolation, the fear of drowning within sight of land, the discrimination of four different human responses to absolute danger—all these in any account of any such disaster, maybe from Nordhoff and Hall. But here, as with Conrad, something else is occurring at the same time. This something is the humorous language-game called "survival," and, through it, the journalistically cool Crane plays a completely gnomic game of narration, which subverts the optimism of an adventure story. The subversion goes deep; the surreal dance of the stranger on the shore, a man who perhaps has seen them, but may not have, forces a question: is this not pushing irony into a special darkness?

> "I'd like to catch the chump who waved the coat. I feel like soaking him one, just for luck."
> "Why? What did he do?"
> "Oh, nothing, but then he seemed so damned cheerful."

In a way the whole story is buried in this bit of dialogue. To show a covert line of connections between the items in a linked series of gnomics, we need only list a few examples, drawn from the beginning to the end of the tale. The whole story depends symbolically on the power of its opening sentence, which might serve as a classic instance of gnomic uncertainty.

- None of them knew the color of the sky.
- The correspondent, pulling at the other oar, watched the waves and wondered why he was there.
- In the wan light the faces of the men must have been gray. Their eyes must have glinted in strange ways as they gazed steadily astern. Viewed from a balcony, the whole thing would, doubtless, have been weirdly picturesque.
- It was probably splendid, it was probably glorious, this play of the free sea, wild with lights of emerald and white and amber.
- So they were silent.

- "Think we'll make it, Captain?"
  "If this wind holds and the boat don't swamp, we can't do much else," said the Captain.
- No one said that it was so. No one mentioned it. But it dwelt in the boat, and each man felt it warm him.
- Shipwrecks are *apropos* of nothing.
- Then there came a stillness, while the correspondent breathed with open mouth and looked at the sea.
- But the thing did not then leave the vicinity of the boat.
- A high cold star on a winter's night is the word he feels that she says to him. Thereafter he knows the pathos of his situation.
- It merely occurred to him that if he should drown it would be a shame.
- The coldness of the water was sad; it was tragic. This fact was somehow mixed and confused with his opinion of his own situation so that it seemed almost a proper reason for tears. The water was cold.
- The correspondent did not know all that transpired afterward.
- When it came night, the white waves paced to and fro in the moonlight, and the wind brought the sound of the great sea's voice to the men on shore, and they felt that they could then be interpreters.

The story "The Open Boat" is a narrative suspended between two poles defined by the first and last sentences: "None of them knew the color of the sky . . . and they felt that they could then be interpreters." We return always to the question of the unknown foreshadowed in the opening line ("None of them knew the color of the sky"), as it comes to the men struggling against the elements. The story is told as a third-person narrative, but the narrative point of view is that of the correspondent, the gnomic historian of this fate of consciousness. The story begins by speaking of the blank color of the sky, and etymology tells us that *obscurity* and *sky* come from the same Sanskrit root, which means a covering. Translated this way, the opening sentence says that none of them knew the exact nature of an overarching obscurity, "the color of the sky." Similarly, throughout his account, the narrator uses conditional terms like "probably," "might have," "possibly," and "if."

One effect of the uncertain conditionality of the words of perception and cognition is that the story almost succumbs to mental paralysis. In its extremest form, such a paralysis is death. Crane's task is to place the ideas of knowing and interpreting in an extreme testing situation. The story asks what it means to survive and answers this question in a variety of ways. However, of all the ways that the story understands survival, none is more striking than its emphasis on the survival of consciousness. Based on Crane's own experience, the story presents a test which occurs when tension stretches the thinking process to the limit of its capacity for order, or pushes thought into a state of arrested liminality. (The liminal character of the story is established as soon as we learn that the four men are hoping to cross the threshold from sea to land, by successfully crossing the shoreline with its wild and dangerous surf.) Through the perceptions of the narrator, which move fitfully among different perspectives on the situation, Crane gains access to the sublime, which Kant identified, psychologically, as an absolute overstraining of the faculties. The elements in this story are overwhelmingly powerful, the stakes are life and death.

Thinking the Poem

The gnomic expression of Crane's story is a significant model for the critic of obscure and secretive aspects of literature, because gnomics express the fundamental conditions of life or death. The critic needs a method that deals with language on the one hand and the conditions of life on the other. This requirement is met by Wittgenstein's later philosophy in the *Investigations* and elsewhere; it concerns itself precisely with what may be called the context of the gnomic. This context is labeled by Wittgenstein "forms of life" and is associated with his idea that language is not to be derived from perfect logical "atoms" in propositional shape, but rather is a vast network of language-games linked with each other by "family resemblances." The gnomic is just one among myriad elemental forms of language-games.

In Section 23 of the *Philosophical Investigations*, a list of 23 separate and varied language-games is given, ending with the beautiful final two lines:

> Translating from one language into another—
> Asking, thanking, cursing, greeting, praying.

Scholars such as Anthony Kenny and P. M. S. Hacker have pointed out the extreme heterogeneity of all those practices that Wittgenstein calls language-games. Hacker says:

> The term language-game is notoriously equivocal in Wittgenstein's later work. It sometimes designates primitive simplified forms of language, whether natural or notional. Occasionally it designates the totality of language and the actions and activities into which it is interwoven. Frequently it is used to designate a *fragment* of language or linguistic activity. The latter use encompasses a highly heterogeneous class [partial systems; speech acts of specific kinds . . . language-games with color words, or cardinal numbers, etc.] . . . A concept ranging over so wide and disparate phenomena is not obviously perspicuous or useful.[9]

Wittgenstein's extension of language-games, then, is rather like the map in Lewis Carroll, the map which is the same size as the country of which it is a map. As Hacker is aware, the objection to the term "language-game" might seem strong and clear and decisive. Wittgenstein and his commentators are, however, aware of this objection. At the end of Section 23, Wittgenstein suggests that we compare the multiplicity of linguistic tools and their uses, the multiplicity of kinds of words and sentences, "with what logicians have said about the structure of language." Wittgenstein then includes himself as author of the *Tractatus* among the logicians who have not understood language.

The whole point of a vast heterogeneous set of language-games is that such a conception fairly and naturally fits the facts of natural language and linguistic usage. The fact is that possible uses of language are innumerable. In the present context, this fact allows a place among language games for the expression of extreme conditions and forms of life. We have already seen such extremity in our account of the gnomic.

Wittgenstein's terse and often gnomic style of writing has an affinity with the chief characteristic of his fundamental unit of analysis, the language-game. As gnomics express questions about life itself, Wittgenstein tells us that the language-games are "forms of life," and he does philosophy in a particularly exemplary fashion. His written thought is divided and parcelled out in the form of the *zettel*, one file-card at a time, that is, one moment at a time. This writing gets its form not as representation of philosophy, but as the voicing of the living of that philosophy. The phrase "forms of life" includes the sense of staying alive and of being lively. The relevance to literature is immediate, in that imaginative authors do not, in the ordinary sense, care if what they say is true or not. They just want the poem or story or play to be credible. A rigorous truth-value system of analysis such as the *Tractatus* provides will scarcely ever be useful to the literary critic. The notion of the language-game takes the center away from true/false issues and moves criticism toward a life-centered approach, drawing attention to the spirited *activity* of language used in a particular context. Literary authors and their language-games are seen as more or less "alive," and, one is tempted to say, more or less full of spirit. In one of his notebooks Wittgenstein jotted down four lines from Longfellow's poem "The Builders":

> In the elder days of art,
> Builders wrought with greatest care
> Each minute and unseen part,
> For the gods are everywhere.

Under these lines, in parentheses, he wrote: "This could serve me as a motto." The idea of the liveliness of the language-game is virtually the same as believing that "the gods are everywhere."

The sense of an animated universe is as true for reading as it is for writing and speaking. Wittgenstein imagines reading machines and humans who read as if they were machines. Programmed to read, both machine and human being would be made to appear to be "reading," even though neither understood a word of what was being said. As usual, Wittgenstein is pointing out the role of conscious understanding in the activation of language and is suggesting the difficulty of knowing what it is that we are conscious of, when we read, with or without "understanding."

To elucidate the picture of our capacities as readers, let us suppose an activity that we may call "thinking the poem." To think the poem will be the goal of our studies.

Thinking the poem implies such things as taking the poem as an occasion for thought; thinking through the poem; being aware of one's thoughts as one reads the poem; looking for some logic in the poem; allowing a poem to trigger certain lines of thought; looking in the poem for what Coleridge called its "implicit metaphysic"; asking if what one is experiencing is Heidegger's "what is called thinking"; thinking about whether the poem is getting one to think. If you can interpret a poem, you can also think it. Yet how odd it sounds when we say: "Well, I have just been thinking *An Ordinary Evening in New Haven*, or *Love's Labours Lost!*"

The trained critic will treat the poem in a variety of ways, all of which concern ideas *about* the poem. Among these approaches might be comparing a poem to other poems, and noting some special linguistic or poetic or rhetorical feature, and describing the historical genesis of the poem. In short, the critic articulates a rich sense of its context, intertext, subtext, as well as its lexis and its tradition. These are all learned and technical responses, which permit us to go round and about the poem. What I mean is a more neutral, more naive kind of response, as if one were looking for some order or rhyme of thoughts that, of itself, the poem might disclose to the thinking mind, the mind that looks for logics and underlying rhythms. A mind that would know what kind of thing the particular poem is, *before* the thinker were able to say: "Well, this kind of poem (this sonnet, this short story) resembles that kind of poem"; or, "This one is like *that* one, in kind."

For the critic of linguistic activity in the poem, each poem is, initially, somewhat estranged. As a theorist, I habitually act as if I knew nothing about critical theory and practice. In this light each poem asserts its own strangeness, its own identity. Here "poem" means any imaginative artifact, regardless of genre or medium. As always, when doing theory, the fundamental response is to the rhythm of the work. It has been said that among the many subtle shades of meaning Aristotle gives to the term *logos*, one is rhythm. A poem has a rhythm, not primarily because of the way it may relate to other works, but owing to some properties of its own internal organization. Nor is this view the statement of a mere Romantic prejudice! The rhythms are there.

Wittgenstein's notion of a language-game is particularly useful here, because it suggests that significant language, for example a poem, is played. The play of language in the poem is essential to its thought.[10] When the critic is alerted to the notion that some kind of literary language-game is being played, he begins to think the poem. The critic becomes gnomical and begins to wonder about the thinking that inheres in the text at a given moment. As Wittgenstein put it, the critic lets the language-game "guide" his sequence of thoughts. The guide does not control the direction of one's reading, rather the guide, which is the "played" aspect of language, is simply there *with* him. This philosophical belief that in some such fashion the poem and its rhythm are guiding him requires that he think the poem.

In retrospect we may say that allegories use obscurity in a ritual rhythm, to veil and reveal hidden meanings. In most cases, the allegorical secret is decipherable and thence becomes an open secret. In some cases (the example given was Kafka's *The Castle*), ultimate secret meanings may remain impervious to analysis. Moving away from allegory, we find that all literature can be more or less cryptic and obscure. The secret, along with lesser forms of obscurity, will evoke the interpretive response. This hermeneutic response is most profound when the secret results from a simple obscurity. Such ontological obscurities are sublime, and stylistically they are deepened by the use of gnomic utterance. A gnomon is that moment of experience where the writer and then the reader encounter a barrier to understanding: namely, that possession of the gnomon demands a virtually impossible combination of general and particular knowledge, as with a concrete universal. By thinking the poem, moving through its thought patterns, we catch moments of gnomic obscurity. These we interpret. Such language and the language-games that go with it occur in a context I have called the extreme situation.

Extremity, we need to remember, is a variable notion, dependent upon circumstances. It might mean the situation of Arctic explorers or the situation of someone facing death, *in extremis.* On the other hand, an extreme condition occurs when a writer is attempting to verbalize exotically new, or exceedingly numerous, pieces of information: in short, the writer faced with an encyclopedic task. In all cases, extremity means an approach to some limit, and, in turn, it tests the powers of expression to their limit. Criticism needs to be able to describe thought occurring under extreme conditions and, in different ways, such is the purpose of the chapters that follow.

In case after case, one sees that the powers of expression are required to deal with some ultimate demand; whether it is the need to prophesy or to envision "mere being," whether it is the need to theorize all history or to combine history and ethnology, or whether, in the most general sense, there is a quest for new forms of mental activity that accompany new forms of intellectual discovery.

6. The Language-Game of Prophecy in Renaissance Poetics

Poets and prophets use inspired words and word orders, but poetry and prophecy seem to be heterogeneous notions, so that we need a method to discriminate them. Wittgenstein's *Philosophical Investigations* (#203) warns us that "language is a labyrinth of paths. You approach from *one* side and know your way about; you approach the same place from another side and no longer know your way about." It was in this context that Wittgenstein invented the descriptive notion of a language-game. This concept permits us to decrease the intricacy of the labyrinth of language, thereby attaining a viable and essentially nonreductive simplicity.

Inspiration is a notably obscure phenomenon. Nevertheless, it is possible that some idea or experience of "being inspired" is connected to the differing use of words that mark language-games of one type or another. The *Investigations* tells us that, like chess, every language-game has its defining rule or system of rules. Wittgenstein finds that deep uncertainties pervade the very idea of following a rule. Yet, loosely, literary conventions have a rule-following character, in which case we shall say that, as language-games, poetry and prophecy follow different rules of inspiration. It may be objected that inspiration is precisely a part of language that escapes the constraints of rule-following. It carries the work of utterance beyond conventional and standard usage and in that sense would seem to evade obedience to a rule. Yet it is a given of poetry and prophecy that they *must* be inspired. Our way out of this contradiction will be to examine the case of inspiration in both linguistic domains.

Throughout history names for the poets and the prophets have varied, but both are known to speak with a certain authority. Their inspired combinations of words come to be considered the finest, the strongest, the most perfect word-orderings for a culture at some moment or period of history. The origin of authority is authorship, and authorship in some sense is always an augury, an augmenting of order in the world of words. If poets and prophets do achieve that, their power to increase order and their power to overcome disorder differ to the extent that their sources of inspiration differ. The difference of source leads to a variance, if not rivalry, between two familially related language-games.

In the *Phaedrus* both types of word-players are said to suffer from a divine mania. They are ecstatic, beside themselves, and Socrates even puns on "mantic" and "manic." Plato discriminates four kinds of divine mania: "The divine madness was subdivided into four kinds, prophetic, initiatory, poetic, erotic, having four gods presiding over them; the first was the inspiration of Apollo, the second that of Dionysus, the third that of the Muses, the fourth that of Aphrodite and Eros." Two thousand years later in *A Midsummer Night's Dream*, Duke Theseus was to speak of "the poet's eye, in a fine frenzy rolling." Similarly, in the Old Testament the early seers, the *nebiim*, were ecstatics. Max Weber was not a theologian, and so he felt free to observe that the prophets, the *nebiim*, with charismatic furor delivered to their followers an "ecstatic victory magic." In the Song of Deborah we see what a great cultural distance separates Weber's "charismatic berserks" from the author of that remarkable chant of victory.

This ancient Song is epochal, because in it, with exemplary power, poetry and prophecy converge and flow together, if "flow" is not too serene a word. "Rush together" might be better. Here the shaman is a poet, the poet a shaman. The form of the Song makes it hard to follow its inner leaps, as it shifts from historical recounting, to present praise, to a fluctuating inclusion and exclusion of Deborah, the prophet. She is both in and out of her own song, it being partly sung *for* her as the scribe records, interprets, and embeds it in a historical context. Martin Buber describes the Song as follows:

The singer of the Song of Deborah is not only near the event [Jael had driven a nail through the forehead of the enemy captain, Sisera], but stands in the midst of the actual occurrence; he calls to the actors, stirring them up and encouraging them, he blesses and curses not on account of something previously done, but in the midst of the tempest of events not yet subsided. His heavily galloping rhythm he feels as a pacing in the midst of the event; the singing *nephesh*, the breath-soul, rises and falls heavily, like the step of the heavily armed man.[1]

The event celebrated in the Song of Deborah is for Israel cataclysmic: perhaps only an ecstatic singer could do it justice. With wild anticipation the song promises other future victories for Israel over her enemies. But it is the mixing of that portentous "barbaric yawp" with the prophet-scribe's larger framing attitude (he is part visionary, part historian) that gives to this document its special authority, and confers upon the Song itself its problematic relation to the prophetic mode.

The Song of Deborah and other works like it raise the question of literary hybrids. We can ask, how does a song fit or fit into a larger prophecy? The obverse question is equally critical: how may a prophecy fit or fit into a poem? Geoffrey Hartman approaches these questions in his "Poetics of Prophecy," where he shows how Wordsworth as poet had cause to question his own prophetic gifts.[2]

The long-developed traditional sense of the term *poem*, as it comes down to English poets of the sixteenth and seventeenth centuries, holds that poetry is pleasing. George Gascoigne spoke of making "a delectable poem." Sir Philip Sidney's *Apology for Poetry* allows the mixture of poem and prophecy, and asks: "And may not I presume a little further [that is, even beyond his example of the Delphic and Sybilline oracles], to show the reasonableness of this word *vates*, and say that the holy David's Psalms are a divine poem." Louise Schleiner in an article on "Spenser and Sidney on the Vaticinium" shows that Sidney is less sanguine about the poet's vatic pretensions than is Spenser, who followed Scaliger's Platonic claim that the poet is divinely possessed. In either case, the issue concerns a possible conflict between rational and inspired thought. Schleiner shows Sidney disagreeing even with Plato, denying to poetry in general "its divine name of *vaticinium* for any but explicitly religious poetry."[3] Here poetry and prophecy are conceived to differ in their manner of being inspired. Hence, paradoxically, we need to reconsider the poetics or language-game of prophecy.

One property of the traditional sense of *poem*, going back to the Greeks and Romans, is that the poem is ideally a completed *making*, a thing fully made. That is, in principle it defines its own borders. Everywhere in the history of poetry one sees this driving tendency to produce closures upon actions; whether these actions be of story or of expressive lyric self-definition. The actions might be those "a man might play," or symbolic actions which a mind might ruminate, recollect, or meditate upon. Kinaesthetic and cathartic actions would allow the singer to go through a song of joy or despair or sadness, singing of victory or defeat or peace. Closures mark all such poems in our tradition. They do not all succeed in hitting that mark, but generally before the later eighteenth century we do not usually consider that the fragment of a poem *is* a poem in itself; it is only the fragment of one.

Even the episodes in oral or literary epic are merely what they are—pieces of a whole story which, as partial language-games, are themselves whole stories. Such is the classic ideal that even the parts must in themselves have the beauty of wholeness. After the Renaissance unsettling changes occurred in that ideal, but these changes were only beginning with the Renaissance to assume their early modern shape, a secular shape. Meanwhile the medievalist always reminds us that whenever we have romance forms, we find a tendency to upset ideals of closure. Arguably romance never breaks, in a single poem, with the ideal of closure. Romance persistently defers closure by appearing to extend the boundaries of a "whole story," about Arthur and the others, to an ever wider circle. In romance, the problem of closure becomes an obsession.

If one clings to the classic idea of poem, one must then hold that the role of prophecy as it enters poetry will be to destabilize the discourse in a radical fashion. Prophecy breaks in yet another way with the ideal of poetic closure. On the plane of temporality prophecy forces poems, which as unities partake of the ideally recurrent and timeless, into a partly historical mode. By history here I mean events to which we give proper names and dates, whenever possible. History in principle records things that happen *only once*. (For example, there are only three contemporary persons in *Paradise Lost:* Columbus, Galileo and Milton himself. Their co-presence permits our entry into the prophetic aspect of that poem.) Historically inter-polated events destabilize, because they lead the readers out of the fiction of oneness which the poem, as such, presumes.

Another way to describe the destabilizing role of the historical intrusions the prophet makes would be to say that, whenever a piece of eventful history (so named or signaled) is introduced into a timeless poetic structure, there is a strong call to action. To name a historical person or event is to evoke a world of decisions, where decision itself is critical. Yet decisions are never wholly certain of their ends. To its quest for closure the poem now admits the voice of decisive uncertainty, the prophet's doubt.

Prophetic interpolations shake up the poet's assured mode of in-spiration. Plato's fourfold classification holds that poets are to be inspired through their invocations of the Muse, as when Milton invokes the Heavenly Muse, Urania, and then invokes the Holy Spirit:

> And chiefly thou, O Spirit, that dost prefer
> Before all temples th'upright heart and pure,
> Instruct me, for thou know'st, thou from the first
> Wast present, and, with mighty wings outspread,
> Dovelike sat'st brooding on the vast abyss,
> And mad'st it pregnant: what in me is dark
> Illumine; what is low, raise and support;
> That to the height of this great argument,
> I may assert Eternal Providence,
> And justify the ways of God to men.

Milton's practice here, by which he calls upon two separate muses or spirits, seems to indicate that the harmony of his epic requires the twin forces of poetic and prophetic inspiration. By twinning this double source, he saves the strictly poetic inspiration; he is not solely a prophet. He retains a strictly Platonic source for *poetic* divine madness, "the blessed rage for order."

Leaving aside the effects of prophetic powers, one asks: why does the poet's divinely inspired ecstasy not destroy his own poem? Why does this shaking of the mind not render closure impossible? Be-cause, I think, the classic appeal to the muse invokes an internally ordering model—the game of playing the poem to its close. The muse, mothered always by Memory, authorizes the inspiration provided by the game itself. In fact poets tell us that their poems inspire themselves, in their playing. The perfection of the playing to a close is the source of inspiration. The sense of authority the poet experiences comes from his being beside himself, but inside the rule of the poem in the making. The poet seeks the inspiriting rules of the form of the sonnet, the elegy, the epic.

As maker or *poietes*, the poet is inspired by the formal problem of his poem, as a composer might be inspired by the form of the minuet. To make a poem in this classic sense is then to discover its own rule, its own language-game, which will always involve complexes and crisscrossings of inner moves. Finally, the poet does not so much look for his own voice, to speak the poem, as he looks for the voice of the poem, to speak him. Few poets can write with inspiration, through more than a few different rules of poetic form; poets in general choose to be inspired by the forms they deeply know.

The inspiration proper to prophecy runs counter to the classic ideal of poetic, muse-like inspiration. Whereas a poem such as Keats's "Ode on a Grecian Urn" strives for the timeless, prophetic utterance always seems to refer us to future events. This is a crucial guise of prophecy, for its futuristic aspect in fact often leads it to become debased and trivialized. Vulgar prophecy is a magic travesty of science, like predicting the horses through astrology. The prophet as predicter and fortune-teller feeds the human craving for a guaranteed result, somewhere off in the future. A historian's tact will be needed, as we reckon with predictive prophecy, whenever it occurs in chiliastic or messianic movements found in the religions of the oppressed. In principle, however, prophecy need not be focused on the future: its interpolation of the once-occurring event or events could be a presentism. Such events will intrude upon the aesthetic calm of the classic poem.

Questions arising about poems like Keats's "Ode" suggest that some prophecy can indeed, as Elizabethans and Blake perceived, be interwoven in a poetic texture. Hartman quotes Wordsworth: "Poets, even as Prophets, each with each / Connected in a mighty scheme of truth, / Have each his own peculiar faculty, / Heaven's gift . . ." (1850 *Prelude* XIII, 301–4). The fact is that the Greek term, prophecy, means that the prophet "speaks for" something. True prophecy has a high calling, to immerse us in the historical factness of the timeless, which Goethe in *Faust* calls *der Tat,* and which recently Harold Bloom has called "facticity." All the most powerful prophecies concern present attitudes toward present decisions, while remaining aware of both past and future.

In either case, whether prophesying in the present or for the future, the prophet is not moved to inspiration by anything like the closed *form* of a poem. Something quite different occurs with the prophet.

Imagine the ancient Pythoness. She speaks the inscrutable hexameters, having intoxicated herself with the "exhalations" of her cave (those vapors which Plutarch and his friends discussed at length, while trying to discover why the oracle no longer spoke in verse). The Pythoness finds her words by sacred intercourse with the divine, with the daimon, as it was believed. The impersonal mania of oracular Hellenic prophecy was mediated by intervening priests, who were not autointoxicated; their role was specifically to mediate between the oracle and the suppliant. They were interpreters. Many centuries later, after the Reformation, the so-called "liberty of prophesying" meant the freedom to interpret Sacred Writ.

The critical point is that with the oracle and with other interpretive prophecies, the inspiration is thought to come from a distinct other. This is most powerfully true of Old Testament prophecy. Yet the daimon of pagan culture is scarcely less other. The God of the Old Testament, however, is a being utterly other, even though He intervenes in the world He has created. In the "presence" of this awesome progenitor the prophet takes upon himself or herself the harsh task of speaking the Word of God. This prophet claims not to speak his own word—what we hear is, "Yahweh told me this," or: "Yahweh says to me that I must tell you that," or merely the phrase, "The word of Yahweh." Geoffrey Hartman informs us that the Hebrew term for words in this case, *divre,* "indicates something closer to 'acts' or 'word-events'."[4] When the King James version says "to whom the word of the Lord came," the original Hebrew says "the God-word was to him." It is but a short step from word-events to the large scale event we know as the language-game of prophecy. True, we get the Old Testament in the form of a scribal overlay whose layering is perpetuated in the commentaries of later interpreters, but the aboriginal prophetic encounter is ecstatic in the most absolute sense. One could put it crudely this way: what can you do with the voice of God, except to transmit it? For its rules are undiscoverable, its language-game finally unknowable (which is one message of the Book of Job).

As a result the prophet *makes* nothing. He does, however, *do* something. He voices the words of the Other. The ancients called him also a seer, a visionary, but what the prophet sees is entirely controlled by the words he thinks God is giving him to report. The images that the prophet evokes—and Abraham Heschel and others have stressed how trivial they can be—are images so loaded with moral imperatives that in effect they are the mere signs that go with the driving message of the voice of God, which is always a voice of absolute, arbitrary, inescapable divine power. This power seems to have one rule, that it penetrates all parts of the believer's life, and no less the nonbeliever's life and world. Hence prophecy in this form can sustain the most extreme variations from the sublime to the ridiculous. Nothing is too grand, nothing too trivial, to concern the deity's divine attention. The prophet has to be willing to let God be; he must transmit anything that comes to God's mind. One's heart goes out to Jonah, when he was called to come out of comfortable retirement to prophesy doom to the citizens of Nineveh. The Book of Jonah is the comedic counterpart to the Book of Jeremiah, which must end in lamentation. Both prophets are called to leave home and its comforts. They go far away, to move no distance at all. For the prophet the far is near. So, in the Christian tradition, preaching on the text "A Virgin Shall Conceive," John Donne said that "there shall be a messiah, a Redeemer Given. Now, how is this future thing (There shall be a Messiah) a signe of present deliverance from siege? First, in the notion of the Prophet, it was not a future thing for, as in Gods own sight, so in their sight, to whom he opens himself, future things are present." God speaks always in the present tense, though the prophet discerns a future meaning. Paradoxically, nothing could be more fraught with implications for the future, then precisely this deep concentration on the present moment.

Two questions arise concerning the prophet's moment: what is the nature of access to the divine? what is the form of the present moment? Throughout history these questions keep changing somewhat in form and substance. Quite obviously, as to the first question, our world is more secular than Chaucer's or Shakespeare's.

The Prioress's invocation to the Virgin was central to the life of Chaucer's time, but we have to reimagine that centrality, trusting to every tone and nuance in the poet's wording. The Divine Poems of Donne could hardly be written today, one imagines. Things change, and the access to the divine changes.

Similarly with other areas of sensibility—Parmigianino's self-portrait was painted in the year 1524, we think. On the one hand, surely no Renaissance poet could have written John Ashbery's poem, "Self-Portrait in a Convex Mirror." On the other hand, the original portrait is an index to one change of poetic outlook that does seem to mark the Renaissance, its explosive concern with the artist's "creative" role in the making of the poem. Montaigne's essays (as he matured) are not only modern works, but are also products of their own time, as are many other documents of increased poetic self-awareness. When Montaigne says that he "portrays passing," he speaks for a whole culture. But where Montaigne is most intensely modern he goes one step further, and this I regard as close to a prophetic sensibility. He portrays passing and change, to be sure. But he then goes on to portray the way ideas of change are themselves changing.[5]

Here the idea of the present moment is seen not as fixed and eternal, but as subject to alteration over time. Montaigne anchored his thoughts to a strong idea of humanism and its self-discovery. He anchors the nullity of an always passing moment to the stability of a system of inherited values, which might be called "Plutarchan humanism." Such a vision marks his discourse with ideas of stability in change.

Writing about Edmund Spenser in *The Prophetic Moment* (1971), I wished to show that in the Renaissance a prophetic sensibility would have to entertain subtle ideas of change. In *The Faerie Queene* these ideas are presented through a liminal poetic. The poem is liminal in that it depends upon complex arrays of threshold situations, whether of image or of narrative. For his inspiration Spenser draws variably upon the authorizing voices of the Bible, Virgil, Arthurian lore, Ovidian metamorphic beliefs, and even Hermetic thought-experiments. All these are prophetic sources of inspiration, a divine madness held subject to the control of the Spenserian stanza, which permits the poem to assimilate such a wide variety of prophetic sources.

The example of Spenser is central for his own time and for the Miltonic and then Romantic tradition that issues from his epic vision. Spenser develops an archetypal structure of narrative, such that the poet may envision changes in the idea of change. Throughout *The Faerie Queene* Spenser counterpoints visions of temples inside labyrinths, labyrinths inside temples. The purpose of this polyphony is to create for narrative a dilated threshold, an instantaneous crossing from labyrinthine confusion and excess to a templar clarity and restraint. Spenser's stanza is the poetic mechanism by which this instantaneous crossing is paradoxically enlarged and dilated, as if the instantaneous prophetic moment could be reduced to extreme slow motion. The Spenserian stanza, by interlacing its rimes and rhythms, becomes the locus of the oscillating change of temple to labyrinth, labyrinth to temple.

The temple and the labyrinth, with the threshold between them, indicate a path that the poet may follow as he engages with the forces of prophecy. Roughly speaking, we may say that the labyrinth is the archetypal space of historical time, while the temple (as its name suggests) is the home of the timeless. The liminal crossover between these two "spaces" marks the moment of prophetic vision in which the poet sees life from the joint perspective of passing and immutability. The poet's task includes preventing either archetypal space from freezing into a fixed idea. The truly prophetic poem allows maximum access to change, at the threshold.

If, as Hartman suggests, "the relationship between *poetics* and *prophetics* cannot be so easily accommodated,"[6] then it will always be necessary to examine for cases of prophetic liminality. The example of Shakespeare's history plays should prove decisive. Let us, therefore, consider *Henry VIII* and *Richard II*. Both works include major prophetic speeches, which relate problematically to the idea of history.

Henry VIII ends with the christening of the infant Elizabeth, Henry's child and future Queen of England. Archbishop Cranmer begins his prophecy thus:

> Let me speak sir:
> For heaven now bids me; and the words I utter
> Let none think flattery, for they'll find 'em truth.

Cranmer recites the glories of an Elizabethan reign which he says many times "shall" come. (Cranmer uses the word "shall" twenty times.) When the play was performed, in 1613, its prophetic prediction could be seen as having been fulfilled, even down to the final vision, that Elizabeth would die a virgin queen:

> A most unspotted lily shall she pass
> To the ground, and all the world shall mourn her.

The "shall's" are contagious—Henry himself picks up the habit of this game.

> This day, no man think
> He has business at his home; for all shall stay;
> This little one shall make it holiday.

Thus the play ends. It closes, rounded upon a promise of permanent and continuing political stability.

We might call this official prophecy. As usual, Shakespeare intends a more self-doubting reflection on the fact that it is an optimized piece of history—Elizabeth has been gloriously dead for ten years. Cranmer's speech gives a frame of reference to the whole action, gives it a "prospect." As perspectival device, the speech is superadded to the dramatic *poem*, as a mechanism of enclosing self-awareness. The speech does not in any way change the action of the play. The prophecy does not enter the poem deeply, but merely comments upon it. Indeed, as a prediction, Cranmer's speech slightly debases its own prophetic force.

With *Richard II*, however, the case is different. When the dying John of Gaunt pronounces upon England's sufferings, he goes deeper than Cranmer, that other spokesman for official Tudor messianic propaganda. Gaunt speaks, like all major Old Testament prophets, for himself, and he is himself inspired to speak a higher vision: "Methinks I am a prophet new inspired." The weight should fall on the "I." Much in Gaunt's speech is traditional and Biblical: the sense of a chosen land, a chosen people, a covenant, a providential history, a royal dereliction from the higher laws of God and nature, and a sense of the prophet's highly individual role in the speaking of the prophecy.

Unlike Cranmer, with his guaranteed vision of the future (it had already passed into a nostalgic haze by 1613), Gaunt speaks in the prophetic present tense, about a crisis where the right decisions are not *now* being made. But Gaunt touches the springs of the greater prophecy in yet another way. If we ask what, leaving aside his dynastic claims for the moment, he really wants from Richard, surely the answer is that he wants Richard to be a prophet like himself, to *see* as he does, to *hear* as he hears, to speak out as he speaks out. Perhaps like Moses he wants all of the children to be prophets. But he is cheated of this hope: Richard is offstage and does not hear the prophecy, and would not hear it anyway if he were present.

A deeper assimilation of the prophecy occurs here, however. Gaunt's dying, mantic presence becomes the ground for the subsequent tragic action, and Richard ends by indeed becoming a prophet—prophesying his own doom, but prophesying nonetheless. It is as if, following Gaunt's speech, the whole play had been prophetized. Gaunt has spoken the rule of the language-game of prophecy, its form of life, which holds that one cannot escape one's destiny, because one is what one is. Richard is the solitary tragic hero, whose prophetic gift is to have the power to listen to the broken music of time, and to speak for its tragic implication.

There is nothing extraneous or superadded about Gaunt's speech. It yields to the play its tragic energy, as if that energy came at once from a source both outside and inside the world of the play. Because this is a Renaissance drama, we are not surprised to find that the alienated source of inspiration of Gaunt's words is to be found within himself and again, more strongly, within Richard's own ruminations—as the poet said elsewhere, "ruin hath taught me thus to ruminate." The play stages a transformation of viewpoint, from that of Gaunt, who is traditional as Biblical and oracular prophet, to that of Richard, who is the truly new prophetic type and who draws his vision from within the selfhood of what is almost a modern sense of alienation.

John Milton was later to write of the deep impression made by Shakespeare's "Delphick lines." Delphic can merely mean mysterious; it also means "prophetic," and correctly sets the pattern of Shakespeare's plays in their true light. Joseph A. Wittreich has said that "From the standpoint of literary history, prophecy is a link between Milton's poetry and Sidney's poetic, and an absolute bond between Milton's poetry and that of Chaucer, Langland, and Spenser—their poetry, in its generic mixtures, rhetorical strategies, and labyrinthine structures, finding major analogues, if not a primary source, in prophetic tradition. But prophecy is also the bridge thrown up over time, uniting Milton with Romantic poets and modern ones."[7] To these poets who interact with Milton we may add that of his predecessor, Shakespeare.

There are then movements in Shakespeare's plays which are double, in the sense of doubly inspired. Gaunt's speech is very much *in* the play and contributes to its plot, which seeks poetic closure. But it also exists in the play as marginal to that tragic plot and closure. As such it suggests a higher law than that of dynastic politics. Richard does not hear Gaunt; at the critical moment he is offstage, waiting to enter. But it is as if, being king, or being Richard, he does hear it—or somehow knows it without hearing it. Gaunt's speech lets prophecy loose in the play, and after that, all is subject to the shadow of those higher laws. What is odd about this process is that in Shakespeare it does not intrude, it seems to flow naturally from his ways with speech. If one were to guess what underlies these ways, perhaps one might say that, like Milton and Wordsworth after him, and Marlowe and Spenser in his own time, Shakespeare allows ordinary language to find its way among the gorgeous ornaments of high rhetoric. He lets words and phrases resound without undue control, trusting that linguistic overtones will permit him to move toward and away from the numinous, as freely as air. In this hybrid art the wind blows where it will, stirring and touching all things. The play escapes the diminishing effect of arbitrary, unearned closure.

The paradox of Gaunt's prophecy is that it invokes two contrary archetypes at once. Ideas of the temple and of the labyrinth interact within this prophecy, to create in us and for the play a most acute sense of the liminal tension of the prophetic moment. In its inspired duality, Gaunt's speech catches the pathos and the enigma of all major prophetic insight into history. Events have their structure, which we grasp and do not grasp. Providence is and is not a pattern to follow. Prophecy commonly foretells and does not foretell the future. Prophecy sees and does not see into the present moment. Owing to this paradoxical situation, it becomes evident that of all the types of prophetic thinking, literary prophecy requires the thinker to have greatest insight into the riddling web we call "history."

7. *The Father of Lies*

In Oscar Wilde's *The Decay of Lying* young Vivian announces the "final revelation . . . that Lying, the telling of beautiful untrue things, is the proper aim of Art." Vivian regales his friend Cyril in the following way:

> We need not say anything about the poets, for they, with the unfortunate exception of Mr. Wordsworth, have been really faithful to their high mission, and are universally recognized as being absolutely unreliable. But in the works of Herodotus, who, in spite of the shallow and ungenerous attempts of modern sciolists to verify his own history, may justly be called the "Father of Lies"; in the published speeches of Cicero and the biographies of Suetonius; in Tacitus at his best; in Pliny's *Natural History*; in Hanno's *Periplus*; in all the early chronicles; in the Lives of the Saints; in Froissart and Sir Thomas Malory; in the travels of Marco Polo; in Olaus Magnus and Aldrovanus, and Conrad Lycosthenes, with his magnificent *Prodigiorum et Ostentorum Chronicon*; in the autobiography of Benvenuto Cellini; in the memoirs of Casanova; in Defoe's *History of the Plague*; in Boswell's *Life of Johnson*; in Napoleon's despatches, and in the works of our own Carlyle, whose *French Revolution* is one of the most fascinating historical novels ever written, facts are either kept in their proper subordinate position, or else entirely excluded on the general grounds of dullness. Now everything is changed. Facts are not merely finding a footingplace in history, but they are usurping the domain of Fancy, and have invaded the kingdom of Romance. Their chilling touch is over everything. They are vulgarizing mankind. The crude commer-

cialism of America, its materializing spirit, its indifference to the poetical side of things, and its lack of imagination and of high unattainable ideals, are entirely due to that country having adopted for its national hero a man who, according to his own confession, was incapable of telling a lie, and it is not too much to say that the story of George Washington and the cherry tree has done more harm, and in a shorter space of time, than any other moral tale in the whole of literature.

Cyril: My dear boy!

Vivian: I assure you it is the case, and the amusing part of the whole thing is that the story of the cherry tree is an absolute myth. However, you must not think that I am too despondent about the artistic future either of America or of our own country. Listen to this:—

"Listen to this!"—the eternal appeal of the story-teller to his immediate gathering of listeners. To proceed along such lines of rhetorical art, it may be that the author must be a *speaker*, working within a culture still deeply oral. High conversation still remains a cultural ideal. The telling of "beautiful untrue things" serves to arouse and hold the listener's interest and tireless attention to the flow and turbulence of a fine story. Dullness is the enemy.

The truthfulness of Herodotus turns out to be a subject of lively debate in the ancient world. Wilde knows this and plays upon the idea in his version of the Persian Wars. His dramatic intuition leads him to see the narrative importance of Herodotean untruth and to observe the irony of most historiographic pretensions to the truth, an irony he embodies in the conceit that our American tale of the truthfulness of our founding father is "an absolute myth." The joke has various parallel lines. Herodotus not only writes what we call history; in effect he writes the first book of history in the West. His account of the Persian Wars exists as a book, supplanting the fragmentary or lost remains of his shadowy forebears, a Xanthus or Hecataeus. "There was no Herodotus before Herodotus," says Arnaldo Momigliano.[1] Herodotus, like George Washington, is a founding father.

Herodotus gives us the operative term, "history." When Wilde's Vivian speaks of "absolute myth," he means a total lie or complete fabrication. Myth certainly can have this sense, but originally it was closer to the words "story" or "tale." Our word "history," by contrast, comes from the Herodotean Greek term *historia* (researches): it is what Herodotus named his writing of the story of the Persian Wars. He gives us the narrative of a research project, and in so doing forces a collision between his form of thinking and the greater forms of myth, as they were known from Homer in his own time. For surely the historian held somewhat different ideas of truth than the author of the *Odyssey.*

Indeed when the ancients called Herodotus a liar, they probably meant that he was a spinner of yarns. A common Latin word for him is *fabulosus,* which is different from *mendax,* deceitful by design. Cicero observed that his work was full of "innumerable fables" (*innumerabiles fabulae*). Defining a liar as a fabulist would help us if we knew exactly what a fable was, but that is exactly the issue raised by the method of *The History.* There seems to be no convenient single word for a truthful story. And a *mythos* can be true or false, depending on one's point of view. Very likely Thucydides was thinking of Herodotus when, in the Preface to *The Peloponnesian War,* he said that he would exclude "the mythical" (*to muthodes*) from his fictively literal record of what was said and what was done. This was a severe change, with important consequences for the later repute of Herodotus. "It is only too obvious," says Momigliano, "that Thucydides ultimately determined the verdict of antiquity on his predecessor. He carefully read (or listened to) his Herodotus and decided that the Herodotean approach to history was unsafe."[2] Herodotus failed because his materials could not be tested for their veracity, and that was the case for two reasons: the sources were often too remote, that is, they were not contemporary; and they were often too muddled in their content. Though writing on a war which occurred in the generation before him (he lived from about 484 to 435 B.C.), Herodotus had wanted also to delve into the distant past. Given the heavy reliance on oral reports for his data, the temporal distance between the event and the historian was too great for factuality to be weighed. Secondly, Herodotus wanted to relate his account of the war to a wide variety of events. The problem was not merely temporal; it was conceptual in a broader taxonomic sense. Thucydides thought that only those events which were politically determined could be studied in a more or less critical fashion. Folklore, for example, lacked the logic of Athenian and Spartan politics and thus could not be treated historically.

This brief account suggests that Thucydides' polemic against Herodotus and the other story-tellers, the *mythographoi,* has immediate force—the more impressive because it yielded a great narrative, the history of *The Peloponnesian War*. On the other hand, we begin to see where the polemic itself is vulnerable. Unable to ask questions about the logic of myth, it ends by depreciating the intellective value of mythology. As critical historian, Thucydides holds that a myth is a mere tale, signifying very little. A myth to him is any old story that Herodotus or other fabulists use to get their listeners or readers to pay attention, as Homer had told stories in earlier times for similar rhetorical reasons. The early critical historian believes that myths are entertaining anecdotes, beautifully improvised by a bard, but deserving banishment precisely because they belong to the an-ecdotal, literally the un-published, the *inédit*, the unofficial and historically dispensable property of the poet and dramatist. Thus Aristophanes would parody a Herodotean account of the causes of war in a burlesque Rape of Helen, in *The Acharnians*, where the whole affair is reduced to a tabloid scandal.

In modern times myth has reacquired the dignity it held for Homer. Philip Wheelwright, for example, gives this definition of myth: "a story or a complex of story-elements taken as expressing, and therefore as implicitly symbolizing, certain deep-lying aspects of human and transhuman existence."[3] Such a definition points to the psychoanalyst's equation between myth and the unconscious, myth and dream. Such equivalences may be traced back to Vico, for whom man's earliest poetic and imaginative creations are a mythic protophilosophy. We have discovered the buried transcendencies of mythic structure, and with Lévi-Strauss or Northrop Frye we understand the logic and thinking of the mythmaker. As a means of ordering their perceptions of existence, primitive cultures are seen to mythologize the actions of daily life. "This process, too, is determined primarily by the lines which activity takes; so much so that the forms of mythical invention reflect, not the objective character of things, but the forms of human practices."[4] Form here has a sense of the underlying structure, which it shares with its parallel use in Wittgenstein's phrase "the forms of life." To a degree, the forms of life found in postmodern technologically advanced societies possess this depth, and display it, in the field of popular culture.

Postmodern analysis takes a generous view of the apparently imaginative constructions that sprinkle the pages of Herodotus.

Myth has reached the Vichian status of a complex, if primal, structure of language and thought, on which we depend to see through and beyond the developmental obscurity of life as, in all its confusion, life is lived. In particular, we often prefer to *begin* analysis of a set of events by simply accepting their story, their mythos. Testing the veracity of men, for example, in an endless ordeal of public journalistic exposure, a newspaper in a sense speaks for modern man's complete acceptance of myth as a mode of truth-telling that will be tested through a continuously warring Miltonic contest between different "unimpeachable sources." We have seen how fragile, yet necessary, this process can be.

In similar fashion, while not precisely writing news of the day (his anecdotes may refer to the remote past), Herodotus is creating something new—his collection of stories is "news" to the reader. In short, Herodotus prizes novelty of information. Dionysius of Halicarnassus cited Herodotus as giving greater pleasure than Thucydides perhaps because, besides the optimistic ending of the Persian Wars, the book gave a narrative "varied by pauses,"[5] that is, an endless string of novel situations.

Dionysius, who settled in Rome about 30 B.C., seems to give emotive reasons for preferring Herodotus over Thucydides. In particular he fails to understand Thucydides' method of close political analysis. He is distressed that the later historian wrote of a war disastrous to Athens, as if to say all history must end on a rising note. Yet Dionysius seems vaguely aware that Herodotus has a method in his seeming lust for the anecdote. As he puts it, "What it comes to is that the writer who has taken a single subject has succeeded in breaking a unity into fragments, while the writer who has preferred a miscellaneous plurality of subjects has created a harmonious unity out of the congeries."[6]

Dionysius was writing against current opinion, for Herodotus went into partial eclipse for many centuries. Readers believed, with Thucydides, that Herodotus should be classed with "the poet's exaggerated rhapsodies, or the entertaining rather than accurate compositions of the genealogists."[7] A climate of thought persisted in which it was hard to value the poetic "harmony" of The History.

It was not until the Renaissance that this climate altered and the negative judgment of Herodotus could be reversed. This period of history saw the beginnings of a rudimentary comparative ethnography. Herodotus could now play the role of historian as comparatist. Momigliano describes the change:

> In the sixteenth century historians travelled once more in foreign countries, questioned local people, went back from the present to the past by collecting oral traditions. In some cases they acted as ambassadors, in others they were missionaries and explorers: they were seldom professional historians. But they wrote history—a history extraordinarily reminiscent of Herodotus, both in style and in method. The new diplomacy required careful examination of the traditions of foreign countries; religious propaganda made urgent the production of objective accounts of the peoples to be converted. Above all, there was the discovery of America with all that it implied.[8]

If the representation of thought is a complex matter for prophecy as well as poetry, it enforces a yet more critical test for the narrator of history which, by definition, emphasizes the otherness of its subjects. Historical fact is alien to the present. Whenever such chronologically alienated fact includes the thinking, or *mentalité*, of foreign groups and cultures, the historian necessarily has to imagine how *someone else* is thinking. The logic of the historiographic makes extreme demands upon this imaginative process, for such discourse strikes the solipsistic wall of mind. It would seem that history cannot rest with the scientific constraints that determine the facticity of events, but must seek to free itself for research into alien mentalities. Just such a freedom began to be felt in England in the later sixteenth century.

Queen Elizabeth claimed that "the use of the sea and the air is free and common to all." Richard Hakluyt called his countrymen "stirrers abroad, searchers of the remote parts of the world." Shakespeare's Ferdinand cried out in *The Tempest*, "Oh Brave new world, that hath such creatures in it!" Despite narrow-minded religious conflict, this was a time for the expansion of mental horizons. The first two Books of *The History* had appeared in English in 1584. Both Hakluyt and Herodotus share an enlargement of perspective. They delight in pointing to the foreign customs which may be compared with native Greek customs or native English customs. The historian must now begin to deal with the otherness of native custom, and for ethnographic compilations curiosity becomes a principle of composition. As Momigliano observes, one could now "travel abroad, tell strange stories, inquire into past events, without necessarily being a liar. One of the standard objections against Herodotus had been that his tales were incredible. But now the study of foreign countries and the discovery of America revealed customs even more extraordinary than those described by Herodotus . . . Here the impact of the modern *relazioni* from distant countries is obvious. What we might call the comparative method of ethnography had been vindicated."[9] Above all, the idea of a *world* of related customs and peoples was, in present works, now recalling the view Herodotus had originally taken.

A wide, more or less global perspective marks *The History*, even from the opening words of its preface: "Herodotus of Halicarnassus presents the results of his researches in the following work, with the twofold object of saving the past of mankind from oblivion and ensuring that the extraordinary achievements of the Hellenic and Oriental worlds shall enjoy their just renown—particularly the transactions which brought them into conflict with one another." This is to be the account of a "world war," as it was for a Greek "world-shaking." The historian is searching for the grounds of the feud between Hellenic and Oriental peoples. The preface states the method of preserving past events in memory—the historian researches transactions between different peoples, or groups of people.

Before him Herodotus had the example of the two Homeric epics, both of which contributed to the development of his method. By the close of the *Iliad* we know a great deal about the attitudes and allegiances that brought Achilles and Hector face to face, in tragic duel before the walls of Troy. By the end of the *Odyssey* we have passed through fables of cultural difference and, in a sense, come home with Odysseus to Ithaca, to reclaim not only his wife, but even more, his kingdom. Both great stories are memorable, with (for us) the exception of notably remote genealogical myth and also the otiose profusion of hackings, spearings, choppings, assaults, and batteries that occur in the *Iliad*. Dionysius of Halicarnassus believed that Herodotus' "hero and example" was Homer. Both poet and historian wanted to tell a memorable story, with deep cultural resonances. A dependence upon oral report is native to both authors, and both authors are clearly able to improvise upon the unity of their themes. Herodotus clearly stands at the borderline between oral and writing cultures; his history shares a certain laxness with epic, as it shares the forms of improvisation.

The History is formally divided (by its Alexandrian editor) into nine Books, each of which came to be named after one of the nine Muses. The largest structural division of the whole is roughly that between Books VI and VII. Books I through VI give a panoramic tour through all the prior transactions that Herodotus believed contributory to his *epos*, the main Persian War itself, which begins effectively in Book VII, where Xerxes prepares for war and invades Greece for the second time.

Book I, although it has the effect of a prolegomenon, belongs conceptually with all those other preliminary matters that antedate the final onrushing climax of the whole research narration, a climax occupying the final three Books, VII, VIII, and IX. It is only in this final triad that Herodotus shows the complete victory of the Greeks over their Persian invaders, and the vindication thereby of the animating Hellenic idea, freedom, *eleutheria*, within the polis. The war is fought on land and finally at sea, but the essential combat is shown by Herodotus to take place between opposed ideas of freedom and tyranny.

The drama of isolated, onrushing climax in Books VII through IX depends upon the characterization of the archetypal Persian tyrant, Xerxes, whose antagonism to the Greeks is so monolithic that their defense against him acquires a memorable grandeur. Many embattled underdogs have seen such a destiny, and have documents to go with it. In such circumstances the historian must recreate an adequate antagonist, which the ruminative, brooding, impulsive Xerxes certainly is. If among the many remarkable Herodotean touches of portraiture we were to isolate one, it would not be the famous scene of Xerxes' tears at the shortness of life, as he looked upon his army poised at the Hellespont. It would rather be the persistent, delicate rendering of his paranoia, as when he discusses his violently oscillating dreams with his uncle Artabanius. He is memorably paranoid. When a storm smashed one of the Persian bridges over the Hellespont, Xerxes went into a rage. Immediately he "gave orders that the Hellespont should receive three hundred lashes and have a pair of fetters thrown into it." Such behavior delights Herodotus the raconteur, and he goes on about the lashing of the strait: "And I have heard before now that [Xerxes] also sent people to brand it with hot irons. He certainly instructed the men with the whips to utter, as they wielded them, the following words: 'You salt and bitter stream, your master lays this punishment upon you for injuring him, who never injured you. But Xerxes the King will cross you, with or without permission. No man sacrifices to you, and you deserve the neglect of your acrid and muddy waters'—a highly presumptuous way of addressing the Hellespont," Herodotus adds, "and typical of a barbarous nation . . . In addition to punishing the Hellespont Xerxes gave orders that the men responsible for building the bridges should have their heads cut off. This unseemly order was duly carried out, and other engineers were appointed to start the work afresh." Herodotus then counts out the exact number of boats used to support the floating bridge, describing the method of anchorage in some detail.

What is so striking here, and throughout the *History*, is the rapid juxtaposition of the plausible and the strange, both recounted with complete *sang froid*. Another quite striking property of Herodotus' *History* is its assymetrical form, as a whole. We are not simply given the final triad, Books VII and IX, which is meant to be offset by the counterbalancing, if unequal, bulk of Books I through VI. Rather, Books I through VI *prepare* for the triad, conditioning us to read it in a certain way. They train us to read it not as an epic, but as a history. Not only is the vast prolegomenon of I through VI not an epic, but even more critically, the increasingly condensed and concatenated and, we might say, increasingly Thucydidean triad of VII through IX—the account of the war itself—is not an epic. It does *not* have heroes. Xerxes and Themistocles possess epic stature, but they finally lack the power to concentrate the action upon themselves, to draw the fate of the whole mass of their followers into their own single, all-consuming heroic lives. Oddly, the more their subtlety and grandeur work on us, the more convinced we become of their lack of heroic selfhood. They become less and less like Achilles and Odysseus, Hector and Diomedes.

Herodotus questions the nature of the hero, especially the one necessary characteristic of heroic action, its concentrative power. In epic the hero may even do the thinking for the group. He does more than embody a great passion or great system of values, though he may do this as well. But the final effect of his "heroism" is that it leaves him not merely isolated or brought back victoriously to his proper place in the world (like Odysseus), but individualized in a positive, synecdochic way. As part, he stands for the whole. The *hero* of an epic narrative, not his setting, comes finally to be our main interest in epic narrative. In the end we do not care much about what happens to the Achaians and the Trojans; we do care about Achilles and Hector. Epic is designed, despite all ancillary anthropological concerns, to separate out this heroic identity.

The importance of Books I through VI in *The History* now comes into focus. Their effect has been, through their tissue of accumulated anecdotal background for the main climactic encounter between Greeks and Asians, to disperse the concentrative force of epic heroism. Time after time, in the earlier Books, Herodotus creates a violent "infiguration" (as F. M. Cornford would call it),[10] through which the tales of Persians, Lydians, Medes, Scythians, Egyptians, and so on combine to frustrate our belief in individual heroism. What is left is the heroism of the group, a group conceived un-Homerically. By contrast, Homer's heroes belong to a cohort of noble friends and relations on either side of the war. They never lose their soleness before death and adversity. They go off to war and into battle as a group; but they meet death singly, alone with that sense of self which, in its noblest form, we call the heroic.

Quite the opposite is the effect of defeat and victory in Herodotus. He embeds the individual's great actions, or his casual deeds, in a matrix of endlessly concatenated influences. He narrates to evoke thoughts and questions about thought and custom. Thus the bulk of his story consists of tales about groups of people, frequently ethnically differentiated, which are described in a plural and general way, such as, "the Lydians do this" or "another Indian tribe does that." Such an anthropological distribution of the individual human act—so that it is seen to characterize social, religious, political, ethnic, and especially geographically distinct groupings and is not the exclusive property of heroic protagonists—is the net achievement of Books I through VI. This is particularly true in Book II, where Herodotus seems at first to employ the Persian King Cambyses' invasion of Egypt as a mere excuse to justify his lengthy compilation of data gained on his own journey to that country. Instead, besides showing more deeply than ever the extensiveness of Persian ambitions, he is able to provide a theoretically complete anthropology of important aspects of Egyptian life. Book II is often said to be only the most egregious of Herodotean digressions. If we assume, however, that it is not extra, but integral, and then ask, integral to what? we have an immediate and satisfactory answer. The broad excursus on Egypt is a virtuoso demonstration: if any king wanted to *possess* Egypt, he would have to reckon with encountering the thoughts and traditions of the oldest of Mediterranean cultures, with all the hidden but still acting forces this Egyptian culture must eventually let loose upon him, the alien invader. As if to say, to a Cambyses, "Sir, if you knew what you were invading, you might think twice about your power to invade successfully, for you would see that some things in that country are alien to you and your understanding, and you will lack the natural power to possess and to hold that country."

This piece of fictional advice to Cambyses is intended to show what Herodotus' stories suggested to him, and why possibly he recounts them. Their sheer extent shows him pondering the difficulty of adequately "covering" the story of any complex set of events and their causal nexus with each other. He holds the view, skeptically exercised, that men are no less men because their customs differ. Greek and barbarian are both equally human. Conflict arises from the blind forces of nemesis and from the ways members of the same species come to exist in very different configurations of the world. The history of such conditions must perforce be comparative and, as we shall see, discursive.

To this end Herodotus seeks to anthropologize a large-scale narrative, the main model for which had to be the Homeric narratives. While in a loose sense anthropology is potentially strong in all epic, Herodotus wanted to enhance that strength even further. He wanted to examine the problem of treating men in the mass, in the group matrix. To this end he not only subtly took heroism away from his chance-ridden protagonists, his creatures of nemesis, but he also tried to present another type of protagonist to replace the Homeric hero.

Herodotus himself was this other protagonist. He was that person signed or called by name in his preface: "Herodotus of Halicarnassus presents the results of his researches in the following work." The hero of history, if we must have one, is the story-teller himself.

A few examples will show Herodotus' controlling presence in the narrative. Early in the book, having recounted the rape of Helen and other assorted outrages of early Near Eastern politics, he launches into a revelation of his own thoughts about his material:

> So much for what Persians and Phoenicians say; and I have no intention of passing judgment on its truth or falsity. I prefer to rely on my own knowledge, and to point out who it was in actual fact that first injured the Greeks; then I will proceed with my history, telling the story as I go along of small cities no less than of great. Most of those which were great once are small today; and those which in my own lifetime have grown to greatness, were small enough in the old days. It makes no odds whether the cities I shall write of are big or little—for in this world nobody remains prosperous for long.

On other occasions Herodotus will simply mark his approval or disapproval. He will say, "I admire also the custom of such and such," or "In my view this is a sound practice" (when discussing a certain Persian child-rearing method). Sometimes he seems to insist violently on the surety of his research: thus, about such matters as that the Persians have a profound reverence for rivers, or that the best Persian names end in the letter S, he will say "Inquiry will prove this in every case without exception," and then immediately add, "All this I am able to state definitely from personal knowledge." Again, at times he will relax into a musing mood: "Well, it is an ancient custom, so let them keep it." He is quite aware that anthropological description slows the action of his narrative, and brings himself in to say, "I shall now take up the thread of my story," or, "I shall return from this digression," or the like.

The truth-value of his statements is constantly reviewed if there is any doubt about the veracity of an informant. Concerning the myth of the "Egyptian Helen," Herodotus remarks that his informants "told me that they had learned of some of these events by inquiry, but spoke with certain knowledge of those which had taken place in their own country." Having commented on the external reliability of his sources, he then continues, "This, then, is the version the Egyptian priests gave me of the story of Helen, and I am inclined to accept it for the following reason . . . " Potentially fabulous Egyptian material seems to have been Herodotus' test case, and at one point he states that "anyone may believe these Egyptian tales, if he is sufficiently credulous; as for myself, I keep to the general plan of this book, which is to record the traditions of the various nations just as I heard them related to me."

The self-revelations of the historian as researcher clearly serve a variety of functions. When he says, "I have myself seen the mines in question," he is giving the strongest possible grounds for the reader's belief in the truth of his narrative. When he says "Concerning the nature of the river, I was not able to gain any information either from the priests or from others," he is reporting on a critical gap in his information. Herodotus is well aware of the problem of bias and prejudice; he will say, "and here I feel constrained to deliver an opinion which most men, I know, will dislike, but which, as it seems to me to be true, I am determined not to withhold." One effect of such statements is to defuse unexamined antipathies, disarming them beforehand. While such rhetorical devices are needed for the art of persuasion, Herodotus tends, in his self-revelations, to focus on the author's role as an information-processing agency in the narrative.

Strictly ("purely" one might say), the narrative of events could proceed entirely without authorial interjections. It is critical therefore that as early a theorist as Aristotle should hold strongly developed views on the role of the story-teller in the rhetoric of history. He is concerned with the unity of a recounted series of events. Aristotle notes that history, which is less "philosophical" than poetry, has a more dispersed form than epic. "History," he says in *The Poetics*, "has to expound not one action but one period of time and all that happens within this period to one or more persons, however tenuous the connection between one event and the others." He objects to the way most epic poets adopt the historical structure of tenuously linked, multiple actions. He identifies the unity of purpose in epic as one of its ties with tragedy, in that both seek the ideal within the concrete event, through the "imitation of a single action." He also finds a purity of form in the perfect epic narrative stance or voice, as always epitomized by the immortal Homer. Among the varied praises of Homer is that "he alone realizes when he should write in his own person. A poet should himself [that is, in his own voice] say very little, for he is not then engaged in imitation . . . . Homer, after a brief introduction, straightway brings on a man or woman or some other speaking character."

In his article "Frontiers of Narrative," Gérard Genette distinguishes between narrative (or story) and discourse.[11] The latter comprehends a "vast domain of direct expression," whether this is Hesiod's advice to farmers or Parmenides' theory of the universe. Roughly speaking, discourse *tells* rather than represents mimetically. Genette shows that there is a grammatical distinction between narrative and discourse, which he takes from Emile Benveniste. Benveniste had shown that discourse uses

> certain grammatical forms, like the pronoun "I" (and its implicit "you"), the pronominal (certain demonstratives), or adverbial indicators (like "here," "now," "yesterday," "today," "tomorrow," etc.) and—at least in French—certain tenses of the verb, like the present, the present anterior, or the future, are confined to discourse, whereas narrative in its strict form is marked by the exclusive use of the third person and such forms as the aorist (past definite) and the pluperfect.[12]

Discourse is "subjective"; it is spoken by someone who calls himself "I." Further, as Benveniste says, "the present, which is the tense *par excellence* of the discursive mode, is not defined other than as the moment when the discourse is being spoken." Conversely, "the objectivity of narrative is defined by the absence of any reference to the narrator." Aristotle's Homer produces greater objectivity in this sense, by referring to himself as infrequently as possible. Benveniste took his observations to the extreme: "as a matter of fact, there is then no longer even a narrator. The events are set forth chronologically, as they occur. No one speaks here; the events seem to narrate themselves."[13] Hayden White has observed that the intrusion of discourse into narrative is related to the question of whether historical events are real or imagined: "narrative becomes a *problem* only when we wish to give to *real* events the *form* of story."[14] White wishes to argue that " 'the true' is identified with 'the real' only insofar as it can be shown to possess the character of narrativity."[15] In his book *Metahistory* White had shown the power of "mythic" emplotment to control the reader's expectations of truth-values.

Questions of epistemology must arise here for the philosopher, but in practical literary terms what emerges is the idea that history constantly tests narrative for its handling of the truth or fictiveness of narrated events. With Herodotus the process of self-regulation and testing produces those seemingly innumerable instances of the intrusion of the authorial "I." Herodotus exemplifies exactly the grammatical phenomenon of "discourse" that Benveniste described and Genette situated at the "frontier" of narrative.

Part of Genette's argument is the idea that narrative can absorb only so much discourse without ceasing to be narrative, whereas discourse has an almost unlimited capacity to absorb narrative. Unlike narrative, discourse can be as impure as it wishes to be. So much is this true, that Herodotus can endow his own first-person existence with an active part in a drama of its own making. As an "I" he represents himself in the person of a mind fully participating in the narrative of its research capacity.

As researcher, this "I" takes upon itself the role of interpreter. Through this impersonation Herodotus comes to belong to his own history; he belongs as the interpreter of his methods of selection and compilation. This rhetorical situation appears graphically in what may be the most celebrated of his authorial interjections.

In Book VII Herodotus discovers himself debating with himself about two different accounts of the way the people of Argos reacted to a certain display of Spartan pride. The Argives, he says, claim that they simply could not stand the Spartans' arrogance, so they preferred joining the enemy rather than fighting under Spartan command. "So much," says Herodotus, "for the Argive account of this transaction; there is, however, another story current in Greece," a story to the effect that Xerxes himself made an early overture to the Argives, wooing them to his side with an appeal to a common ancestral kinship. This argument, the story went, was powerful with the Argives. There then follows the famous Herodotean comment upon his own search for historical truth:

> For my own part I cannot positively state that Xerxes either did, or did not, send the messenger to Argos; nor can I guarantee the story of the Argives going to Susa and asking Artaxerxes about their relationship with Persia. I express no opinion about this matter other than that of the Argives themselves. One thing, however, I am very sure of: and that is, that if all mankind agreed to meet, and everyone brought his own faults along with him for the purpose of exchanging them for somebody else's, there is not a man who, after taking a good look at his neighbour's faults, would not be only too happy to return home with his own. *My business is to record what people say, but I am by no means bound to believe it—and that may be taken to apply to this book as a whole.* There is yet another story about the Argives: it was they, according to some, who invited the Persians to invade

Greece, because their war with Sparta was going badly and they felt that anything would be better than their present sufferings.

The idea of relevance is here, in the words italicized, so stretched that any and all reports need to be recorded, a requirement in no way constraining the researcher's beliefs regarding "truth." The extension of relevance is furthermore a principle of composition for the whole book. Herodotus hereby openly grants the ultimate self-revelation: he admits to an almost universally willing suspension of disbelief. If a narrating self would seek to override interpretation, the interpreting self, by declaring its views and biases, overrides the claims of pure and pretended neutrality of narrative style. The story encounters, but does not succumb, to attack from the forces of negative skepticism.

The mind behind such narrative technique is thus actively neutral, if such a state can be imagined. The story-teller drives always onward toward a wider and wider circle of information and anecdote. Yet his drive to comprehend does not subvert the authorial admission of doubtful certainty. Skepticism is controlled, not prohibited. Herodotus' refusal "to believe it all alike" does not mean that he will change the story to fit a more plausible pattern. Nor will the researcher transform his materials to "infigurate" them into a predetermined schema of historical sequences. Instead, he lets his materials stand in an almost synchronous jostle, strung together, not by time, but if anything by space. Time passes in *The History*, but strangely it can seem as if no time passed at all.

Ancient geographers such as Hecataeus are known to have influenced the Herodotean method of travel and reporting. Herodotus perhaps overdetermines space. His method certainly suggests a tendency toward taxonomic classification, a drive toward comparative ethnography. Herodotus is partly the doubting taxonomist who also recounts loosely strung sequences of events. In this role, Herodotus the interpretive narrator is the hero of his own story. We may call him the protagonist, because he plays such an active part in his own person. He is the voice of exploration. Unwilling to lose any piece of the memory of the past, he wants to save that one last but intractable, odd but telltale, reminiscence that might lead the history of greater things onto the correct organizing path. The interpretive spatializing of *The History* is really the space of thought that allows room for the dispersed variety of human life to find place in a matrix of overlapping actions and points of view. In what seems a very modern way Herodotus allows his reader to see into the workings of the historian's mind, as well as method. He is astonishingly open in this regard, unless it is held that such displays of candor are bound to be hiding something. But it is hard to doubt the active neutrality of the narrator of the history, if only because that neutrality is such a powerful rhetorical device. The narrator is speaking for research, and not for any sort of prefabricated mental construct. Herodotus is unabashedly enthusiastic about the questions his inquiries raise in the skeptical reader or listener.

Almost the last word in *The History* is the word "slaves." The exhilarating ambience of Herodotean researches derives from its narrative of Greek freedom. Later, when the Greeks found that freedom had to be *within* their linguistic culture and *within* the mind, as well as without, it was time for Thucydides to criticize the Herodotean achievement. It was time for the historian to close the shutters on the mind and its methods. Thucydides, with his diagnostic technique of assessing symptoms and causes, will remain one of the masters of historical thought. Yet he rarely lets his reader see into the workings of his mind, with all its doubting, assessing, classifying, and sifting of reasons and facts. Instead, we are allowed only to see the fact or reason Thucydides has decided is the sole telling one. How different this art is from that of Herodotus! Yet we cannot have one historian without the other, as we cannot have the *Odyssey* without the *Iliad*.

Highlighted by this contrast with Homer is a broad question as to how we shall assess the neutrality of historical judgment. Where the poet is free to invent, the historian is pledged to a certain involvement with fact. As we know, what counts as fact depends very much on what fiction is thought to be, as well as what is considered a sound basis for distinguishing the true from the false. Hence it is of some general importance that from the time of Thucydides all the way to the sixteenth century, Herodotus was not always found to be reliable as a chronicler of fact. Whether it is Cicero speaking of "innumerable fables" or Wilde ironically speaking of "beautiful untrue things," Herodotus the father of history has courted the other name, the father of lies. He is in part perhaps the author of this doubtful reputation, for his own authorial intrusions constantly draw open attention to the questionable nature of his information; he is the first to interrogate the reliability of his sources. His attitude seems to be, "I tell you an important story, but I leave to you the judgment of its truth or falsity, since I myself (who collected the story) cannot be absolutely sure if it is fact or not."

This skeptical attitude is virtually synonymous with the enunciation of the Herodotean "I." Such a formulation of skeptical presence signals the operation of a controlled system of language-games, those Wittgenstein called "reporting an event." The authorial "I" is the chief mechanism of control, for it always alerts the reader to the need for tracking the ensuing "story" with an appropriate caution.

The question of truth or falsity quickly becomes the more critical question of factuality versus fictionality, the real versus the imagined. This shift of focus points away from the supposed essential properties of story (truth or falsity somehow inhering in certain aspects of story) and points toward the original Greek sense of the term "history," meaning research or inquiry. For what then comes to the fore is a transaction between reporter and informant. One asks, what is the mental terrain of this transaction? Surely, to begin with, the questing historian encounters, as researcher, all sorts of ways of wishing to doubt or to believe his informant. Then, as the larger historical account is developed, the historian encounters another source of doubt, namely the effect of his own bias as a mere constructor and developer of the broad historical picture, in this case the whole of *The History*.

In the case of this particular history the most obvious source of error or doubt arising from bias would be the fundamental nature of the conflict being described—after Homer the first recorded conflict centering upon East versus West. Herodotus is dealing with what Edward Said has taught us to recognize as Orientalism. It seems that Herodotus was in part quite aware of the possibility that as a Greek he might *pre*judge an issue in the context of Orientalism— hence a large number of his authorial intrusions. Certainly these intrusions or interventions are the signal of a mind skeptical of its information, a mind aware that all the information refers to conditions of disputed rights and possessions. This mind, the historian's, represents itself as "explaining" events. In his *Analytical Philosophy of History* Arthur Danto, following C. G. Hempel, holds that "to (empirically) explain an event is to connect that event with a condition, and by means of a law."[16] This would be the Herodotean assumption also, as understood in a loose fashion, to be sure.

The law of Herodotus' universe is the force of nemesis, which works as if (doubtfully) by chance; it works to reduce man's pride in temporal achievement, as Herodotus' prefatory remarks indicate. In the spirit of Danto's formulation Herodotus gives narrative shape to "conditions," permitting the reader to see how the fortunes of the Greeks and the Persians were intertwined by a great conflict on land and sea.

It remains only to insist once again that Herodotus does not rely on an essentialist philosophy of right and wrong, truth and falsity. He knows the power of masterful mythmaking; he knows the power of Homer. But he also knows that he has a different kind of narrative to give his reader. The language-game of history is designed to recount or report an accumulation of story, which means to describe the mental conditions of doing research within the field of that accumulation. The historian, the researcher, is concerned to define the kind of certainty that may lodge in his chosen "fiction of factual representation," in Hayden White's phrase. "The kind of certainty," Wittgenstein reminds us, "is the kind of language-game."[17] Herodotus works with his materials in the large-minded spirit of a late Wittgensteinian sentence: "We might speak of fundamental principles of human enquiry" (On Certainty, #670).

The Herodotean view is that, without a revelation of authorial doubt, the mode or kind of the historian's certainty cannot emerge in the same family as "the kind of language-game." Without expressing the mixture of authorial curiosity (an imperious if not imperial drive) with authorial skepticism, there can be no research deserving of the name. Perhaps because he stood at the borderline between oral and written cultures, Herodotus appears to have wanted to establish the question of certainty on this level as well; what, he asks, is the transaction between the spoken and the written? He is a father of history then in yet another sense: he questions the linguistic conditions of his utterance. In all respects he seems to have wished to engage in a negotiation of meaning, between himself and his informants, between his information and himself as interpreter, and finally between himself as interpreter and his reader as interpreter. There is much activity at all levels. Doubtless this activity is what imparts to The History its air of complete and confident narrative elan. There is nothing in literature more confident than Herodotus' avowals of complete uncertainty.

8. Dipintura: *The Visual Icon of Historicism in Vico*

The third and final edition of *The New Science* appeared in 1744. Its text begins with an allegorical picture, the *Dipintura*, which is followed by an extensive gloss that looks in two directions at once. This gloss, "the Idea of the Work," explains symbolic details in the picture and looks ahead to the ensuing verbal text. Reading *The New Science* in its natural order implies that the *Dipintura* guides and informs our interpretation of the printed text.[1] The arresting presence of a picture at the inception of the text suggests forcibly that Vico himself thinks in terms of images and figures. The purpose of the *Dipintura* is to show the reader how to think about the structure of Vico's visionary science of man.

Taken as a whole, the structure of *The New Science* is designed to be seen from a number of different perspectives, such as wisdom, metaphysics, logic, morals, economics, all of which are functions of the major perspective, which Vico calls "poetry." All these perspectives are described as having a real or putative historical course: thus, "Within Greece itself, accordingly, lay the original East called Asia or India . . ." or "From the Thrace within Greece must have come Mars, who was certainly a Greek divinity; and thence too must have come Orpheus, one of the first Greek theological poets." Vico always holds that man is the maker of his "gentile" world and, in this sense, poetry is a general, cultural productivity. Man is a poet in many domains of social and political and theological

Dipintura, the original frontispiece for Vico's *The New Science*, 1744.

thought. The disparity of these domains, their seemingly infinite variety, is synoptically brought under a single heading by means of the governing term, poetry. This term names a general hermeneutic, a master principle of interpretation.

The most important aspect of this Vichian hermeneutic is that it identifies *homo sapiens* with *homo faber*—cultural thinking is cultural making. Man, for example, not only thinks through issues of law, but must make or unmake laws as "poetic inventions."

The large result of this vision of history is that many human activities are gathered under the heading of poetry which normally are not so conceived. The variety, or even excess, of such disparate "poetries" exerts powerful centrifugal force upon *The New Science*. We may well ask: what holds the book together? Our answer can only be that it is written in the manner of a complex syncretic allegory, which allows the disparities to be contained.

Three cardinal allegorical features adorn the main body of the text. First, Vico's "Homer" is a personification. The poet is specifically depersonalized, denied specific human identity, to make way for a re-personalization of the archetypal figure as the voice of a whole culture. As such Vico's "Homer" is no longer a single poet whom someone might have known at some given historical moment in time. He becomes a collective voice and is personified as such, alerting us to the presence of allegorical thought.

Second, Vico uses etymology in exactly the way this "logic" has always been used by the great allegorists. They use Vico's method of false etymology, and they use it as he does, to bind together elements in the argument that cannot possibly be conjoined on the basis of modern scientific etymology. The play of language here is heuristic. Many of Vico's beautiful etymological games are based on proper etymological interpretation. He enjoys the best of both worlds, like the good syncretist he is.

Third, Vico prefers to put any sequence of change, or any structure of fixed relations, in triadic form. It is not enough to refer this practice to his deep and abiding Christian reverence for the Trinity, with its providential overtones. Of all the number symbolisms imagined by man, none has more powerful iconographic energy than the triadic vision. Students of the Renaissance have shown in detail that the neo-Platonism of that period gave special privilege to the number 3. Vico mythologizes his materials, to fit a system of triadic permutations.

To a Hegelian who knew nothing of the Renaissance iconographic tradition, Vico's triads might appear to foreshadow the Hegelian dialectic of thesis-antithesis-synthesis. But it is not Vico who foreshadows, it is the whole Renaissance Hermetic enterprise which foreshadows both Vico and Hegel. Vico knew his own intellectual origins, and by preferring Bacon to Descartes he evinced a preference for the method by which a true Baconian (*contra* Descartes' classic demonstration of the mathematics of the three "dimensions") will tend to resist triadic forms of truth or illusion. Instead he starts from the broader position of epistemology, namely, the tetradic structure negatively defined by Bacon's "four idols." Vico perceived that once the Baconian breaks the iron grip of triadic "pagan mysteries," he can then use such mysteries freely, with complete emblematic elan, because he knows them to be merely a useful fiction for universal order. Taking the sacred triad as the central iconological fiction, Vico is free to move backwards and forwards within the whole developed sequence of number symbolism, from the godlike One to the infinitely pluralistic "myriad," that indeterminate final permutation of the integers of the decimal system. What gives Vico confidence in this magic labor is the confluence of the ultimate one-two-three with "the One" (the Trinitarian dance of ideas). What gives him enthusiasm for his numerology is the way in which traditional Pythagorean numerology permitted extension beyond the triad into the rich symbolism of all numbers beyond three.[2]

While the infrastructure of *The New Science* is based on an ordering of numerous sets or cells of triadic cultural development, the whole book is given its external form by the number 5. This is traditionally the magic number of marriage and betrothal—as shown in works like Spenser's *Faerie Queene* or Sir Thomas Browne's *Garden of Cyrus*, works which derive their pentadic symbolism from Renaissance discourses like Ficino's *Expositio circa numeram nuptialem*, if not directly from the original Ficinian source, Plato's *Republic*. The pentad is often modulated, in number symbolism, into what might be called "the beginnings of a circle"—as we know from the post-Renaissance rule of five-act dramatic structure, the pentad is conceived as perfectly closing off an extended action. Vico achieves this same "five-act" closure by dividing his 1744 *New Science* into a pentad of triads, that is, the five Books permutate their evolving three-celled discourse without loss of order or energy, because, on this plan, the resolving number five has the power to hold the triad in a state of relatively fixed syncretic closure. The book allegorizes its own symbolic structure of ideas by confining that structure within the bounds of number. "Number" here is endowed with magic properties, toward which, as Corsano has shown, Vico takes an ambivalent attitude in his complex response to the acceptance and rejection of Renaissance Hermeticism. As Corsano notes, the demystification of the untrue Homer owes much to Casaubon's proof that the *Pimander* is not an authentic Hermetic document, as the adepts had claimed.[3] Corsano's "Vico e la tradizione ermetica" shows an extremely ambivalent Vico who is fascinated by, and suspicious of, the Hermetic philosopher's magic. If this reading is correct, then we find ourselves once again facing a Vico for whom the syncretic mode of High Renaissance allegory is congenial. The finest practitioners of that art, or science, trust and distrust their exquisitely visionary magical games.

The ultimate source of Vico's subtle anti-Cartesianism, so often directed not against Descartes himself but against his redactors, is to be found in the fact that a wholehearted acceptance of Cartesian rules and method would entail a draconian banishment of the allegorist's *serio ludere*. The toys and devices of the magician, be he *magus* or charlatan, must end in the Cartesian junkyard.

And that, for many good and fortunate reasons, Vico is unwilling to allow. He may be the last complete Renaissance *magus*, as he may be the first of the pre-Romantic *magi*. He stands, like a colossus, between two worlds and will abandon neither world. Heroically, he mobilizes almost every known device of high allegory, which he further strengthens by making new and scarcely tried instruments for thinking afresh the positive facts of language, culture, religion, and politics. He is a model instance of a figure at the threshold, with each foot planted in a radically different "space," poised at the doorway between two epistemically distinct worldviews. Like all allegorists whose final aim is to attain prophetic vision, Vico is acutely aware that his book must issue from its own iconic threshold, since prophecy is precisely vision at the threshold.

The best schema for such visionary play will be a six-fold epitome of Vico's work as a whole. We may say that it has the six following dimensions of method.

- It is allegorical. Thus it mythologizes both ideas and facts.
- It is syncretic. Thus it seeks to harmonize its materials even though they are mutually contradictory or roughly discordant.
- It is philological. Thus it tries to uncover new facts, for instance in the history of language, or of custom.
- It is speculative. Thus it persistently looks for metaphysical relationships within its body of fact and theory.
- It is historicist. Thus it looks for patterns and paradigms of change within history, as opposed to producing an annalistic tracery of detailed sequences of historical events.
- It is prophetic. Thus it refers its historicism to such puzzling mysteries as the Christian idea of Providence, particularly by an emphasis on the *presentness* of the enigmatic "now" embedded in the courses and re-courses of the "ideal eternal history."

This schema shows that the allegorical is only one of six procedures used throughout the text. Together the six imply burdensome complexity, unless, of course, we acquire a method of easily shifting between the six perspectives. This method, indeed, Vico supplies to his reader. He begins the complete text of the 1744 *New Science* with the powerful symbolic threshold of the *Dipintura* and its prose explication. The reader is thereby enabled to move freely amid the various planes of Vico's historicist "science."

W. J. T. Mitchell has analyzed the mutual stress between the verbal and the pictorial. His remarks would pertain to Vico's use of *Dipintura.*

The dialectic of word and image seems to be a constant in the fabric of signs that a culture weaves around itself. What varies is the precise nature of the weave, the relationship of warp and woof. The history of culture is in part the story of a protracted struggle for dominance between pictorial and linguistic signs, each claiming for itself certain proprietary rights on a "nature" to which only it has access. At some moments this struggle seems to settle into a relationship of free exchange along open borders; at other times (as in Lessing's *Laocoön*) the borders are closed and a separate peace is declared. Among the most interesting and complex versions of this struggle is what might be called the relationship of subversion, in which language or imagery looks into its own heart and finds lurking there its opposite number. One version of this relation has haunted the philosophy of language since the rise of empiricism, the suspicion that beneath words, beneath ideas, the ultimate reference in the mind is the image, the impression of outward experience printed, painted, or reflected in the surface of consciousness.[4]

If Vico begins *The New Science* with an engraved frontispiece or "Table," the *Dipintura*, he also at once provides an extended verbal "Explanation of the Picture Placed as Frontispiece to Serve as Introduction to the Work"—twenty-three pages in the English text. The Explanation shows verbally that the *Dipintura* pictorially *reduces* the twenty-three pages and by extension the whole of *The New Science* to a single complex image. In so doing the *Dipintura* doubles a temporally extended verbal construct, by synchronous emblematic means. Picture schematizes text, apparently without subversion.

Various ways of classifying the emblems, the pictorial units, are possible. Most are traditional, but the most important iconographic touches seem to have been devised originally by Vico himself and then communicated by him to "the ingenious" artist. (The preciseness of the instructions, the degree to which they were carried out to the letter, the clarity of the engraver's rendering, are all matters of considerable importance, but we can assume that the picture gives us a generally accurate rendering of Vico's intent.) One could classify the emblems as Pagan, Hebraic-Christian, and Other, or, as technical versus mysterious, or animistic versus mechanical, or natural versus artificial, or intellective versus emotive, and so on. One would then have developed a complete system of binary cuts, resulting in a complex structural matrix of symbols.

Nevertheless, it may be helpful to observe one singularly graphic binary cut. The largest number of emblems would seem to refer to Vico's theory of *corsi* and *ricorsi*, that is, to the curve of "poetic" development of civilization. Examples would be the fasces, the purse, the altar, the plough. Let us call them, Type A.

Set off against these iconically separated elements there is a second, superordinate group of connected units: God's triune Eye, the winged figure of Metaphysic, and the figure of Homer. Although these are abstractly and statuesquely presented, these three emblematic figures (Type B) do not directly refer to the whole course of human development. Rather they refer to Vico's theory and method for understanding that whole course. It is difficult to draw a sharp distinction between this cardinal triad of magic figures and the more numerous cluster of historicist units comprising Type A. After all, does not Homer play an absolutely essential role in Vico's vision of the semiotic transition from the age of the hieroglyph to the age of true linguistic competence? Yet despite this apparent confusion, there is still a fairly clear difference to be drawn. Homer does not epitomize an extensive catalogue of beautiful objects or cultural changes in the ancient world, although hints of these exist in his poem. Rather, Homer stands for a visionary, linguistically powerful, heroically energized *medium* of expression of all those objects, events, and changes. Dependent upon the wisdom of "poetic metaphysics," Homer is seen to embody a complex human capacity, the capacity to make the "true poem." If this mediating role defines Vico's Homer, then his goddess Metaphysic is even more grandly the daimonic mediator of knowledge and understanding, while on the highest level the Eye of God stands for the perfect, ultimate, radiant clarity of Divine Truth itself. On this basis we can draw a working distinction between the Type B triad and the approximately forty emblems of Type A, all of which point to objective facts in the whole historicist fable of the West. If one had then to epitomize Types A and B, one might say that all elements of Type A are understood to lie within the domain of *things seen*, whereas the triad of Type B lies within the domain of *powers of seeing.*

Such a distinction is crucial to reading *The New Science* in its natural order, because it enables us to move intelligently back and forth between what Edward Said has called the Vichian principles of *parallelism, adjacency,* and *complementarity.* The Table alerts us to questions of "what things are collected and known by means of what method." Stirred by the imagery of the Table, we can move from questions of Vichian fact to matters of theory, from historiography to metahistory. We move easily between different modalities of semiotic speculation, as Vico passes from the ages of theological wisdom to the ages of positive knowledge. The governing triad of the Table fixes a triadic limit for the method of the poetic historian.

The interplay of the three statuary elements of the Triad provides our best picture of Vico's historicist method.

The controlling indicator in the Table is its spatial organization. Like many allegorical pictures of its period and tradition, the *Dipintura* mixes proper perspective with willful disregard of such perspective, whose laws it obeys and disobeys. Thus the Eye of God is drawn with crude realism as a human eye, as if to emphasize that it is too large to fit a true perspective drawing, whereas most of the foreground elements are drawn with clear insistence on receding orthogonal lines. While such visual mixtures are typical of cruder pictures in Renaissance emblem-books, and while they assume sophisticated form in the Florentine tradition of pictorial allegory, they are particularly useful for the creation of baroque or mannerist effects in the post-Renaissance era.[5] The mixture of spatial orders (perspectival and nonperspectival) is extremely difficult to describe systematically. However, one can say that the mixture tortures the containing space of the picture-plane, as if it were twisted. The space is thus made more natural and less artificial, with the result that Vico's artist divides the picture into symbolically linked iconic zones.[6] Vico describes these zones triadically in his final summary in The Idea of the Book:

> Last of all, to state the idea of the book in its briefest summary, the entire engraving represents the three worlds in the order in which the human minds of the gentiles have been raised from earth to heaven. All the hieroglyphs visible on the ground denote the world of nations to which men applied themselves before anything else. The globe in the middle represents the world of nature which the physicists later observed. The hieroglyphs above signify the world of minds and of God which the metaphysicians finally contemplated. (Sec. 42)

This brief summary scarcely tells us enough about the artist's actual rendering, which structures and fills space according to a principle of asymmetry. If space is twisted, so are the two major figures placed in it, Metaphysic and Homer. Both figures, especially Metaphysic, conform to the well known mannerist shape of the *figura serpentinata*, which Lomazzo in 1584 described as "like the twisting of a live snake in motion, which is also the form of a waving flame . . . The figure should resemble the latter S . . . And this applies not only to

Dipintura 155

the whole figure, but also to its parts."[7] Lomazzo states further that "nature is favourably inclined" toward such figurations of living bodies, and his authority for this view owes something to Michelangelo's example and precept, a typical model being Michelangelo's statue of *Victory*. In Lomazzo's view the strongest use of the *figura serpentinata* results from its incorporation into some composition containing pyramidal shapes, such as are clearly apparent in the *Victory*. These torsional forms are familiar also in the statuary of Giovanni Bologna, for instance the *Astronomy* or the bronze *Mercury*. Marghareta Frankel has maintained that, if Ripa's *Iconologia* provided Vico's artist with the model for the goddess Metaphysic, then the figure is not, as Rossi claimed, a combination of Metaphysics and Mathematics. Rather the image is a more or less direct rendering of Ripa's *Contemplative Life,* which Ripa described clearly as standing in a serpentine pose: not only is her face twisted up toward the heavenly light, but "she keeps the right hand high and extended, and left low and closed, and has two small wings on her head."

If the two most prominent figures contribute to a general effect of the serpentine, the Table as a whole is filled with secondary forms that produce a matrix of crossing diagonals which bind foreground to middle ground to background, as if a carpenter's folding rule were opened up, leaning backward and upward from front to back in the picture. If this zigzag pattern were rounded off at its turning points, the final result would be a picture of several intersecting or overlapping S-curves. Simply as a spatial form, the Table fits mannerist expectations. This would be merely the concern of art historians, were not the S-curve format understood to suggest not only a line of beauty, but, more strongly, the flame-like freedom of the living forms of natural growth. The imagery establishes thoughts of *conceptual* figuration. The space of the *Dipintura*, like the "space" of written concepts, is truly as Salomone suggests,[8] subject to a temporal warping such that while a perfectly constant spatial recession into depth (with consistently true perspective) would be the picture of Vico's *storia ideale eterna*, the actual distortions of the space in the Table correspond to the turbulence of actual, "relative" rather than "absolute" human history. Both the Table and its pendant written text, whether text of the "Idea" or text of the five-act expanded discourse, are pressed and dilated into the visually defined shapes the reader encounters before she meets any other element of *The New Science.*

Let me correct a common misapprehension about the nature of allegory. While it is true that simple or naive allegory tends to miss the living plasticity of actual human existence, the great allegories maintain the closest possible contact with the world that men have made, both as they have changed it and have slowly learned more about it. This contact is achieved in many ways—consider the variousness of Dante's allegorical technique in the *Vita Nuova* or the *Commedia,* or consider the astonishing range of symbolic devices employed by Spenser in *The Faerie Queene.* Somewhere at the heart of all such works we discover a central point of contact with the deeper questions of human destiny—such points of contact I would identify with prophetic insight.[9] Such vision pushes historicism to its limit. It invites the reader into a sense of the fullness, the pregnancy, of the present moment—a fullness that is inevitably uncertain in its dimensions, not least because the present moment is always disappearing with infinite speed of transition into the past, as the future disappears into *it.* This section of time dividing past and future is mysteriously simultaneous. The great allegories seem to aim at conveying as much of this mystery as possible; their intensifications of a sense of time are prophetic in character. Such an attempt equally characterizes *The New Science,* a work of historicist vision.

Like Dante and Spenser, Vico uses data gathered from the past by mainly philological means to show something critical about the continuing presentness of historical experience, that is, its fluxional oscillation of *corsi* and *ricorsi.* Vico invents contemporaneous and "new" ways of finding significance in the past—hence his historicism. Yet he is rarely the narrative historian in *The New Science.* (In a sense historicism may be understood as the historian's self-conscious and critical reaction against narrative history.) Given Vico's concern for moments of historical transition occurring in an elusive presentness of time, we must look again at the allegorical *Dipintura* for signs of this concern.

One iconic element of the Table has not been mentioned or subsumed in this argument: the reflected ray of light from the Eye of God. While it had been customary to show light emanating from the Divine Eye, Vico may be suggesting that he agrees with Descartes' optical theory presented in the treatises *Le monde* (ca. 1630) and *Principiae philosophiae* (1644), to the effect that light is an emanation of the eye; we see surrounding objects as a blind man feels them with his stick. While this may not be good neurophysiology, it is extremely natural protopsychology. Poetry attempts to express this truth in phrases like "he darted a glance of ferocious hate at his savage opponent." Such extravagant language attempts to suggest a deeply Vichian thought: seeing, in the intellectual sense, is an active illumination of the objective world by the organ of sight, the mind. The Table thus sets up an analogy. As the Divine Eye emits divinely radiant light, so the human "eye of the mind" emits a humanly (socially) radiant light—its science.

In The Idea of the Book Vico tells us how this providential gift of emanation works to illuminate the prophetic darkness of actual human life. The ray of divine providence first illuminates "a convex jewel that adorns the breast of Metaphysic," and this part of the symbolical optics has more than one emblematic sense: a) it denotes the "clean and pure heart that Metaphysic must have," thereby avoiding the errors of Zeno the Fatalist and Epicurus the randomist; b) the image suggests to Vico that truly, veritably, providentially-illuminated metaphysics will not serve the private intellectual delight of the philosopher, but will aid him in a more socially applied science, that of "public morals or civil customs, by which the nations have come into being and maintain themselves *in the world.*"

At a second stage of its transit the Divine Light is reflected off the breast of Metaphysic onto the statue of Homer. Having passed though the refining intermediation of metaphysics, the divine ray finds a secondary receptor in the illuminated mind of the poet, "the first gentile author who has come down to us," an author seen to have intense theological wisdom.

Such an iconography gains interest as soon as we stress the compass-form of the light ray, as it is reflected onto Homer at an acute angle. If we notice this compass-form, and notice its visual extension to the plough below, we may remember the compass held in the right hand of Dürer's *Melancolia.* The Dürer recalls to us that the compass is the emblem of true measurement, is the means of drawing the perfect circle and (as in Donne's *Valediction*) is an image of the lover's approach or departure from the beloved. Here in the Vico it follows that reflected light is the source of all measurable truth; it is the means of closure (the circle, whether drawn by the geometer's compass or cut into the ground around the original *urbs* by the sacred plough); and it is the living essence of the life-force that animates man's social affection for his fellow man.

On the negative side, Vico is insisting that true knowledge cannot be direct; it must at least be mediated by metaphysics. It must obey the reflective rules of proper speculation. To clarify this mediated aspect of wisdom and science, Vico invents a remarkable iconic unit, the convex mirror adorning the breast of Metaphysic.

The mirror and its convexity hold the secret to the inner life of Vico's method, both in its range and power, and in its ultimately enigmatic withdrawal. Several things may be said about the convex mirror, to interpret it as the crux of meaning in the Table. To be sure, there are other enigmatic elements, such as the *selva oscura*, which may be read also as a *selva ingens*,[10] or the teetering globe which is not simply (as Vico says) "supported by the altar in one part only, for, until now, the philosophers, contemplating divine providence only through the natural order, have shown only a part of it." Such statements are puzzling and not unimportant.

The convex mirror, however, raises questions having to do with the schematic structure of the Table as a whole, questions which in turn reflect upon the written text of the whole book. For instance, why is the mirror a jewel? Why does it adorn the breast of this particular goddess, Metaphysic? Does the jewel have any function beyond its role as a transmitter of the divine light? Does it reflect images of the world, as well as redirect the emanation of the Divine Eye? Taking this last question, if the mirror should serve such a double function, then it would be natural to interpret the trajectory of the "divine ray" in reverse direction: Vico, standing somehow in the shoes of Homer, could then see his own image in the mirror of metaphysics. The image of the poet-thinker would then resemble the mannerist work of Parmigianino, the famous *Self-Portrait in a Convex Mirror*, a work which has been recuperated in the lyric poem of John Ashbery, his "Self-Portrait in a Convex Mirror."

The use of convex mirrors for self-portraiture is critical for any theory of pictorial realism, since the mirror does two things: like any mirror, it provides the artist with a reflection (of either a real or virtual image), which he can then transfer to canvas, but unlike a flat mirror, the convex mirror severely distorts the shapes and sizes of objects lying out toward the edges of the mirror's surface. Thus, in the Parmigianino, as Pope-Hennessy observes, "the mouth diminishes in the same disconcerting fashion on the right, and the eyes, just as they do in Dürer's sketch [his 1484 self-portrait "copied from myself in a mirror"], appear to rest on two quite different planes."[11] If then the mirror permits autoportraiture, it does so only under conditions of spatial torsion such as we have already discovered at work in the Table as a whole. To be sure, Vico does not explicitly state in the Idea that his mirror is placed so as to reflect his own mind and method, via deflection of thought from, and through, the mind of Homer. Yet in the Idea he never mentions the winged helmet of Mercury (an almost solitary omission in the gloss), so that we may assume some things in the Table are allowed to go unglossed. There is a temptation at least to discern a metaphysical game being played with and around the mirror.[12] If the reader is intended to read the divine emanation in reverse order, as an allegory of imagination and image-making (Vico's "poetry"), such an approach will increase the general emphasis on Vichian speculation.

Vico's *speculum mundi* is, like the self-portraitist's, convex. It remains nonetheless a *speculum*, a convex mirror which, following Parmigianino's painting as our model, is suffused with a strange shadowy light emanating from the same position as that of Vico's Divine Eye, at eleven o'clock. The critic's task becomes one of rather subtle reading, so as to determine, for example, the Vichian relationship to the monadism of Leibniz. The jewel-mirror resembles nothing so much as a monad, of which E. G. Boring writes: "The *monad* is the element of all being and partakes of its nature, and being is activity. If we ask further concerning the nature of the monad or activity, we can only be told that it is most like *perception*. *Activity* and *Consciousness* are thus two words for the same thing and lie at the bottom of nature."[13] To highlight the approach to Vico via Leibniz, we might observe that Vichian method is at once manifestly hyperactive and hyperconscious. He always enlivens the perception of whatever questions he raises.

To emphasize the jewel-aspect of the mirror means to emphasize the life-giving, symposiac side to Vico's science. He would as etymologist have delighted in the fact that a jewel is a *jocus*, a plaything. But he never denied, indeed he stressed, that his lifework could be interpreted as the effort of a baroque *magus*, sharing with thinkers like Kepler what Michael Polanyi has called the "heuristic passion." Did not Kepler say he had "prophesied" the truths of his astronomical theory, did not the invention of analytic geometry come to Descartes in a dream, did not Bacon conceive his "advancement of science" in the mode of a brilliant oration? Even the later Newton, like Leibniz, allowed himself a freedom of speculation that can only be called prophetic. All such thinkers appear to have wished to lift at least parts of their "science" to the level of prophetic vision.

Vico is no exception to this pattern. What is common to thinkers conforming to the Renaissance and Baroque model is that they never allow their work to become too narrow in focus. Tending to expand their theories beyond an original mathematical or positive core of provable assertions, they encompass remote relationships between distant elements of the *plenum*. Such thinkers descend from Plato and the NeoPlatonic example, with an inevitable tendency toward allegory and syncretism, as if they were all children of the *Timaeus*. Thus Vico himself depicts an opening out of speculative method as the consequence of a *convex* reflection of the divine light. The convexity of the mirror "furthermore . . . indicates that the knowledge of God does not have its end in metaphysic taking *private* illumination from intellectual things and thence regulating merely her own moral conduct, as hitherto philosophers have done. For this would have been signified by a flat jewel, whereas the jewel is convex, thus reflecting and scattering the ray abroad, to show that metaphysic should know God's providence [i.e., our "world"] in public morals or civil customs, by which the nations have come into being and maintain themselves in the world." (*Idea of the Work*, sec. 5)

For prophetic vision the "scattering" is a crucial idea. Concentrating on the impregnated fullness of present significance, the prophet is led to deal conceptually with a certain excessiveness, a continuous expansion or dissemination of relevant data. He cannot withdraw into narrow, positive proofs. Rather he has to accept the inevitable bafflement engendered by what Foucault has called the "plethoric" nature of reality—the same Foucault who follows Vico's example by introducing his own work, *Les mots et les choses*, with an allegorized picture, Velasquez' paradigmatic depiction of

Las Meninas. The bafflement of the generalist's mind, Vico seems to be saying, need not defeat the aims of cosmic vision. But some bafflement needs to be recognized and accepted as given, by the scattering of light.

Vico begins the Idea of the Work by noting that the traditional model for the Table is the famed Table of Cebes, which it seems likely, despite Wellek's demurral, Vico had read about in Shaftesbury's *Second Characters*.[14] Another parallel to Vico's Table is the greatest of all such pictures, Dürer's *Melancolia I*, the so-called "*Great Melancholy*."[15] The tone of the whole is muted, darkened, saddened, while the visual structure of the picture obeys a rule of single, rather than the Vichian double, perspective. The vanishing point falls exactly on the distant sun in Dürer, whereas such a vanishing point cannot be located at any single point in Vico's Table. Thus the Table may lack the beauty of the Dürer, may lack its *aesthetic* complexity and power, but it does not lack intelligence. Vico has gone beyond the Renaissance, rather his vision is Baroque, if not Mannerist. Such an advancement into the world of multiple, yet controlled, zonings of space is an essential intellectual move, if the increasing awareness of relativism is to find its method of ordering. To achieve such an advance Vico had to remember Baconian cautions while adopting a Cartesian geometry. Where Bacon's precepts call for an awareness of the *thingness* of this actual world, Descartes calls for techniques of measuring quantity, given our awareness of the pragmatic relationships. Vico shares Descartes' view that we can control two, or perhaps only three, dimensionalities at once, unless we engage in exceedingly complex mathematics. Vico's triadic structures are thus probably more Cartesian in spirit than they appear from the perspective of NeoPlatonic speculation, which, as I have suggested, plays a strong role in his thinking. One has to go back in time, perhaps to Ibn Khaldun's *Introduction*, before finding a social scientist as profoundly Cartesian as the Vico of *The New Science*—or indeed as Baconian.[16] If the need to accommodate the two philosophies of Bacon and Descartes is the force producing the Vichian syncretism, the idea seems unavoidable that Vico is a genuine hybrid. If the aim of Vichian humanism is to discover "analytic geometry" for analyzing cultural change, a complementary task also confronts Vico, producing an adequate prophetic speculation. We must learn to read *The New Science*, not only as a prospectus for empirical research, but as a visionary meditation on the human consciousness of what it is "to be human."

The twin demand placed upon the reader cuts two ways: it encourages a depth of research, attending to small factual details, while at the same time it proposes an almost unprecedented largeness of historicist vision. Demanding an awareness of two opposing perspectives leads to Vichian syncretism. Scholars attempting to "make sense" out of Vico have shown many ways in which Vico fully grasps the complexity of human history, often at the moment when he is most patently fanciful, as with his typically allegorical etymologizing. Seeing the pervasive *allegoresis* within the body of the book and seeing the rhetorically determining force of its opening use of the Table have a positive implication. Vico has the merit of showing us discursively, as his Table shows visually, that a large-scale order of historical thought will require a conceptual space for tortuous uncertainty. The peculiar thing about *The New Science*, from this perspective, is that, with all its allegorical schematism, it never fails to carry the pulse of human life in history. Vico is a powerful rhetorician, who makes a strong poem, a "serious poem," of his own meditations. He has a grip on the mysteries of time sufficiently active to permit him a vision of corporate human destiny which would later appeal to Romantic thinkers. By the same token his Renaissance predecessors, including Pico and the Neo-Platonists, including his beloved Bacon, would have respected his preeminent capacity for "vision." They would have admired his lonely conquest of a new world of intellectual activity—and they would never have felt the need to deny the figurative energy that was making this conquest possible. The emergent Vico is deeply involved in many strains of post-Renaissance thought. Vico is peripheral and independent enough to anticipate new forms of PreRomantic speculative philosophy and philology. What seems always to abide in Vico is a taste for the excessively particular, commingled with a taste for the equally excessive generality (e.g., the history of cycles). Vico's book must then be read paradigmatically, as Thomas Kuhn has developed that notion for the history of science. In *The New Science* Vico creates a new paradigm for humanistic studies, a paradigm envisioning intellectual, political, social and religious activities and changes as occurring within a general *schema* of human creativity. This creativity Vico calls "poetry."

A natural reading of *The New Science* is thus aimed, like Vico's book itself, at a new paradigm for the analysis and evaluation of Vico's great work. To say that he writes a syncretic allegory which reveals its interest through four complementary "terministic screens"—philology, speculation, historicism, and prophecy—names a basic dynamic principle of *The New Science*. The human mind undergoes "modifications." Such a modifying capacity is precisely what the allegorical mode expresses and tests, when defined in the six-fold paradigm given above. If it is observed that the six Vichian modifications of his own allegory depart from, fuse into, mutually support, or mutually contradict each other, then it should equally be observed that such is the standard procedure for the allegory which the Table and its Idea introduce to the attentive reader's mind. By reading *The New Science* in what I have called its "natural order," the reader is alerted to what is most striking and most valuable in Vico, his remarkable powers of symbolic transformation, from one matrix of thought to another. Introduced to the imperious role of the Table and its Idea, the reader is enabled to appreciate the force of an art that Vico made his life-long study, the art of rhetoric. This is not a rhetoric which made its way at once into the intellectual world, as had Bacon's oratorical prose, or Descartes' lucid austerity of style. But it is a rhetoric that, given the passage of time and the growth of the human sciences since the Romantic period, has not only made its way into European intellectual consciousness, but into the hearts of men and women as well. Putting all other considerations aside, Vico remains vividly *human*, as a thinker.

To this end, none of Vico's rhetorical devices counts more heavily than his initiatory use of the prophetic and hieroglyphic device, the convex mirror, by which he depicts the opening out of speculative method. Through the pictorial device and it explication, he engages the reader in the task of thinking about philosophic (he would call it scientific) thought. While the iconography of the *Dipintura* serves a schematic and mnemonic purpose, its major function is to introduce the reader at once to a series of relational questions, which the ensuing discursive text will attempt to answer. A complex icon thus becomes the key to an even more complex verbal text. The enigma represented by the *Dipintura* suggests the intellectual perspective of the entire work, beginning the work with a pictorial outline of Vico's larger strategy. The *Dipintura* and its exegesis are models of metalinguistic power, as they generate the thinking of what is to follow, and at the same time allow the "ingenious" picture to serve as what W. J. T. Mitchell has called the "hypericon."[17] In this role the *Dipintura* belongs, like Foucault's *Las Meninas,* among "figures of figuration, pictures that reflect on the nature of images." By thus beginning his text of *The New Science,* Vico insists on our attending to the iconic aspect of any large vision of human affairs. The *Dipintura* raises the profound question as to whether it is possible to think at all without employing imagery. Among various rhetorical strategies of *The New Science* none is more effective than the way this visionary treatise begins its natural sequence of reading itself, by the foregrounding of a richly enigmatic iconological device.

9. Threshold, Sequence, and Personification in Coleridge

"It was, I think, in the month of August, but certainly in the summer season, and certainly in the year 1807, that I first saw this illustrious man, the largest and most spacious intellect, the subtlest and the most comprehensive, in my judgment, that has yet existed amongst men." Thus, in an article written some twenty-seven years later, Thomas De Quincey recalled his first encounter with Coleridge. The encounter was somewhat uncanny. Coleridge, one might say, *appeared* to his young admirer.

> I had received directions for finding out the house where Coleridge was visiting; and, in riding down a main street of Bridgewater, I noticed a gateway corresponding to the description given me. Under this was standing, and gazing about him, a man . . . . his eyes were large and soft in their expression; and it was from the peculiar appearance of haze or dreaminess, which mixed with their light, that I recognized my object. This was Coleridge. I examined him steadfastly for a minute or more; and it struck me that he saw neither myself nor any other object in the street. He was in deep reverie; for I had dismounted, made two or three trifling arrangements at an inn door, and advanced close to him, before he had apparently become conscious of my presence. The sound of my voice, announcing my own name, first awoke him: he started, and, for a moment, seemed at a loss to understand my purpose or his situation; for he repeated rapidly a number of words which had no relation to either of us. There was no *mauvaise honte* in his manner, but simple perplexity, and an apparent difficulty in recovering his position amongst daylight realities. This little scene over, he received me with a kindness of manner so marked it might be called gracious.[1]

Coleridge appeared to De Quincey in the hovering stance of "a solitary haunted by vast conceptions in which he cannot participate," Hartman's romantic "hero of consciousness."[2] He stood on the threshold between a building and a street, a palace and a highway, a temple and a labyrinth. This threshold is an edge at which simultaneous participation in the sacred and the profane becomes available to the hero of consciousness.

Thought has been our term for the active aspect of this consciousness. To emphasize the conscious is to emphasize an awareness of thinking in all its dimensions, a global self-awareness. The critical terms applied to Coleridge will be formal ones such as threshold, time, sequence, figuration, and personification. All such terms refer simultaneously to the shaping of literature and the operations of mind. In essence, what follows is the topography of a salient development of post-Enlightenment thought.

Coleridge inherited and developed ideas about the mental faculties which combine to produce the organizations of poetic form. He attempted to observe in his criticism "the component faculties of the human mind itself." The exercise of the imaginative power that most impressed him as essential to poetry was the capacity to reconcile opposed and discordant perceptions of the world and of nature. Such imaginative powers are required for the highest poetry which in turn exemplifies poetical thought itself. One major consequence of M. H. Abrams's celebrated study, *The Mirror and the Lamp*, and its sequel, *Natural Supernaturalism*, is the clear implication that Romantic thought pioneered all aspects of the psychology of imaginative process. What Abrams called "a productive tension" between spontaneous feeling and the impulse for order is the tension and source of excitement in all those works of Coleridge which give a large place to their own subjectivity. Coleridge, like Wordsworth, achieved his most spectacular successes in this pursuit of the subjective, whenever he had a *mise-en-scène* of an extreme character as in "The Rime of the Ancient Mariner" or "Christabel." Therein he intensified the rendering of poetic thought, especially by inventing situations of liminal, or threshold, passage. In a sense, the liminal is the key to the Romantic projection of the most intensely powerful effects of creative thought, including a verbal virtuosity in Coleridge's work. He bases much of his criticism on an acute sense of the semiotic aspect of language. We are not surprised to find that linguistic figurations are tied to the use of liminal settings. We, therefore, will have to examine liminality itself in some detail, if we are to grasp the critical form of consciousness of which the Romantic poet is the heroic master.

Thresholds: A Spenserian Origin

The gateway is a sacred *via transitionae* in all cultures: in our materialist world there are myths of carrying brides over doorsteps, though we no longer break oatcakes over the heads of newlyweds. Thresholds, which are dangerous, have an ancient, rigorous mythography and rite. The Romans consecrated a god of gates, Janus, whose bifrontal face looked opposite ways, in and out of the city, blessing or cursing the passer in his entrance to or exit from the city.

Janus was also a god of beginnings, which suggests that, in any advanced civilization, a genuine beginning always starts from somewhere. Within culture, it would seem, there are no beginnings *ex nihilo*. The scene of the origin is a fountain, a *templum*, a ground made sacred because it is the iconic double of the world conceived as sacred space and therefore, as so frequently in the ancient civilizations, a space formally demarcated by a sacred limit, the so-called *mundus*—the world-wall. Within culture, also, deaths and endings seem to belong to what lies outside the sacred inner-space, an outside archetypally structured as "the labyrinth."

Ancient religious traditions descend and enter into English poetics largely through the imagery of a dialectical opposition between temple and labyrinth.[3] The Romantic fascination with these two great images of life seems to gain its power from the hybrid nature of classical and Christian mythography, as a Christian Humanist combination. The temple and labyrinth are the paradigmatic mythic structures for Biblical as much as classical, historicity and prophecy. The hybridization of pagan and Christian myth is, at least in this area, entirely conventional.

If temple and labyrinth provide the models of sacred stillness and profane movement, the threshold is the model of the transitional phase that links these two fundamental modes of thinking and being. Mythographically thresholds take many forms: Homer's Cave of the Nymphs, Virgil's twin Gates of Horn and Ivory, Dante's Limbo—or, leaping into the modern era, Wordsworthian "spots of time," Conrad's shadow line, Forster's Caves of Marabar. While epic tradition supplies conventional models of the threshold, these conventions are always subject to deliberate poetic blurring, and this shift from the distinct limen to the indistinct serves a double purpose. On the one hand, poets, like painters, may delight in the softening of outline because it permits an intensification of medium: thus Turner's mastery of the indistinct expresses a technical interest in medium which is remarkably parallel to that of his near-contemporary, Coleridge.[4] On the other hand, and this is perhaps the fundamental and more substantial point, poets have wished to subtilize, to dissolve, to fragment, to blur the hard material edge, because poetry hunts down the soul, with its obscure passions, feelings, other-than-cognitive symbolic forms. Spenser, for example, places doormen at the gates of his various temples; Milton stations various guardians of the gates: angels watch over Eden, Heaven, and Hell (including the counterwatch of Sin and Death). Such porters actively frame their universes. Yet despite this hard and obvious utility of suggesting the security force watching over mythic borders, few poets of major stature remain long interested in the material aspect of the threshold. If not always before, at least with the Renaissance there is a poetic commitment to a blurred psychologized threshold. Earlier authors like Virgil and Apuleius appeal to the Renaissance poets partly because this psychological element had been so strong in their earlier rites of passage.

Spenser's thresholds are often occurrences in the minds of his protagonists, changes of mind, rather than transitions of body or thing. At his most powerful, as at the end of Book III of *The Faerie Queene*, Spenser may accommodate a physical and mental crossover, so that the two merge in one single, unbroken psychosomatic drama. Scudamour cannot pass the threshold of Busirane's castle-prison, because his "mind" will not permit the passage, but Britomart can pass over, and when she does, as with her other marvelous psychological breakthroughs, she achieves for Spenser an originating shift within English Romantic sensibility. She enacts the exchange of psychic energies.

From Spenser, Milton learns the iconographies of mental shift. Milton takes the mind to be the locus of the symbolic threshold, and he begins his career (after saluting Shakespeare, Donne, and the other Metaphysicals) with shorter works on various rites of passage, among them the "Ode on the Morning of Christ's Nativity," *Comus*, and "Lycidas." The later epic works dramatize cosmic threshold scenes, but the same sense of dawning animates the prose works of Milton—his *Areopagitica* breathes light as the form or medium of truth. Milton places dramatic action at the cosmic threshold. For English Romantic rites of passage he is a most vocal prophet.

Where this prophetic voicing becomes problematic, however, is not in the discrimination of our Romantic interest in it: that we recognize. But threshold becomes a more elusive concept when we stress, as such, the prophetic speech that marks its liminal apprehension. Here both sight and sound tend to create a sense of time, and time is enigmatic.

Betweenness and Time

In poetry, as in the Scriptures, one notes at once the temporal aspect of the threshold. Measures of the precise amount of natural light (or artificial light, if you take *The Invisible Man* as the contemporary model) specify the experiencing of a shift from one period to another. The archetypal liminal scene occurs at dawn or dusk (Baudelaire's two *crépuscules*), at the end of a departing year or the start of a new year (January), the end or beginning of an era, a millennium perhaps. Whatever the magnitude of the joined time-frames, however, there seems to be no reason why thresholdness, which its chief modern theorist, Heidegger, would call "betweenness"—*das Zwischen*—could not minimally refer to a crossing from one instant to another. Montaigne, in "Repentance," when he says "I do not portray being, I portray passing," is assuming the possibility of instantaneous change—"from minute to minute," he says, "my history needs to be adapted to the moment. I may presently change." Indeed, in high Coleridgean fashion, he can conceive that since all things in the world are in constant motion, "stability itself is nothing but a more languid motion."

Montaigne is the philosopher of modern poetry, and the one thinker whom we at once associate with the Shakespearean (and by an extrapolation, with the Coleridgean) enterprise. Montaigne records the way things more and more seem to be staggering with "natural drunkenness." Remarkably, while more extension-conscious than even Descartes himself, Montaigne can speak to Shakespeare because he shares the sense of the dramatic confusions wrought upon us by the "petty pace" of diurnal time.

The slow Cartesian scientific development of a system opposed to Montaigne, the "elimination of time" which Whitrow has shown descending earlier from Archimedes, flowering with Descartes, and culminating with Einstein's "geometrization" of all time and space, makes war upon the poet's sense of time as lived duration, lived succession. "Physics endeavours in principle to make do with space-like concepts alone, and strives to express with their aid all relations having the form of laws."[5] Here "space-like" means, or may be translated to mean, "dimensional." Einstein is not monogamously wedded to space—the great fiddle-player allows time into the cosmic system as long as it can be "space-*like*." The wars of space and time in modern science are no more monolithic than any other wars fought since the Renaissance. Yet time took refuge, after Descartes and Locke, in the arms of the poets.

Time, of course, had never even seemed neatly or conveniently dimensional. Dimensionally, in terms of measurement, despite natural clocks like the human pulse or the moon and artificial clocks like hour-glasses, time had always been mysterious, as Augustine admitted in Book XI of the *Confessions*. To take only one Augustinian paradox of temporal nondimensionality: "In other words we cannot rightly say that time *is*, except by reason of its impending state of *not* being" (that is, its falling away into the disappeared past, out of an empty future that is not yet). Rather in the manner of Hamlet, Augustine has just made his famous aside: "What, then, is time? I know well what it is, provided that nobody asks me."

Augustine's epistemological jest reminds us that it has never been difficult for Western man to perceive time as the model of nothingness, with space the model of somethingness. Time in our world displays an instantaneity so perfect in its slippery transit—its slither from one temporal fix to another—that there is nothing to mark, let alone measure, its being, its at-homeness. Like the doomed brother and sister of Coleridge's "Time Real and Imaginary," time's arrow dissolves finally before us into nothingness, as it flies forever outward toward the infinitely going-away horizon we call "space." Time as the creator and destroyer of space is relatively easy for us to imagine. Time, as becoming, is then whatever is not space. Yet the heart only painfully accepts this divorce.

Coleridge, whose heart is so full, if sometimes only of its own emptiness, its desire to be filled, seems fully aware that the betweenness of time-as-moment, pure thresholdness, barren liminality, at least in what Einstein would call a "space-like" way, must be a nothingness. Between the temple and labyrinth there must be a crossing which, viewed from the perspective of time, does not stand, stay, hold, or persist. Yet the poet craves persistence and duration—like Spenser and Milton, Coleridge would dilate the prophetic moment; unlike them he takes opium, with what effects of temporal dilation we can only surmise. So he is caught in a psychosomatic paradox: though the threshold is temporally nonexistent, a phantom-place, the passage across this no-man's-land seems to be more intense, experientially, than life either inside or outside the temple, inside or outside the labyrinth. The threshold unmakes the dialectic of inside and outside, replacing it by an unmediating passage between. Its motto: Readiness is all.

The intensity of the rite of passage, or simply, of Montaigne's "passing," seems with Coleridge to raise an accompanying liminal anxiety—the existential vertigo that led Herbert Read to associate Coleridge and Kierkegaard. This anxiety characteristically feels like a border-crossing emotion. It manifests itself as uncertainty, as fear approaching paranoia, the fear that what animates life—thinking— will be blocked, that one will be arrested, pressed down, or suffocated in the manner of Poe's heroes (with whom Coleridge shares the terror of suffocation). As one approaches the border, this anxiety rises; as one crosses it successfully, the anxiety recedes. While anxiety may also be "free floating," here it tends to focus on the border-scene itself, the moment of crossing the border, with its guards. The moment is finally a dramatic event. The special, painful uncertainty of thresholdness should first, in a theoretical account, give rise to a connected problem, the problem of sequence, and to this we must now turn in our search for the Coleridgean readiness.

Sequence

In the present context, "sequence" means the process and the promise that something will follow something else. Spatially, sequence means the contiguous placement of events which, when they occur "in sequence," will display a one-after-the-otherness. If events occur "in rapid sequence," they come right next to each other. This neighborly aspect of sequence does not necessarily mean that events will always follow one next to the other in a crowded way, each event as it were jammed right up against its neighbor and "predecessor." Predecessors and precursors get linked to their successors. If anything, because there is a strung-out, stretched relation from earlier to later. A sequence is like a line; it has length. Tempted as we may be to argue that two points or events may make a sequence, we perhaps should question whether sequences do not need to be constructed out of three or more points. The initial statement might be made that a sequence is not likely to be a *straight* line or shortest distance between two points. Common experience suggests that sequences are wavy lines, strung out like the linked chains of logical sorites.[6]

Words like "line" and "string" imply a necessarily spatial or "rhopalic" definition of sequence, and yet sequence can also mean what follows logically, and here space is ideal. This logical concatenation might, for example, be represented by the theoretical circles of Boolean algebra or the thickness of lines and points in geometry, that is, a thickness known by its own theoretical absence. Logical space is the space which, "In the beginning," was occupied by the Logos of the Apostle John. Although the readiest terms by which we understand sequence are spatial, there is a question as to what kind of space sequences may be occupying if, as so often in the thought of Coleridge, they are sequences with logical, theoretical, or visionary form.

There is a further difficulty, which almost defines the problem of sequence so far as it relates to Coleridge: the fact that serious concern with "what follows" will have to entertain a temporal factor, whether science wishes so or not. Can a poet imagine a sequence that is devoid of any passing of time, when the poem shifts from space to space, point to point, as long as there are more than two points in the diagram? From this question arises the Sisyphian labor of modern philosophy, whether a Jamesian, Bergsonian, Husserlian, or any other phenomenological attempt, to define the role of time-consciousness in the grasp of logical wholes. Under this structure of analysis, our phrase "next door" would have to be replaced by "and then" or simply by "afterwards." In spite of the fact that, in dealing with sequence, we begin spatially, we end on a note of temporal description. God alone has the power to be absolutely timeless. All His acts occur at once. To begin with, "The Infinite I Am" names an entirely spatial mode of being, set off against man's relativistic temporal nature.

The Fourth Gospel counters the utter timelessness of God. To this text Coleridge intended to devote a critical study (which, in effect, he sketched in *The Confessions of an Inquiring Spirit*). Paradoxically, John's doctrine of the Logos is the most powerful philosophic machine within Christian culture for the counterattack against the logical annihilation of time. The Incarnate Word is a theoretical notion of man-in-time, and thus Coleridge mythologizes The Word when he reads the Fourth Gospel.

Time and the Logos are, no doubt, violently yoked together. Coleridge, the diachronic thinker, believes in the Johannine Incarnation, *even though* the mystique of The Word sometimes shifts ideas of sequence into a mystique of stillness, which is stated as a numerological mystery leading to the static number symbolism of Revelation. In such static symbolism a sequence "follows" because each element of it is like a natural number, the larger numbers "following" because they contain the smaller numbers. Numerology, if not number theory, suggests a timeless ontology.

Yet the *poetics* of number accept, and do not, under pressure from logic, reject man's time-bound duration. Augustine's *De Musica* conceived poetry as the art of right proportioning (*bene modulandi*), and ultimately as the mirror or *speculum* of the world—an apparently stabilizing, if not static, symbolic system. But poetry moves, and verses turn, as Augustine knew well (the first five books of *De Musica* discuss rhythm and meter). Poets use spatial terms to control changes in time. They spend their lives measuring lines of poetry—we still study metrics—and Coleridge was a notable metrical experimenter, like almost all metaphysical poets in the English tradition. We may conclude that the poetic pursuit of the logos demands a measuring and time-feeling poetic activity. This runs counter to the *contemplation* of number, as the unchanging pattern of the Logos, and instead embraces an incarnational notion of the poet as a living, moving, breathing, uttering prophet. Incarnation brings the Logos into the world as a living, and dying, man—the Son of Man. It temporalizes and historicizes number.

Pater on Relativism: A Digression

The Coleridgean homing on the Fourth Gospel reminds us further that incarnation is a relativistic concept and that, with it in mind, the philosophic poet can introduce relativity—in the form of causal conditions—into the otherwise absolute and timeless mysteries of a Platonic system. It was Walter Pater, the next great English critical theorist after Coleridge, who saw this problem most clearly. His essay "Coleridge" observed by way of introduction to his subject that "modern thought is distinguished from ancient by its cultivation of the 'relative' spirit in place of the 'absolute.' Ancient philosophy sought to arrest every object in an eternal outline, to fix thought in a necessary formula, and the varieties of life in a classification by 'kinds,' or *genera*. To the modern spirit nothing is, or can be rightly known, except relatively and under conditions."[7] Then follows an exquisite description of the delicacy of true scientific observation, which reveals "types of life evanescing into each other by inexpressible refinements of change." We are listening to the doctrine of Impressionism in its most exact refinement. Coleridge, we expect, will be its chief relativistic progenitor.

Yet Pater proceeds to argue the converse: he finds Coleridge the defender, in a lost cause, of the older absolutism. As the greatest English critical Impressionist, Pater could make the point. Perhaps today he would speak differently if, like us, he had access to Coleridge's *Notebooks*. Yet he almost seems disingenuous. Pater seems blind to the real Coleridge who appears to us in so many ways the first hero of critical relativism in English literature. When Pater says that "the literary life of Coleridge was a disinterested struggle against the relative spirit," we may wonder if the follower has not falsified his paternity. Pater to the contrary, there is plenty of "the excitement of the literary sense" in Coleridge, and is this sense not relativistic? But what really matters is the framework in which Pater placed his precursor: the conflict between the absolute and relative spirits.

This digression will have reminded the reader that the deep Coleridgean interest in the incarnation of genius amounts to a concern for the activity of man, inspired man, *in time*. Genius for Coleridge is nothing if not relative, and this includes a causal dimension of temporal sequence. Sequence attains relativistic form when it is allowed to show its causal enlinkedness. If sequences of events are "causal sequences," their temporal nature is hedged by those conditional limits which can only be known to Pater's spirit of relative perceptions.

Poets, of course, have always shared with story-tellers the knowledge that mythic time is not an absolute and causally blank dimension. Mythmakers know that if you tell a story confidently, no matter how strange its materials, sequence as a causally relativistic set of conditions will begin to arise all by itself. Sequence will arise from the metonymic next-door placement of event after event. The reader imports a hidden causality, though none be present on the surface. If, in a story, one event is told after another, a causal conditionality is very hard *not* to imagine. The imagination, in short, manufactures causes. *Post hoc, ergo propter hoc* is one principle of myth.

What distinguishes Coleridge from Pater is then not a priority of absolute over relative spirit, but rather a different attitude—which Pater did not sufficiently discriminate—toward sequence. Pater displays a synchronous method, while Coleridge is heroically diachronic in his relativisms. Coleridge begins his poetic career wishing to preserve the mythmaker's "story line," because its implicit metaphysic reaffirms his sense of diachronic order. He wants this exactly in proportion to his immense anxiety about its being possible.

Sequence and Survival

Coleridge appears to have suffered from a particular fear that sequence might not organize his world. This is not to say that his lifelong interest in, and study of, logic is a mere defense against a malaise which logic should have had the magic power to undo. Nor, necessarily, that his fascination with logical sequence implies the paranoia which Freud supposed might underlie philosophic thought in general. We need not go so far. We can, however, observe that Coleridge appears comforted and reassured by the contemplation of "method," as various recent students of his life and work have shown. His criticism adopts method as a liturgical ideal; for him method is the expression, and the experience, of grace as it appears in a life of thought. Conversely, like Hamlet he is terrified lest events simply may not follow. His work can be conceived as an intensely interested struggle against this fear.

The great sequences of this struggle are to be found in works of prose, not verse. Prose articulates sequence in grammatical form. The theoretical center for Coleridge is the prose treatise contained in the essays of *The Friend*, where the critic develops his theory of method. Most perfectly exemplified by Shakespeare, method implies, as a kind of providential order, that the mind keeps moving and shaping simultaneously the conditions of its movement. Thus in methodical sequence the poet may wander narratively or dramatically with great range, yet will always project the sense of overall design, a sort of implicit city-plan for his own development in the myth. Shakespeare the model author achieves a balance, since "without continuous transition there can be no method," while "without a preconception there can be no transition with continuity." Method is survival through and beyond continuous uncertain eventualities, achieved because its progression is vital, the reverse of "dead arrangement." Method is inevitably somewhat dramatic and unafraid in spite of the underlying fear that one will lose one's way. Or, more bluntly, method is the expression of courage in the presence of that fear. The literary model of a superordinate structure built on this courageous plan is the whole Shakespearean canon, which for Coleridge has the precise status of a Bible. The model of a subordinate structure of methodical sequence will be the dramatic texture of the poems and plays of Shakespeare, whose genius carries the action careering forward, while judgment continually checks the "Fiery-Four-in-Hand."

The second great document in the Coleridgean pursuit of method is the *Biographia*. Whereas the *Essays on Method* describes the wayward yet ordered sequence of thought that gives Shakespearean drama its "implicit metaphysic," the *Biographia* is more ingenious and ambitious. It does not just describe. It embodies. It enacts, while it narrates, the series of learnings that went into the final providence of the poet's own critical and poetic life. In a way Coleridge one-ups Wordsworth, since his own *Prelude*—the *Biographia*—is written in prose, whereas Wordsworth exploited the method-making powers of the medium of prose only to the extent that prose modulates his blank verse. One other clue to the method underlying the *Biographia* is its epic structure and its final settling upon an agon between Wordsworth and the author, in the concluding chapters. The critical analysis of Wordsworth's theory and practice is not just criticism; it is, more adequately considered, a conceptual myth of the confrontation of two great, jarring, fraternal intellects. Method appears in the *Biographia*, therefore, secondarily in the analysis of mind and imagination as such, and primarily in the dramatic impersonation of that analysis as Coleridge wrestles with his essential adversary, Wordsworth. The critique enacts the biography, and does so methodically, because this is a *literary* biography. In a sense the critique is Shakespearean, since it personifies the critical issues at stake. The *Biographia*, like its double, the *Prelude*, is a myth of the life of imagination as style.

Such an imagination has two possible poles, one of which might be called operatic. It leads to the plan for the impossible *magnum opus*. Its chief yearning is sublimity and unbounded power over vast mentally-projected domains. The magnum opus mania drove Coleridge to plot endless impossible projects, most of which envisage the ultimate transformation of some vast labyrinthine body of inchoate materials into an equally vast, but now perfectly lucid and structured, temple of ideal order. With intuitive grace and genius, Coleridge managed to dictate the *Biographia* and to write a number of other extended prose works, so that, in spite of himself, especially through the *Biographia*, he achieved his desired scope—largely because in that and other works he escaped his compulsions, and just played.

The other polarity of imaginative life-style implicit in Coleridge's "method" is an obverse one, the reduction to the infinitely small, to the instantaneous threshold, where anxiety and uncertainty produce an ideal *reduction* of the magnum opus to an opus minimum. As Coleridge himself was fond of saying, extremes meet, and here the compulsion to overwhelm with sublimity meets the compulsion to pass lightly over the threshold.

The poetics of threshold require an inversion of the ideal of epic containment, such that the poet now strives for lyric concision, *to act for* the epic scope of his vision. The ideal poem depends in this inverted aesthetic on an art of perfect exclusion. The tradition is thus one of brevity, wit, and metaphysical conceit, of the kind that increasingly fascinated Coleridge as he grew older and more deeply pursued the poetry of Donne, Herbert, Crashaw, and others from his favorite century, the seventeenth. No earlier models, however, could quite predict the varieties of threshold-poem which Coleridge was to achieve.

Emotions at the Threshold

To get at this range we need an instrument, the emotive spectrum, which can measure the sense of threshold iself. If readiness is the stance within the doorway, then a mindset of confidence or courage is the ideal mode of readiness. This contrasts with the labyrinth, where the natural emotive state is terror or a generalized anxiety; or perhaps, if life is a Spenserian Wood of Error, then the feeling there is a specifically competitive anxiety, to which Marvell draws attention: "How vainly men themselves amaze / To win the palm, the oak, or bays." Conversely in the temple (or garden) one need not fear, though upon first entering from the labyrinth, one may experience an irrelevant, leftover fear. This is opposed to the controlled sense of trial which often the hero is ritually and penitentially, though not experientially, led through, before his final triumph within the structure of the temple. In the temple, at last, one learns confidence; one's faith triumphs.

At the threshold—between temple and maze—there is a possible range of normal threshold-feelings: anxiety, readiness, blind hope. This continuum measures the degrees of dread, and it refers specifically to a range of feelings aroused by the *sacer*, the taboo, the holy. If within the temple the holy seems triumphant, in the labyrinth the holy is either lost or irrelevant, whereas at the threshold these differences are exactly what is put into question. The threshold tries the sense of the holy.

Thresholds in Coleridge range widely in the degree of confidence or fear they may generate. "Frost at Midnight," with its emphasis on silence and ministry, identifies the ritual transition with the "secret ministry" of frost hanging up its silent icicles, "Quietly shining in the quiet Moon." Poised, the poet—in his threshold *persona*—may bless the child, asleep in his arms, and while meditating on the "stranger," the film of flame glowing in the fire, he prophesies a hopeful future for the child; he sees the child poised also, but on the threshold of a happier life than what the poet had known when he was a child. "Fears in Solitude" balances liminal feelings, so that it suspends war and human conflict within the scales of "Love, and the thoughts that yearn for human kind." "This Lime-Tree Bower My Prison" suspends the poet on the edge of a perfect templum, yet there is a double threat implicit in his suspended state: the bower, as in Spenser, imprisons, while the beloved friends depart from it, leaving the poet alone. Their leaving him has the effect of making the bower a Goldengrove; the poet still utters a hope: "Henceforth I shall know / That Nature ne'er deserts the wise and pure"—but friends may leave their friends, quite innocently, though accidentally, alone.

The danger in being optimistic about Coleridge's visions of threshold is quite simple: it is absurdly wrong for him, in general. The typical case, for example "The Ancient Mariner," is infused with terror. This is a holy dread, not useful caution. The poem is an exercise in what Hartman has called the "spectral confrontations" which are the essential moments of liminal experience.[8] The Mariner's tale is set against the framing doorway before the marriage feast—the basic threshold, of house and home—but its myth sweeps us and the Mariner along the corridors of death and time in a terror-driven sequence of liminal passages, as the ship becomes the first vessel to "burst" into the silent sea of transformational rites. Similarly, in "Kubla Khan," there may be a "sunny pleasure-dome" for optimists to dwell on, but the finality of the poem is a meditation on the terrors of prophetic vision as it confronts theological ultimates and the naïve simplicity of templar rituals ("Weave a circle round him thrice"), leaving us in some doubt as to how much poison there is in the milk of Paradise. "Christabel," in another direction, romanticizes erotic anxiety at the moment of most fearsome sexual initiation. Perceived conventionally, the poem is a gothic tale, full of graveyard atmosphere. Within the convention, one notes the importance of the metric invention, to the hesitancy implied by the theme of demonic eros. But "Christabel" denies the catharsis of its gothic convention. It almost immediately insists on the sacred separation of castle and forest. Christabel reaches her fatal crossover, having brought Geraldine back to the Castle with her.

> Christabel with might and main
> Lifted her up, a weary weight,
> Over the threshold of the gate,

and from this moment the poem scarcely pauses in the exploration of the transit between dream and wake, control and abandon, eros and death, taboo and free sexuality, through a vicious regress of antinomies.

"Christabel" fascinated its early readers especially because it foresaw the world of Victorian inhibition. Isolating sexual boundaries and metamorphoses, it also isolated a growing sexual anxiety. It anticipated the Tennysonian eros. For many years Coleridge insisted that he would finish the poem, but it may be that he hesitated, not because no story could be machined to follow upon Parts I and II, but because the two parts had already adequately set forth their real tenor, the threshold phenomenon itself, and to move along from their unfinished liminality would have been to destroy their perfect readiness by a useful, but merely conventional, narrative ending.

There are times, of course, when Coleridge openly confronts terror as a pure state, that is, as nightmare. In "The Pains of Sleep" the "wide blessing" of deep sleep is subverted by an interim condition of labyrinthine dreams: "For aye entempesting anew / The unfathomable hell within, / The horror of their deeds to view, / To know and loathe, yet wish and do!" As one reflects on these terrible moments in the poet's visionary life, one values more deeply his attachment to the moon, which sustains him in a most extraordinary way, not least because the moon is a primary natural clock older than any chronometric device.

Prayer and the Journeying Moon

The moon has always been known to poets for its changes, its continuous waxing and waning. With Coleridge the moon, among many meanings, enjoys status as an angelic messenger of the possibility of safe crossing, and safe standing at the threshold. As angelic messenger, the moon brings news to the poet by reflecting the sun's light, and other messages depend upon that primary mirroring. Reflected, moonlight is benign, the opposite of that lurid sunset-red Visconti used everywhere in his film *The Damned*, which in its original version is called *The Twilight of the Gods*. Female, or androgynous, the moon brings happier messages of confident augury. Thus the marginal gloss upon the moon in "The Ancient Mariner": "In his loneliness and fixedness he yearneth towards the journeying Moon, and the stars that still sojourn, yet still move onward; and everywhere the blue sky belongs to them, and is their appointed rest, and their native country and their own natural homes, which they enter unannounced, as lords that are certainly expected and yet there is a silent joy at their arrival."

The journeying moon is the harbinger of the return of the hero of consciousness. The celestial bodies are like lords "certainly expected," the prodigal sons of heaven. Coleridge, I suppose, wanted to create a myth of expectation. He praised Shakespeare for achieving plots which work, not through surprise, but through fulfilled expectation. His own criticism is more alive than most, mainly because it stands poised and ready to notice, to respond where there is no standard response. He can observe the most delicate verbal, especially syntactic, shifts. Coleridge is the poet-critic of expectancy. Perhaps in order to intensify this method of response, he shifts, in later years, to a mode of poetry quite unlike that practiced in "The Ancient Mariner" or "Christabel," a poetry, even so, which derives partly from those early poems. As Coleridge the poet becomes increasingly liminal, he seeks poetic prayer—praying being the liturgical form of crossing over once again. The climax of "Mariner" occurs when the Mariner prays—this climax is to become the modal pattern in several later poems, where, however, there is little narrative. Coleridge finally seeks an entente with George Herbert, and especially with the poem "Prayer." Generally *The Temple* creates a structuring dramatic scene of prayer, but in that one lyric the maximum expectancy is reached through a total annihilation of all verbs. No single predominant turn of thought forces itself upon the reader, because the poet allows no constricting verb to push the reader here, there, or anywhere. Verbless, the poem and its reader kneel down, waiting, devoted. Herbert has a formalist importance for Coleridge which Donne, whom he so admires, could never have, for *The Temple* explores the pressures preventing prayer, as much as its amenities and glories. Studying Herbert (and Donne too, one must grant), Coleridge would appear to have sharpened his own skills in addressing the absolute. That, not Pater's notion of "tracking of all questions, critical or practical, to first principles," is the problem solved by *The Temple* and then by Coleridge's later poems. He has to address himself to a frightening sacredness—his "deity."

"Limbo" and the Metaphysical Mode

It is a systematic consequence, therefore, when the poems of threshold, "Limbo" and "Ne Plus Ultra," derive from a Herbertian poetic and state the limits of the powers of prayer. "Ne Plus Ultra" is directly imitated from "Prayer," and it too lacks any verb, with the same liminal intensification accruing to it as a result of a syntactic stillness. Yet Coleridge is not easy or very calm in this stillness; it threatens, with short, weighted, magical phrases that portend storms of spirit and destiny. Like Herbert, Coleridge is rather more dramatic than lyrical as he adopts the attitude of prayer. Bate has observed further that "in the better verse of Coleridge from 1817 until his death we find a denseness of thought embodied in an odd, original imagery, frequently homely, occasionally even grotesque."[9] This reborn Metaphysical Wit manages such "amalgamation or fusion under pressure" that its philosophical words and phrases become "almost substances for him, thick with emotion and meaning. In these poems, with their dense reflectiveness, their odd, often crowded metaphor, their allusion to the technical vocabulary and conceptualizations of Philosophy, Coleridge creates a mode of poetry entirely his own."

Perhaps the finest example is "Limbo," thought to have been written in the same period as the *Biographia.* "Limbo," more complex in form than its companion piece, "Ne Plus Ultra," is a strange mixture of personification, dramatic monologue, and visionary fugue. Its most prominent feature is a dramatic or melodramatic gesture of thought, while its iconography is variously allusive, including echoes of Dante, Milton, perhaps Shakespeare (Hamlet calls the Ghost "old mole"), more probably Henry Vaughan's "Night" and its portrait of Nicodemus (who could be the model for Coleridge's Human Time). The sense of varied poetic origins reveals the essential Coleridge. He is eclectic, yet single-voiced. Nor does the poem assert a doctrinal or dogmatic view of human salvation. The poet seems mainly interested in the transition between this world and the next. A hesitancy throughout conveys anxiety over the liminal condition itself, rather than a theological debate.

Despite this evanescence of doctrine, however, "Limbo" attempts to define an indefinable, ultimate limit, which the poet calls "positive negation." In so doing he justifies his bizarre method of metaphysical wit and prayer: he personifies a bulk of nothingness. His declamatory style, solidifying horror and anxiety, recovers the primitive, or primary, sources of poetic animation. If to personify is to give soul to an idea or thing, then here the poetry is gaining soul through personification.

Coleridge, we are informed, designed his shorter pieces and then read them in such a way that "the verses seem as if *played* to the ear upon some unseen instrument. And the poet's manner of reciting is similar. It is not rhetorical, but musical; so very near recitative, that for any one else to attempt it would be ridiculous, and yet it is perfectly miraculous with what exquisite searching he elicits and makes sensible every particular of the meaning, not leaving a shadow of the feeling, the mood, the degree, untouched."[10] This searching, inflecting recitative expresses the animation of the personifying thought.

Personification and Negativity

A new or renewed Renaissance mode of personification would seem to be the main yield of the poetry of threshold. The need to renew personification was inherited directly from most eighteenth-century verse, except for the greatest. During that period the older, conventional personified abstractions slowly froze to death, and now poets had to bring the statues back to life. Frank Manuel, like Hartman in his studies of genius, has shown that the pre-Romantics could reanimate a daemonic universe in the mode of "the new allegory."[11] From another point of view personifications could come alive again because there were once again adequate conditions of rumination. As Michel Foucault has said, the celebratory religions of an earlier time now gave place to "an empty milieu—that of idleness and remorse, in which the heart of man is abandoned to its own anxiety, in which the passions surrender time to unconcern or to repetition in which, finally, madness can function freely."[12] Madness is complete personification. Poets need not, though some in fact did, descend into this generative void.

Yet the conditions of madness and a renewed animism still demand the appropriate poetic forms, which Coleridge had to invent. As Huizinga has remarked, personification is a kind of mental play, and this ludic strain is strong in Coleridge's make-up.[13] Formally, we can say that personification is the figurative emergent of the liminal scene. In the temple there appear to be personified abstractions hard at work, virtues and noble essences, while labyrinths are stocked by an equal and opposite number of vices and personified negations—the lions of the Marquess of Bath. Yet these polar opposites perhaps only gain animate life, if they have it, from their participation in the process of passage. Personifications come alive the moment there is psychological breakthrough, with an accompanying liberation of utterance, which in its radical form is a first deep breath. Poetry seeking a fresh animation is poetry seeking to throw off the "smothering weight" of the "Dejection" Ode. Such a poetry must breathe, showing life coming or going away, as in "Limbo."

This breathing may be explained, in part, if we reckon with the inner nature of personification. An active, vital, person-making figure must not be a moral cliché. It must not be a machine in a materialist sense. It cannot simply parody the *daimon*. It must be a "real ghost," like the spectral presence of a drug experience or a nightmare or daydream. Hartman has finely observed: "In fact, whenever the question of persona arises in a radical way, whenever self-choosing, self-identification, becomes a more than personal, indeed, prophetic, decision—which happens when the poet feels himself alien to the genius of country or age and determined to assume an adversary role—poetry renews itself by its contact with what may seem to be archaic forces."[14] *This* personifying author will find himself listening, as well as looking, for phantoms.

Above all the phantom must not exist. It must resist existence. To envision, to think the phantom person poetically the poet must empty his imagery of piety and sense, allowing in their place some measure of daemonic possession. The one necessary poetic act will be to utter, to speak, nothingness. To achieve this defining negativity, the poem "Limbo" typically seeks to *posit* negation as the ultimate daemon. By asserting the life of this final nothingness, the poet has reinvented the Ghost of *Hamlet*, the Witches of *Macbeth*, the daemonic powers that abandon Antony, Hermione's statue that comes alive in *The Winter's Tale*. This is a dramatic reinvention; it enghosts and embodies the persons of a play.

The logic of personification requires a phantom nihilism and a return to the heart of drama. This achievement in the later Coleridge depends upon the liminal scene, which permits the greatest experiential intensity at the very moment when the rite of passage denies or reduces the extensity of either the temple or the labyrinth. Drama gets its personifying nothingness—its phantoms—from the making of continuous threshold-scenes. Because the Elizabethan period had so fully subscribed to the norms of drama, its free use of personification—unlike most eighteenth-century personification—goes quite unnoticed. But there is scarcely a line in a Shakespeare sonnet that does not breathe this language of the personified force. Coleridge, in turning to the theme of nothingness, was trying to get back some of that Renaissance utterancy and dramatic presence. Half-brother to Hamlet, he almost succeeded.

The Dramatic Personification

The dramatic or, perhaps more accurately, the melodramatic aspects of the personified "positive negation" must fit a general theory of figurative language. Criticism has for some time focused on psychological aspects of symbolic play. As the mind thinks, so it employs figures of thought and language. It should by now be clear that the problem of sequence is also a problem of figurative series.

In the modern era, when not only music but all the arts have tried to hold their balance while experiencing the loss of tonal center, poets and novelists have testified to the complete loss of cadence within the figurative structures provided by traditional poetics. Atonalism and even aleatory procedures are natural, in an era such as ours. But before its radical breakdowns had occurred, poets could still employ the ancient figurative structures, by bending them.

Such was the Coleridgean scene, where the figurative aspect of threshold and sequence was traditional enough. For the temple and its "timeless" hypotactic structures of sacred being, there was the normal and normative use of part / whole relations, figured in synecdoche. For the labyrinth and its unrelieved parataxis the norms were bound to be metonymic, as they are in the modern novel, where life is represented in the naturalistic maze of meaningless eventuality. For the threshold the norms were, as the term itself forces us to believe, metaphoric. This was the great Romantic rediscovery.

Metaphor has always been the figure of threshold, of passing over. Its symbolic function has always been transfer, transference, metamorphosis, shifting across, through, and over. Metaphor is a semantic process of balancing at the threshold. Metaphor draws the edge of the limen with surgical exactness. When we ally metaphor and the dramatic, we accept the momentary adoption of *another self*, which the mask of dramatic *persona* makes possible. Significant human integers—men as unique creatures with endowments of a yet universal nature—demand metaphor, because metaphor provides the freedom (not the chaos) of a momentary masking.

The person-making, personifying, gestures of the dramatic poet thus sink down, or fall, to the level of nothingness and ghosts, because at that level of the *ex nihilo* there is a test of the "too, too solid flesh" of man. If a ghost can exist, then so can the hero. If his father has a ghost, Hamlet can avenge (and destroy) him, and *be* Hamlet. Hamlet must personify his father, as it were, in order to be himself. Admiring Shakespeare and identifying with Hamlet, Coleridge brought the study of figurative language into the modern context, by giving it a psycholinguistic basis. This modern grasp of the metaphoric—which Johnson vaguely anticipated in *The Life of Cowley*—seems to require an awareness of the experiential element in the *discordia concors*, an anxiety and liminal trembling which is the experience of living through a metaphor. I have envisaged this tremor as the emergence of a personification, at a threshold. Perhaps these too are "only metaphors."[15] If so, they may illuminate the ludic view of theory-building. Coleridge was in nothing so modern as in his theoretical playfulness.

His instincts naturally led him to center his critical theories on the career of Shakespeare, that is, upon a dramatic or dramatistic center. In part this was bardolatry. But Coleridge had a cosmopolitan range of thought, and in his critical theory of method the dramatic (if not always the drama) has fundamental force. For him the drama is the saving test by which men are discovered in their personhood through dialogue.[16] Essaying a poetry and a critique of the liminal moment, he took up arms against the excessive mass of problems which the modern critic knows only too well—our sea of information. Coleridge wanted to find an All that could be One, believed he found it in the final personification—the Trinity—and failed, if he did fail, because he no more than any other man could prevent life's perverse atomism. If he failed to control the world with his personifying eloquence, we should grant him that person and metaphor are the utterance of the gateway, and most men do not want to be standing in gateways. They would rather be inside, or out in the street.

10. Silence and the Voice of Thought

Thought, in and for itself, would appear to be silent, or would appear to be private, that is, effectively silent. As Jacques Derrida has shown in *Speech and Phenomena* and elsewhere, the problem of thought is always a problem of linguistic play, which in turn becomes grammatologically a question of inscription. Deconstruction, which is the voice of exile, real or symbolic, asks where the inscription occurs. If the philosopher can ask, can there be a private language, is he not questioning thereby, can there be silent thought? In what sense must thought always be inscribed in the mind, if not outwardly expressed? Derrida has explored these questions in great detail. Yet the questions remain unanswered; perhaps we do not know enough about how the mind works. Nevertheless, there is at least a tradition that thinking is an essentially silent activity. Writing and inscription, as compared with speaking, are at once silent and expressive. To explore some earlier fictive views of silence and solitude, as they subtend thinking, may shed light on the nature of the iconography of thought.

Silence in the first place should be distinguished from quiet, which is the opposite of noise. As such, quiet is a relative decrease in loudness of uttered sounds and especially their combinations, as with street noises or the sounds of war or the delighted shrieks of small children. Murmuring is a quiet sound that resembles low voices speaking. Hence in his *Arcadia*, Sir Philip Sidney's first eclogue says: "Shallow brooks murmur most, deep silent slide away."

There is a strong contrast between quiet and silence. It would seem that, because silence is so deep as to be absolute, one is silent or one speaks.

Yet throughout history this distinction has been hard to sustain, and, in fact, absolute silence is impossible to produce in real-world situations. One has almost to move into outer space to achieve the absolute state of silence. Properly, Sidney began one of his sonnets "With how sad steps, O Moon, thou climbs't the skies! / How silently, and with how wan a face!" Silence appears to mark an absolute lack of utterance, or at least a tendency in that direction.

The history of noise has yet to be written, though Jacques Attali in *Noise: The Political Economy of Music* has defined some effects of musical noise-making and mechanical reproduction for the period of the French Revolution to the present. Attali's political treatise covers perforce only a small section of the history of the environmental problem. In this chapter I shall be commenting on some literary and iconographic aspects of the relation between silence and thought, as these emerge primarily in the mid to late eighteenth century. During this period Renaissance pastoral evolves, as Jay Macpherson and others have shown, into a various poetry of pre-Romantic withdrawal into solitary places.

Pastoral had always addressed an inner condition of mind. Acute mental distress is often felt to be a cacophony, a tempest of savagely strident and conflicting voices. When Prospero abjures his books at the end of *The Tempest*, he tells us that the storm will cease, not in his heart, but in his "beating mind." Pastoral has traditionally provided a scene of relative, that is, socially organized, quietness. Pastoral engages in a shared quiet, which is relative to some ideal of balanced, harmonious social intercourse. This remains a goal even in John Gay's "Newgate Pastoral," *The Beggar's Opera*. Wherever and however pastoral survives, it ministers to a major need, the hunger for quiet that finds a place in any human attempt to think, to contemplate, to study. The modern city appears dedicated to the frustration of such a need.

As befits the absolute character of silence, its quest tends away from the sociability of pastoral quiet, moving toward individual solitude. Hence it follows that silence plays a marked role in the development of pre-Romantic attitudes. Romanticism understands that we humans cannot evade the internalized Other, which is a co-respondent in the mental theater of silence, an other-within-ourselves, an alter ego, a voice of conscience, a listener within.

Traditionally, the inner voice and its background of silence were sought through disciplines of meditation and prayer. George Herbert, himself a pastor, shares the pastoral goal of thinking of his inner life as only one element in a larger divine purpose, a purpose never permitting the poet, as priest, to remove himself from the scene of society and good works. His meditative verse is concerned more with quiet than with silence. A quest for individual silence is anticipated and found before the eighteenth century in the mystical, as opposed to meditative, tradition, and an even deeper devotion to silence marks the mystic's practice. Typically Henry Vaughan understands his quest for "angel infancy" in its Latin sense: the infant cannot yet talk, he is *in-fans*, so that, in a manner resembling Wordsworth, Vaughan says, in "The Retreat,"

> O how I long to travel back,
> And tread again that ancient track!

He is thinking of a time before, as he says,

> I taught my tongue to wound
> My conscience with a sinful sound.

His mystical goal is what another poem entitles "Peace."

> My soul, there is a country
>   Far beyond the stars,
> Where stands a winged sentry,
>   All skillful in the wars.
> There, above noise and danger,
>   Sweet Peace sits crowned with smiles,
> And one born in a manger,
>   Commands the beauteous files.

Vaughan, to rid himself of his own inner turbulence, contemplates unmoving objects, the "dumb urn," or "the happy secret fountain," or the single, wintering flower, or the waterfall admonishing him always to be silent.

> With what deep murmurs through time's
>   silent stealth

> Doth thy transparent, cool, and watery wealth
> Here flowing fall,
> And chide, and call . . .

To permit this appeal, the poet must be alone. Anticipating Words-worth, Vaughan begins one untitled poem,

> They are all gone out into the world of light,
> And I alone sit lingering here.

Such mystical withdrawal into silence is to be seen against a rapidly changing background. Europe and Britain were about to see a marked increase of disquiet, which may be identified with the greatest achievements of the Enlightenment.

Starting in the seventeenth century, England along with all Europe, with unprecedented fervor, sought a cosmopolitan ideal. Leaving aside the substance of Enlightenment efforts, which might best be called taxonomic, or encyclopedic, we find that information, ideas, opinions, and systems were now being shared across national boundaries and transmitted rapidly. Novelty became a product in the form of "news"—to process the news meant to package it. In Great Britain alone more than 33,000 copies of newspapers were sold every day, while serious authors might sell their books on a massive scale—for Voltaire sales over a seven year period amounted to about one and a half million copies. In the Renaissance period French and Latin had linked scholars from different countries, but the new cosmopolitanism of European intellectual exchange went far beyond the scale of humanist communication. De Quincey did not publish his essay "The English Mail Coach" until 1849, but he was looking back at a great eighteenth-century revolution, the speedy transmission of mail. "Through velocity at that time unprecedented . . . [the mail coaches] . . . first revealed the glory of motion."

Surely, this glorious feeling helped to drive the Age of Enlightenment to its prodigious intellectual efforts. Ideas were now made available to the European cosmopolis by improved systems of transport and the result was a new glory. Not only were ideas shipped back and forth, in private letters no less than public media, but it became the fashion to attempt the purchase of famous men: Frederick had to have his Voltaire, Catherine her Diderot. If the case of Voltaire proves anything, it suggests the salability of thought, the trade and commerce of thought, and, finally, the inflation of thought.

A large measure of *counter*-Enlightenment "antirationalism," as Isaiah Berlin calls it, stemmed from an innate desire to defend against mental inflation, spreading too many clever thoughts too quickly.

In England a master of pre-Romantic image, James Thomson, took one step toward the solution of unduly numerous thoughts. His "Hymn on Solitude" advocates the delights of mere escape.

> Hail, mildly pleasing Solitude,
> Companion of the wise and good;
> But from whose holy, piercing eye
> The herd of fools and villains fly.
> Oh! how I love with thee to walk,
> And listen to thy whispered talk,
> Which innocence and truth imparts
> And melts the most obdurate hearts.

Solitude, personified, is the poet's double—his better self:

> Now wrapped in some mysterious dream,
> A lone philosopher you seem.

In this imagined state, lust is tempered and "calmed to friendship." The poet is not, however, deeply committed to his role as "lone philosopher." Dr. Johnson tells that the Countess of Hertford, to whom Thomson addressed "The Hymn on Solitude," would "invite every summer some poet into the country to hear her verses and assist her studies. This honor was one summer conferred on Thomson, who took more delight in carousing with Lord Hertford and his friends than assisting her ladyship's poetical operations, and therefore never received another summons."

Thomson's "Hymn" nonetheless does exalt an idea of luxuriant independence, a controlled isolation, a healthy escape to ease and safety. At Lady Hertford's he can savor "the woodland dumb retreat" and the onset of evening, when "the faint landscape swims away," and solitude achieves "that best hour of musing." Such imagery exemplifies an optimistic, complaisant, charmed retreat, evoking no deep passion for self-analysis. Thus Thomson concludes:

Oh let me pierce thy secret cell!
And in thy deep recesses dwell!
Perhaps from Norwood's oak-clad hill,
When meditation has her fill,
I just may cast my careless eyes
Where London's spiry turrets rise,
Think of its crimes, its cares, its pain,
Then shield me in the woods again.

A transition is seen from Augustan to the Romantic, in its first phase. Along with Miltonic echoes there are touches of Pope's "Windsor Forest," where an endless variety of scene evokes in the poet a wonder at the supreme organized system of the human and natural world—an order in variety one merely needs to seek out and savor, delighted by its reposing effect. The retreat to a quiet, protected natural haven, the gentle murmurings of streams and warblings of the nightbird, the everpresent nightingale, the "silent marble" of a weeping tomb are seen as iconographic renderings of a benign quiet.

Always opposed to the benign aspects of a restorative solitude is the danger of the excesses of a contrary inner state. In the present context, it becomes clear that an iconography of silence and solitude is directly linked with thought and solipsism. A pre-Romantic sensibility seems to require paradox for the statement of such relationships. If thought is always tacit, as in Shakespeare's "sweet silent thought," it follows that a cult of silence would very likely (though not necessarily) include an attempt to improve the conditions for thinking. Solitude is to aid the thinker to think. However, a series of thoughts will be checked against reality only if the thinker utters them, as when, ideally, a conversation monitors the health of thought. Should solitude deepen, the goal of a more unspoken thought-process would reach dangerously close to pathological isolation. Hence the pre-Romantic is driven to hope simultaneously for *more* and *less* solitary thinking. This is the paradox of introspection, which looks ever deeper into the mind, so as to be clear, to obviate the need for this very act of introspection. The metaphor of mental "depth" is a hazardous one, and it belongs to Romantic thought and its modern descendants.

The aesthetically significant aspect of the introspective quest is the path taken in a number of pre-Romantic works, and perhaps in art generally during the late eighteenth century; the problem of inner mind pursued as an aspect of the "silent pause." C. P. E. Bach's music, for example, develops the pause as part of its *Affekt*, its rendering of acute emotive sensibility. The pause is the mark of mental involvement in that expressive technique for creating *Affekt*. The pause in poetry is similarly a device for producing that fragmentation of vision which Philippe Lacoue-Labarthe and Jean-Luc Nancy have described in *The Literary Absolute*. Always, the pause is a momentary muting of the aesthetic stream of sound or image, while the muting is felt to provide the moment of thought, cut from the fabric of continuous expression. We shall not be surprised, therefore, to find that silence and sounding play such a large role in the development of a Romantic psychology. Let us turn to imaginative works by Gray, Sterne, Goethe, and Mozart, all of whom create an iconographic rendering of the relation between silence and thought.

Gray is the most complex of the English pre-Romantics. A great classical scholar, a gifted entomologist, a man of wide general learning, Gray probably wrote, and certainly published only a small number of poems. His several neoclassic Odes are colored by a daemonic use of personifications—take as an example his "Ode on a Distant Prospect of Eton College." As he looks, from a distance, at the young boys at play, he begins to ruminate on their various destinies and turns remarkably morbid.

> Alas! regardless of their doom,
> The little victims play!

He looks ahead, for them:

> These shall the fury Passions tear,
> The vultures of the mind,
> Disdainful Anger, pallid Fear,
> And Shame that skulks behind:
> Or pining Love shall waste their youth,
> Or Jealousy with rankling tooth,
> That inly gnaws the secret heart,
> And Envy wan, and faded Care,
> Grim-visaged comfortless Despair,
> And Sorrow's piercing dart.

Gray is obsessed by the problem of *his* contemplation, his silence, his inability to warn the children. He concludes:

> To each his suff'rings: all are men,
> Condemned alike to groan.
> The tender for another's pain;
> The unfeeling for his own.
> Yet ah! why should they know their fate?
> Since sorrow never comes too late,
> And happiness too swiftly flies.
> Thought would destroy their paradise.
> No more; where ignorance is bliss,
> Tis folly to be wise.

Here the note of inwardness points to a fearful awareness of the dangers of knowledge—"Thought would destroy their paradise." One can almost hear Thomas Gray saying to himself, thought has destroyed *my* paradise. The poem is a study of painful enclosure, the slow imprisonment of the "secret heart," the growth of a private secrecy that can never be revealed. The ancient theme of *carpe diem* has been ruthlessly psychologized by the poet, and his personified Anger, Shame, and Fear are now fully emotive, and daemonic.

The spell-binding freedom of the College playground was to be but a momentary experience of childish quiet, which the boys could never hold unto—for "all are men." The brutal truth about quietude is that it cannot, and will not last. It will give way, after a moment's perfect calm and freedom, to a common doom—for all these children in fact are members of "the painful family of Death."

But Gray, like other poets before and after him, on one occasion was able to surmount the penetrating despair that underlines much of his work, and this occurred when he found his theme—the simplicity of the country churchyard. This is Gray's "Elegy Written in a Country Churchyard," a poem much revised by the poet—composed over several years and finally sent by Gray to his friend Horace Walpole, on 12 June, 1750. Instead of gloomy and passionate attack upon the common doom, the "Elegy" admits that doom, having found its only palliative. The unknown, unheralded, un-noised young poet whose epitaph ends the "Elegy," received one true recompense for all his pain: "He gain'd from Heaven (twas all he wish'd) a friend."

Opening with the famed evocation of quiet in a new key, that of solemnity, the poem records the shutting down of one sensation after the other:

> The Curfew tolls the knell of parting day,
> The lowing herd wind slowly o'er the lea,
> The plowman homeward plods his weary way,
> And leaves the world to darkness and to me.
>
> Now fades the glimmering landscape on the sight,
> And all the air a solemn stillness holds,
> Save where the beetle wheels his droning flight,
> And drousy tinklings lull the distant folds;
>
> Save that from yonder ivy-mantled tow'r
> The moping owl does to the moon complain
> Of such, as wand'ring near her secret bow'r,
> Molest her ancient solitary reign.
>
> Beneath those rugged elms, that yew-tree's shade
> Where heaves the turf in many a mouldr'ing heap,
> Each in his narrow cell for ever laid,
> The rude Forefathers of the hamlet sleep.

Gray is poised at a threshold, ready to castigate a noisy modern world. He knows that, for the dead, the ideals of Honor and Flattery mean nothing, for in no case can "Honor's voice provoke the silent dust, / Or Flatt'ry sooth the dull cold ear of Death."

What strikes him, however, is not that in their deathly silence, now, these simple men and women have reached a haven beyond the clamor of life, which is indeed so. But he feels more deeply that they were gifted and guided by a better fate.

> Far from the madding crowd's ignoble strife,
> Their sober wishes never learn'd to stray;
> Along the cool sequester'd vale of life
> They kept the noiseless tenor of their way.

In his first draft of the poem, Gray had written "silent tenor."

The Romantic attitude does not appear in such lines; they might have been written by an Augustan, but for a certain languor. No, the Romantic attitude appears in what underlies Gray's vision. In the back of his mind, emerging only in fleeting gleams, is an idea that somehow the simple life commits one to a scene of vast emptiness, of being silenced by anonymity.

> Full many a gem of purest ray serene,
> The dark unfathom'd caves of ocean bear:
> Full many a flower is born to blush unseen,
> And waste its sweetness on the desert air.

One day, walking along with a friend, Norton Nicholls, Gray improvised a couplet:

> There pipes the wood-lark, and the song thrush there
> Scatters his loose notes in the waste of air.

That, anyway, is how Norton Nicholls remembered the couplet. The ground of beauty, which as Stevens said of music is "momentary in the mind," is that vacuous "waste of air," that desert into which all beauty disappears.

It is this terrible separateness of beauty which rings the true High Romantic note, rings through all the great Odes of Keats, animates the great poems of a somewhat richer and more evolved nostalgia of Wordsworth and Coleridge. Given that desertion, or more exactly abandonment, is the underlying fear, it is all the more remarkable that a contemplation of final silence should lead a poet like Gray to find the beginnings of a new way to redeem solitude and isolation from the silent wasteland.

Along with the iconography of silence must go a technical or formal invention adequate to shape that iconography into a *poetry of silence*. This precisely is what Gray's "Elegy" shows. The pre-Romantic style finds a way to slow up the flow of the verses—much of the "Elegy" can be reset as rhymed couplets, with minimal loss of sense. What the cross-rhymes give is a suspension and a deceleration that evokes the guiding theme. The "Elegy" ends with an epitaph, and this (natural as it seems in the poem) provided a formal model for Wordsworth and Coleridge, who are fascinated by epitaphs, inscriptions, and other "isolated" genres. The effect is one of sudden, inexplicable intervention in the disorder of nature; if no inscription (on a monument, let us say) exists, they make one, *ad hoc*, as in Wordsworth's "Lines left upon a Seat in a Yew-tree which stands near the Lake of Esthwaite, on a desolate part of the shore, yet commanding a beautiful prospect." These lines are a warning to the stranger not to scorn the common and the lowly. The lines end:

O, be wiser thou!
Instructed that true knowledge leads to love,
True dignity abides with him alone
Who, in the silent hour of inward thought,
Can still suspect, and still revere himself,
In lowliness of heart.

Like his friend of those early years of the *Lyrical Ballads,* just before the turn of the century, Coleridge too knows this vision of a filled quiet. His "gentle Maid" in "The Nightingale" is arrested by such an awareness; she "oft, a moment's space, / Hath heard a pause of silence."

Such a pausing appears to be the critical discovery, not so much the absolute idea of a perfected mental state—ideal solitude—as a mere pausing, a liminality. Alone in some natural setting the poet is set free, in mind, "to the influxes / Of shapes and sounds and shifting elements / Surrendering his whole spirit." These authors have learned, in Shakespeare's phrase, to "defend the interim."

It seems no accident that Coleridge practiced yet another formal device for making silence into a singable modality—his famous sub-genre, which he called "the conversation poem." To this genre "The Nightingale" belongs, and the extraordinary "Frost at Midnight," where the infinitesimal life-cycles of ice crystals provide a new and more perfect clock by which to measure the most subtle gradations of quiet.

Conversation is talk in which there is always a listener; conversation invents the listener, by quieting the noises of unordered babble, what Dr. Johnson once scornfully called "talk."

And conversation is the chief modality of another epochal achievement of pre-Romantic sensibility, *Tristram Shandy.* To mention Lawrence Sterne is to open our discussion into the domain of prose discourse and prose fiction. Suffice it to say that Sterne, perhaps more painfully and comically than any writer before or since, understood that minute or extended gaps occur in spoken interchanges between people. His chief study is those gaps, discontinuities, silences. He studies all the body-motions that go with speech, and finds that story-tellers have been omitting the bulk of what actually presents itself in conversational speech; namely all the silent pauses, the hems and haws, the extraneous background noises, the digressions, repetitions, absurdities of logical unconnexity, the off-the-wall mishearings and missayings, and so on. His *Tristram Shandy* is also, as we now know, prophetic of another revolution. His is perhaps the first novel to focus microscopically. He sees what is happening in the Shandy family with such precision (watching the exact angles at which individuals hold their heads, for example) that, as a writer, he needs specially precise language-games. Exploiting the forces of mere punctuation, Sterne's "musical score" is, as a final note, almost more real than the music itself. So he writes not only a work of complete liminal self-awareness (the gift and goal of "sensibility"), but also a work which is able to refer to itself—thus Bertrand Russell was able to discover in *Tristram Shandy* a perfect case of the famed self-referential paradox, in which a fiction of a fiction of a fiction, and so on, regressively prevents any exit (in the fiction's own terms) from the terms and words of that fiction.

A way to describe *Tristram Shandy* and its infinite regress would be to say that, much influenced by *Hamlet* and *Don Quixote*, it is the first and greatest epic of hypersensitivity, that is, sensibility and sentiment wrought to their highest pitch and finest fiber. In *Tristram Shandy* Sterne discovered the dark side of hypersensitivity in the context of a terrible fear, that of virtually total human impotence, taking the term in an intellective as well as sexual sense. Sterne is seeking an exit from a fate worse than death, the fate of *being silenced.*

Silencing, in *Tristram Shandy,* is always a kind of interruption of the flow of thought. Whereas in realistic narrative our expectations are maintained in the form of causally sequential thought-processes, here the narrative digresses incessantly, frustrating any idea of logical sequence. Sterne uses punctuation to fragment what he calls the "texture" of the novel (Book IX, Chapter 12). In this way, he imagines the human comedy to be an affair of breakages, ruptures, gaps. The drama of such punctuation is so powerful that the discontinuous narrative form becomes the reader's focal point. The narrative is finally to be read as a fictive discourse upon the nature of mind and sentiment. Trains of thought here hang together according to Lockean principles of association. For example, Tristram's name, "the sad one," was intended to have been Trismegistus, "the thrice great." But normal sequences of events, such as one might expect, for instance, in the affair of Uncle Toby and the Widow Wadman, are blocked by Sterne's dominant principle of narrative interruption. Sequence is prevented and silenced by ceaseless detours. Punctuation in all its forms, including the use of the black page, the marbled page, and numerous blank pages and sections, arrests any hope, or illusion, of continuous story-line. Sterne thereby creates a fiction of the actual processes of heterogeneous thought which accompany "real" life. In this sense, through its art of self-canceling digression, the novel imagines the mortality of man as the mortality of any enclosed family of fixed ideas. To the extent that the "story" cannot come to an end, life will continue. Hence *Tristram Shandy* is comic even in its silencing manoeuvers.

Being silenced is the fate of a madman, of Cowper's Castaway, or Gray's ancient bard, who finally can only throw himself to his death. All High Romantic poetry encounters at some point the need to express, in Pope's phrase, "what one really feels"—not just to impress someone else, but to avoid going mad.

The most celebrated and most frightening of all pre-Romantic works has precisely this subject. This is *The Sorrows of Young Werther* (1774; 1787), whose instant influence on the European suicide rate is well known. In later years Goethe admitted that he wrote the novella, rapidly, in order to save his own sanity. The catharsis had worked for him; he regretted what his rhetoric had done to others.

Many things might be said about Goethe's *Werther*; like Mac-Pherson's concocted poems of Ossian—the mythic Celtic bard—*Werther* was an instant best-seller. Like Ossian, it seems to have induced a contagion of uncontrolled, hysterical responses. To give but one case, Victor Lange recalls that "in 1784 a young English lady committed suicide and a copy of the translation of *Werther* was found under her pillow. In the announcement of her death this circumstance was particularly emphasized 'in order if possible, to defeat the evil tendencies of that pernicious work.' " More curious is the fact that Napoleon claimed to have read the book several times—or so he told Goethe in 1808.

A book of this kind becomes a legend in its own time, so it is easy to overlook the artistry of the work. Whether Goethe used his novella to cure himself of an infatuation with Charlotte Buff is part of the matter. Perhaps because therapy was his aim, he brought to the work a special artistry. He and his own life are included in

Werther's story in an odd way—as a shadowy presence that one is vaguely aware of. External evidence of biographical fact indicates Goethe's personal involvement, and one has the impression, more deeply, that only a person who has been through such suffering could have written it. Such an impression is precisely the result of Romantic identifications between author and hero.

That Goethe wanted us to identify his own and his hero's life is seen by naming the heroine Charlotte, or Lotte, exactly the name of her actual prototype, the real Charlotte Buff. There is something uncanny about this and other doublings, and Goethe is well aware of their *unheimlich* character.

What is odd about Sterne and Goethe (might we not include Diderot here?) is that they present accounts of uncontrolled obsession, unrestrained good and bad feelings, and they somehow remain skeptical, critical, and ironic as they make such presentations. They are like schizophrenics who can tell you exactly how schizophrenia works. They seem to enjoy their own complicity in the scenes they render; they are, at the same time, afraid of such complicity. They seem to be walking around the edges of a madness, looking at it, poking it, savoring it, and then holding it away at a safe distance. Such a hovering attitude marks the most triumphant works of the late eighteenth century.

Technically, as *Werther* will show, this maintenance of the narrator at a threshold of his story owes much to a skilled manipulation of silence and "noise," once again. Thus *Werther* begins with the hero imbibing deep drafts of quiet—"For the rest, I am very well off here. Solitude in this terrestrial paradise is a wonderful balm to my mind . . . A wonderful serenity has taken possession of my soul . . . I am alone, and feel the enchantment of life in this spot, which was created for souls like mine."

But Goethe injects the opposite motif of ominous, or *unheimlich*, silence. As Werther thinks about the obligations of science and art, he senses himself cut off, or severed, from himself by those goals, as they in turn transform into illusory prospects "with which we paint our prison walls with bright figures and brilliant prospects." "All this, Wilhelm, makes me silent." But he then meets Charlotte and for a time they share the benign quiet together. Yet the ominous silence of the grave is heard, invoking a portentous disquiet. They fall silent, looking at the enchanting moonlit scene, and "after a while Charlotte said, 'Whenever I walk by moonlight, it brings to my mind my beloved and departed friends, and I am filled with thoughts of death and afterlife.' "

Gradually Werther's bliss intermixes with another obsession. He cannot rid himself of his desire to be with Charlotte forever, and to embrace her forever—desiring her becomes even more intense as its impossibility becomes more apparent.

He tries to leave Charlotte, but cannot. It is not hard to see how such a bind occurs. Goethe appears to have been fully aware of the sources of Werther's driven malaise—he devises the triangle of Albert, Charlotte, and Werther in stridently Oedipal terms; almost on every fifth page he reminds us of some analogy between Charlotte and the mother, Albert and the father. What is interesting is not this pre-psychoanalytic sureness of construction and understanding—Shakespeare had it in *Hamlet*, Euripides in the *Hippolytus*, Racine in *Phèdre*, and so on. Rather what strikes us is that Goethe, guided by the muse of Sensibility, saw that Werther *had* to commit suicide. He could not be with his "mother," Charlotte. An extreme and sharp ambivalence colored every aspect of his response to her, preventing him from acknowledging her maternal appeal. His desire to be with her was literally *unspeakable*. The taboo silenced him, depriving him of the will to live. Silenced, he could no longer think, or conceive, of himself as an independently living being. "I cannot pray, 'Let her be mine!' Yet she often seems to belong to me. I cannot pray, 'Give her to me!' for she is another's. I try to quiet my suffering by all sorts of cool arguments. If I let myself go, I could compose a whole litany of antitheses."

Here the opposition between Werther's favorite reading, Homer and subsequently Ossian, comes into narrative focus. Largely through these readings, Werther has found the language of his heart. With the onset of Ossian's wild rhapsodies and the rejection of Homer, the fragile balance of Werther's mind is tried beyond endurance. Werther finally has no words of his own. He can only forlornly and desperately try to live through the wild language of Ossianic myth. Having tried to live, exclusively, the life of the mind, he finds himself betrayed by the disorder, the Ossianic wildness of a language utterly Other. Ossian alienates Werther's sanity. Playing the piano as she often does, Charlotte only draws further attention to Werther's lack of expressive capacity, which drives him deeper into isolation. He now lacks an adequate language and cannot even express what is conveyed by the wordless tones of the piano.

In his farewell letter, he writes: "I sacrifice myself for you. Yes, Lotte, why should I remain silent?" Such a question implies that either Werther is silenced by the marriage of Albert and Lotte, or he can only speak by silencing himself forever. He is imprisoned by the image of Charlotte as mother. The last words of his farewell letter are: "Your mother . . . I shall see her, find her, and oh, I shall unburden my whole heart to her. Your mother. Your image."

Let us draw back from this case study of overwrought sensibility. To express Werther's extreme situation, Goethe invents a new form of fragmentation, a *Fantasiastücke*. The letters of the epistolary novel are torn, truncated, interleaved with external narration, reduced and expanded in strange torsions—and always pointing, by their arrangement on the page, to the distance of space and time elapsed *between* each letter. Such discontinuity is fantastic and even oracular, not so far removed from the sluicing tides of the Ossianic poetry that finally engulfs the hero and sends him, through a symbolic contagion, into the arms of death. What Goethe has done is to explore the unguarded passage, the unsafe journey across the desert of a mind turned in upon itself, into a dangerous, because unspeakable, utterly silenced, sea of doubt and feeling.

Werther's question—"why should I remain silent?"—resounds through the centuries. At the end of the eighteenth century, it is perhaps the only question, and spheres of its expression differ, depending on the context. In Goethe's *Werther* silence and expression are mainly private matters, even though the novel continuously renders a background of public, socially derived attitudes, including the functioning of the law. Goethe foregrounds his hero's intensely individual state of mind and coolly, if relentlessly, follows this mind down the path of its own destruction. Goethe exposes the paradox of Werther's question. The only way that Werther can make a statement is to kill himself, which means to silence himself, to speak a self-silencing. The power of Goethe's conception seems to arise from Werther's question itself. When he asks "why should I remain silent," it is ambiguous as to the person he is addressing. Is he asking himself the question or is he questioning Lotte and, therefore, her whole society? Who is to tell him what he can say, put into words, and thus think? Such ambiguity remains unresolved at the end of the novel.

If, as seems likely, Werther is asking himself why he should remain silent, the cause of his self-absorption is shown to reside in the forces of a family romance. Werther conspires to become the victim in an Oedipal triangle. Goethe's novel explores the family structure in order to expose the responses of an individual within that structure; we may call it an exploration of private silence. We have already seen an exploration working on a public level. In his book *Literary Loneliness in Mid-Eighteenth-Century England*, John Sitter shows how Gray balances the pathos of a silenced, unrealized potential against the benign serenity of rural life. In this public sphere of almost pastoral withdrawal, the silencing of a "mute Milton" is taken up into the public vision of a world where quiet and silence are believed to be benign social forms. John Sitter exposes the ambivalent feelings of defensiveness and superiority with which Thomas Gray and others expressed the "flight from history."

In France at the close of the eighteenth century one might say that revolutionary politics engaged in a catastrophic embrace of history. The milder ambivalences of a Thomas Gray were replaced by the most violent of political expressions. Now one had to ask how silence was enforced, policed, rewarded, and punished. An example of public control of utterance would be the attempt in 1793 of the French National Convention to shift ownership of all musical production into the hands of the revolutionary state. Such a move to control music was, as Jacques Attali observed, more totalitarian than any previous royal practice.

Not long before this 1793 decree of the National Convention, Mozart and Emanuel Schikaneder had produced an eloquent and magnificent celebration of private and public silence, their *operone*, *The Magic Flute*. Regarding pathos, *The Magic Flute* oddly resembles *Werther*, since two climaxes of the opera center on attempted suicide. The opera, strictly a *Singspiel*, shares and advances upon stylistic features of the pre-Romantic period. As a *Singspiel*, *The Magic Flute* uses the alternate silencing of music by spoken voice, of spoken voice by music. It has many moments of musical empathy, *Einfühlung*, or expressive *Affekt*. Prince and Princess, Tamino and Pamina express emotion in "depth:" they *yearn* in their arias. During the scene of Papageno's attempted suicide, the note of yearning is turned to comical effect. The new expressiveness serves love, longing, and anguish at the prospect of losing the beloved. In its extremest form, romantic expressivity links to thoughts of suicide.

Romantic capacity for the musical devices of expression owes something to the period's awareness of the elemental expressiveness of natural phenomena. This view takes the sounds of nature to be the basic forms of expression, such as the soughing of wind in leafy branches, the whistling of wind, the snapping of twigs, the night-sounds of the forest, roars of cataracts, crashes of thunder. Thunder gives us nature's cannon shots and is important as an extreme of nature's sonic expression, fixing one end of a continuum. Mozart here devises a music that represents natural forces, almost to the point that at certain moments (for example, the Queen of the Night's arias) music itself becomes a natural force. Music is here reduced to elemental aspects of sonic mass, namely, pitch, tempo, grain, dynamic contrast, and dynamic level.

The setting of *The Magic Flute* is not then ordered, as with the Italian operas, to produce an unbroken flux of dramatic action. This music is organized to create metamorphic scenes of transformation, one magic shift after another, with a resulting sense of ritual, or natural, segmentation between and among the scenes. Music as sonority, in its elemental and primal nature, stands forth here as virtually mythic. It then makes a myth of tonal properties—consider the opposition of the Queen of the Night and Zarastro, as defined by the extremes of highest and lowest vocal register.

Silence too can here be felt as elemental. Such is the case with Papageno's first setback—the Queen's three Ladies punish him for telling lies. They padlock his mouth. This comical effect turns the bird catcher into an animal creature, who cannot speak language. When the Ladies remove the padlock in Act I, Scene 8, we learn the more serious point of Papageno's being forcibly silenced. His first free words are: "Now Papageno can chatter again." *Plaudern*, chatter, is what he really desires to do, and lying is just another form of mindless chatter, with an underlying selfish motive. The whole subsequent dramatic treatment of Papageno centers upon his desire to chatter, which everyone except (as later transpires) his future wife Papagena seeks to suppress.

On an exalted plane, the two princely lovers are enjoined to silence, before they may enjoy final union in the Palace of Wisdom. In fact Act II might be focused around the second Priest's ritual question about Tamino: "Can he preserve silence?" Zarastro answers (repeating the same words), *Verschweigen heit*. He can keep silence. Throughout this first scene of initiatory trial, Mozart repeats at intervals the three double-sounded E-Flat chords, which sonically identify and give tonality to this whole Act as a derivation from Masonic practice. Such chords, whenever sounded, introduce another aspect of silence, the marked gap in the sonic plenum. They order a law of segmentation, of stepping by discrete measures. They use marked silent pauses to demonstrate the sonic ground of music itself, that is, the empty silent ground against which music sounds. Significantly, the three chords herald the higher drama of Tamino and Pamina, the princely quest of heroic self-restraint.

Looking through the score and libretto of the opera, we shall find many emplotments of an onset, or breaking, of silence. Stendhal, in his *Life of Mozart*, was impressed by the silken arrival of the moor Monostatos, "coming in the silence of the night, by moonlight to steal a kiss from the lips of the sleeping princess." Or, when the Three Boys intervene to prevent Pamina from stabbing herself to death, she at once asks about Tamino, "Why did he not speak to me?" The Boys reply, doubling the silence of the injunction, "Of this we must be silent, but we will show him to you." It appears that for sacred power and purity to accumulate in the human soul, the soul must obey a bodily law of saying not a word, a law of linguistic self-silencing. When the Two Armed Men announce to the Prince, "It is permitted that you *speak* to her," Tamino and Pamina may then be reunited, which at once they are. Silence somehow accumulates inner strength, almost as if it nurtured, or stored, courage and authority.

Always against the absolute, or ideal, condition of silence, the opera counterpoints the full range of spoken and sung voice. Silence and sound appear in a play of opposition, against the silence of the night is the thunder. Binary structures permit the opera to treat the problem of *mass*—musical mass, as volume and as tonal quality. Everywhere we have pairings of voice, for instance the diabolically nature-driven musical machinery of the Queen of the Night versus the calmly sonorous vocal eloquence of Zarastro and the Priests. Male and female are strictly paired—and Papageno, one might loosely say, has a lower *class* of voice than Tamino, but both are paired along the male spectrum, both are under trial. Paired with Papageno, in a different respect, Monostatos makes the male voice sly, violent, and "Turkish."

Mozart is exploring the force of vocal music as given by the human instrument. He makes the same gesture, of course, more obviously with actual instruments—the quiet, creamy clarinets, the magic bell tones of the Glockenspiel, the purest, most undefended of all instrumental tones, that of the magic flute itself. All the instruments are pictured, emblematically, as the fundamental sounding resources of musical harmony. By massing full chorus and orchestra, Mozart is able to convey effects of irresistible power.

The question of mass at once translates to a political plane of analysis. One can imagine making such a translation in which each instrument implies a level of social or political resonance—of power to exist and act in a sociopolitical world, of power to have a voice.

By Mozart's time, the play of silence at its widest extent was perhaps political, though an earlier age might have said that the silence of widest import was religious in nature. The uncertainty as to the relative command of religion or politics requires that we construct a scale of speaking and not speaking, in order of decreasing breadth (or "population"): religious silence, sociopolitical silence, familial silence, individual silence.

Mozart's time is critical in regard to such a scale, because the scale itself is then put into question. The political ranking of social foundations undergoes immense pressure to keep changing, through the forces of the French Revolution. Furthermore, the Masonic ideology underlying *The Magic Flute* deliberately hovers between religious and political conceptions of social bonding. *The Magic Flute* is a work of pre-Romantic equivocity, though it stresses the ritual foundation of political authority. To a degree the opera shows a conflict of raw power, in the mythic opposition of Zarastro to the Queen of the Night. Yet we are shown, in another sense, that a religious mystery—the Masonic initiation into wisdom—has the force of a higher law to overcome and dispell the irrational powers of the Queen. At every level of societal organization, from the largest and most complex down to the single individual, the import of silence and the power to speak out concern what we may call the "contents of silence," namely thought. Organized religions and massive political structures seek to control speech because they need to control thought. For example, Prince Tamino is constantly admonished to remain silent, because the Masonic ritual is teaching him to possess the courage, self-control, and discipline of thinking *before* speaking. Papageno, on the other hand, always impulsively speaks before thinking, and for that reason will always be a servant, indeed a bird-catcher.

In the opera Mozart and Schikaneder develop one aspect of tacit self-control, ritual silence. By training the initiate in holding his peace amidst all trials, the ritual here gives to Tamino a mysterious inner strength. Zarastro can answer yes to all three questions posed by the Priests of the Temple of Wisdom: "Is he virtuous? Can he be silent? Does he love his fellow-men?" The second question in effect asks, can the Prince remain quiet enough, indeed silent, in order to give mental space to the highest princely act, which is to think in an enlightened fashion. Such a cult of silence as the precondition of thought is absolutely central to Masonic ritual of the period, as Paul Nettl showed in his *Mozart and Masonry*. Archetypally located in the Temple, silence is enshrined as the proper condition of princely mind. The genius of Mozart's librettist is attested by the way in which, through the reuniting of Prince and Princess, the powers of dynastic lineage are affiliated with the cult of universal brotherhood. Tamino and Pamina are tested, so that they will enter upon their royal destiny in the most human of ways, as man and wife. In this sense they are like, are continuous with, Papageno and Papagena. But beyond their humanity lies their power to reflect, which confers authority upon them. It is true that silence, political or religious, familial or individual, may be cultivated as a false front, a facade. There are possible abuses of mystery and silence, as there are terrors when silence is forced at gunpoint. Such terrors are the context of the age in which Mozart and his librettists, Da Ponte as well as Schikaneder, collaborated to reveal the outlines of revolution and its causes. Nonetheless, the intention of *The Magic Flute* seems to be quasi-religious. The opera explores the benign connection between silence and thought, as if it were a splendid commentary on the last words of Wittgenstein's *Tractatus:* "Whereof one cannot speak, thereof one must be silent."

Although the examples of Gray and Sterne, Goethe and Mozart, would seem to indicate an increased attention given in the eighteenth century to silence and thought, it is by no means clear that this topic only then comes into sharp focus. Perhaps we have it, already developed, in *The Taming of the Shrew* and in *Epicoene*, Jonson's masterful comedy, which is subtitled *The Silent Woman*. Jonson the civic poet, as might be expected, is sensitive to the question of intolerable noise, an excess endemic to city life. Yet the chief emphasis in Renaissance poetry falls on the conventions of pastoral quiet, which in a sense provide an ideal against which to measure the conditions of thought in any social setting. Similarly, the meditative disciplines of poetry, as Louis Martz showed in *The Poetry of Meditation*, provides the Renaissance standard for solitary quiet and introspective thinking. Some fundamental condition for such thought seems to change in the pre-Romantic period. Both pastoral and meditation fall victim to what might be called an increased noise of thought, as news and information multiply encyclopedically, heralding the time for a change of perspective. Whereas in general the earlier poets had spoken of a *choice* of silent thought, the later eighteenth century discovers a fear that silence can also be *enforced*, to censor thought terroristically. This becomes the scarcely hidden theme of Gray, Sterne, and Goethe in the works I have discussed.

Silence, as the benevolent condition of thought, is the all-encompassing concern of works other than *The Magic Flute* in the Mozartean canon. We have also *The Musical Joke*, which musically identifies the cacophonous with a mindless travesty of sociable music-making. We have sublime quiet, as only Mozart could provide, in the slow movement of the late Clarinet Concerto. Above all, we have *Figaro* and *Don Giovanni*, where aristocracy is shown specifically attempting to silence the servant class, to render it thoughtless.

Such examples cannot pretend to historical uniqueness. Once again, it is not clear how far back we must trace the notion that thought has a special relation to benevolent or malevolent silence. Nonetheless, it seems clear that whenever there is inner "noise," thought is diminished. Thought calls for quiet in the soul, for inward calm. In this light it seems natural enough that when early Romanticism turns the imagination inward, the need to guard and preserve an endangered inner repose is intensified. Or, putting it the other way round, it may be that at the center of what we call Romanticism stands the discovery of the dynamics of quiet and noise, which attend the process of introspection. The "voice of thought" is the Romantic poet's highest aspiration.

11. Music and the Code of the Ineffable: Visconti's Death in Venice

Any complex literary or dramatic work, including film, is likely sooner or later to present ideas, and this presentation or representation is further likely to be considered "thinking," or intellectual content. In Thomas Mann's Death in Venice such ideas form part of the description of the hero, as when Mann sketches profiles of a number of Aschenbach's famous writings. In Mann's Doctor Faustus many pages are devoted to the form and cultural significance of Adrian Leverkühn's music. The novel of ideas, of course, is intended to permit such discursive passages of presented or represented thought.

Luchino Visconti's film Death in Venice shares this capacity to project thoughts and ideas. Its hero, Aschenbach the composer, and his musician friend Alfred discuss the high philosophic destiny of music, on two separate occasions. These two flashbacks stridently break into a present narrative to combine the hero's life with an ironically grandiose and self-conscious ideological portrait of the artist. One wonders if such discursive episodes are truly where the film is doing its most intense thinking, which is not an easy question to answer. Whereas discursive or dialogical passages are prima facie evidence of intellectual concerns, and hence of active thought, it is possible that Visconti (and Mann before him) could think through problems equally well in a nondiscursive way. This activity would have to occur on the level of narrative as action. Such narrative, if intellectively ordered, would carry an intellectual content more or less implicitly.

If thought is implicit in the way a story is told, we profit largely by examining the symbolic order of metaphors and other tropes linking events in the story with each other, perhaps across unlikely gaps. Tropes always signal the attempt to bring coherence to narrative conception. If such coherence is rigidly and ritualistically enforced, the result is allegory. More commonly in the post-Romantic era symbolic coherence is more loosely contrived. With Visconti's film the combinatorial play of image and symbol evokes ideas about the meaning of the story being told, as well as about philosophical conceptions existing in their own right. While the events portrayed lead directly to the death of the hero, the fact is that *Death in Venice* equally concerns his life, wrought to a pitch of feverish intensity.

The intellectual problem that this story seeks to expose is an almost absurd question, what is the meaning of (this) man's life? Visconti avoids the poverty of an allegorical answer to such a question, as he perceives its virtually unanswerable character in a general sense. It is as if this film recognized that, while the phrase "meaning of life" means nothing very definable as a question, the meaning of a *particular* life is still somehow a legitimate quest. Meaning will be conferred on such a life's worth of mixed experience, as long as the story of that specific life can be told in a certain way, with a certain character, or ethos. The writer thinks through the search for a fitting symbolic method, a symbolic order that confers upon that life a sense of destiny. In the case of Gustav von Aschenbach the idea of heroic destiny is maintained by bonding his career to certain philosophic antecedents. In Mann's originating version, he is a writer. In Visconti's film he is a composer. For him music is a passionate and arduous vocation, practiced in order to bring shape to an understanding of life. The film shows us an artist who wishes above all to believe in the philosophic importance of his work. The strong but partly occluded implication is that the life and death of Aschenbach acquire meaning, the sense of an order, when seen in relation to Nietzsche's thoughts about music, particularly as these thoughts relate to Venice, the Venice where Richard Wagner had died. Such connections provide the basis for interpreting this particular fictional life. Aschenbach is shown seeking to understand his own life, his path, his destiny. We in turn think about him, as interpreters. In this role we seek out clusters of symbols or symbolic series, which extend the horizon of the life-story beyond the contained moments of filmic narration. Perceiving these extensions of horizon is not always easy, and first impressions may be misleading, just as they are in the case of actual life.

The metaphor of horizon points to the immediate scope of a story and its outer edges. The metaphor of depth is equally implicated in the way both Mann and Visconti tell stories. Depth virtually identifies the Romantic Symbol as being an icon which possesses "depth of meaning." Visconti directly alludes to the Romantic notion of depth by giving a central musical position to Mahler's setting of the Second Dance Song from *Thus Spake Zarathustra*. This song, which Nietzsche punctuates with the tolling of the midnight bell and repeats in Part Four with several pages of elaboration ("The Drunken Song" climaxes the book), reiterates the word "deep" over and over, applying it to midnight, the dream, the world, woe, joy, agony, and eternity. As this haunting music from Mahler's Third Symphony fills the scene of the Lido, all the way to the horizon, it insistently evokes the mysteries of Romantic depth of meaning. Here we can say that whatever may be qualified as "deep" will count as a symbol. Such icons will have intensity of value within the story as told, and will carry our thoughts at the same time into domains lying "outside" the story as told. One way for a symbol to point outside a given story is for it to allude or somehow suggest some *source* for that story. Interpretation may become a search for sources and analogues, and at that moment, as in psychoanalysis, the search for meaning seeks to pierce an obscurity hidden in the depths of time, the depths of what came much earlier. Then, by a process of symbolic circulation, what was once outside the work of art (the story as told) and also deeper than the surface of the story now reenters the work by means of allusion, on the higher level which we call interpretation—as the symbol reenters the thinking of the patient, through an interpretation of his dreams. Thus if Nietzsche is initially outside Visconti's film, the philosopher and his meditations on music and Venice circularly return to haunt the action of the film as it progresses. When viewers of the film are ready to experience this infolding of source into the work, they have reached the level on which the film seeks to project its most powerful thinking.

The film calls upon us to think by engaging us in an attentiveness to the boundaries of meaning implicit in the story told. Because the meaning of symbolic clusters is not immediately apparent, their utterance can only be made obliquely, through epiphanies, gnomic statements, and chains of allusion. Such effects are dynamic; they stimulate the viewer's full intellectual powers. Nothing is more mysterious, at times, than the obvious surface of phenomena as these appear to the naive observer. And nothing is more dynamic than this mysterious obviousness. If to the blank face of appearances we add the dynamic effects of enigmatic or gnomic utterance, we reach new conditions for the experience of thought in relation to the work of art. Commonly there is a tendency to speak of thinking as if the full range of an author's ideas (his "thoughts") were exactly stated by a finite number of words, called "the poem" or "the story." This view places thought, somehow, in the text. Yet as various critics have shown, the thinking experience, as experience, also occurs in a reader's mind; the text stimulates or releases such thinking, as a consequence of an encounter between a responding mind and a produced symbolic array. The author designs the text so as to control the direction of readerly thoughts, and when this control is strict and obsessive, the resulting effect will be called allegory. When the control of the reader's response is looser and more liberal, it is hard to find a proper name for the more flexible symbolic procedure. Perhaps we can only speak of a complex mythography, in the sense that loosening the reins of authorial control allows a subtle weighting to be given to any and all elements of the total language the text disposes.

There are then at least two fundamental aspects of the thought of the artwork. Like other artists of major power, Visconti is able to contrapose both aspects of intellectual force. On the one hand his film *Death in Venice*, like his other films analyzing Germanic culture, presents an enacted array of reflections on the aesthetic dimensions of culture and personal destiny. On the other, the very same action will generate thoughts in the mind of the viewer, and these will be extensions of the immediate mental response to the filmic action. As extensions, these generated thoughts will reach out and away from the immediate array of reflections, until a far horizon and an ultimate depth is met. This is not the common experience or expectation of the average moviegoer, but filmmakers like Visconti do not work in terms of average responses. He and his peers wish to generate the sort of mental activity in the viewer one could not predict on the basis of hasty and superficial viewings of the particular film: the simultaneous representation and generation of thought.

In the case of *Death in Venice*, one asks if particular forces allow the film at once to represent and generate thought. A certain literariness provides part of the required force; the film, as we shall see, insists on a variety of oblique links with its literary sources. The chief source of intellective power seems, however, to come from the hybrid treatment of those sources. For filmic purposes an almost magic access to power is achieved when Visconti translates the literary Aschenbach to a musical Aschenbach. The literary is not lost, but simply translated—both Aschenbachs now coexist for the viewer. Beyond this effect of aesthetic doubling there is the further effect of the ability of film, and this film specifically, to employ the visceral power of music itself. Music, that most abstractly ordered of all the arts, is able to close the gap between the objective representation and the subjective generation of thought. Music is hardly the sole stimulus to thought, indeed many would say that music usually lulls thought to sleep. Here, however, music provides the system for the organization of all elements in the language of the film. The opulent use of music leads, for example, to analogous use of the zoom lens and of slow panning shots which are like notes held for longer than one could have imagined possible. Under the synaesthetic control of actual musical pieces which accompany the filmed action, the visual texture acquires what one can only call a musical tonality. All parts of the represented surface of the action begin to refer to all other parts, as if by harmonic design worked out on a large scale. Precisely this combination of the visual and the musical recalls the philosophical writings of Nietzsche, and not only among these the *Zarathustra*. By the same token the mixed purpose of the film, to represent and to generate thought, is a Nietzschean effort.

Visconti's film derives from Nietzsche, whose body of thought may be called its philosophic source. The stream from this source is filtered, however: the immediate story-line comes through Mann's novella and his later *Faustus*. Both literary texts translate into moving picture. Mann's Aschenbach becomes Visconti's Aschenbach. A writer becomes a composer, Aschenbach/Leverkühn, who (somehow) writes Mahler's music. From this cardinal change derives, we may say, a myth of derivation. By reshaping and recombining materials from Mann's text, Visconti opens a path back to Nietzsche, for whom in so many ways music provides the key to a worldview, if not a fairly complete worldview in itself. Searching for the center and the boundary of this worldview, both Visconti and Mann return to the play of music. Visconti uses each proposition or movement of this art as philosophers use the propositional elements of a proof. Like the dithyrambic style in Nietzsche's philosophy, here music is allowed to have the force of destiny.

It helps to treat the unusually complex score of this film as a single, many-sided, polytonal, and especially parodic composition, which makes the spoken word integral to its form. Of this constellation and its musical genealogy, including its relation to *Sprechstimme*, a musicologist might have much to say. However, in line with nineteenth-century beliefs that music is a language—a Romantic belief—we can make a modernist and Nietzschean assumption: here "musical score" means the total soundtrack of the film. Such an assumption fits his global description of the "aesthetic state":

> The aesthetic state possesses a superabundance of means of communication, together with an extreme receptivity for stimuli and signs. It constitutes the high point of communication and transmission between living creatures—it is *the source of language.* This is where languages originate: the languages of tone as well as the languages of gestures and glances. *The more complete phenomenon is always the beginning,* our faculties are subtilized out of more complete faculties. But even today one still hears with one's muscles, one even reads with one's muscles.[1]

Or again, "One never communicates thoughts: one communicates movements, mimic signs, which we can then trace back to thoughts" (S 809). On this view it follows that every single sound in Visconti's film may be scored as a type of music, including whistles, bells, feet crunching on gravel, coffee spoons tinkling on breakfast coffee cups, the sound of the gondolier's oar, and so on; but more important than these normally nonlinguistic sounds, there is scored into the film both the variety of spoken languages and the absence of speech.

Because with Visconti every detail works, this extended under-standing of music permits the artist to organize and express the deeper-lying principles of existence which, in the first place, allow this Nietzschean story to be told, *in the first place.* The logic here is that no sound effect escapes the condition of music; every such element is part of a world. In principle, *aesthetically,* the sound-world is always more perfectly a world than can be any collection of the objects of vision, since, unlike them, music surrounds.

Some literary people were shocked by Visconti's analysis of Mann. He had destroyed Mann's magnificent, granitic literary hero. Aschenbach's mutation had more than a touch of antiliterary sacri-lege about it. It attacked blind reverence for "the immediate literary source." Visconti's reasoning should have been clear: if Mann had seen fit to transform his Nietzschean hero of aesthetics from writer to composer, arriving at Leverkühn/Faustus, why should the film-maker not go one step further, to recombine or hybridize the two arts in his myth of derivation? Recursively, Visconti raised the Nietzschean question of the purity of an origin for speech: "Com-pared with music all communication by words is shameless; words dilute and brutalize; words depersonalize; words make the uncom-mon common."[2] One asks then the very old, the very new question: does literature begin with music, or does music begin with some kind of strange gestural inscription, that is, with the invention of a key word, and thence with literature?

This ambiguity raises, in turn, a philosophic issue somewhat be-yond the question of the hero and his representational origins in some literary text. Suppose we enlarge the concept of immediate, literary, textual sources—suppose that Visconti is trying to probe the question of source itself. What is a source? How does a flow of thought, of philosophy, of poetic vision, of a life begin and then flow onward, transforming as it goes? This is a Nietzschean question.

Its investigation turns here upon thoughts centering on the fic-tionality of biography. For the life of an Aschenbach, what is a reliable source?

Let us see how this line of filmic thought develops. Having jetti-soned Mann's opening pre-Venice pages in the novella, Visconti (by a mathematical substitution) interpolates the substance of chapters 16 and 17 of the *Faustus,* the scene where Leverkühn visits the Leipzig brothel—let us call it the original scene of contamination.

With this single move, Visconti initiates an inquest into the nature of biographical fact. It turns out that no one, including Nietzsche himself, could be sure of the events of his own life which Mann reinvented and realized in this scene, as its "picture" and its consequences were shown to us through the eyes of his narrator, Serenus Zeitblom. Nietzsche's own account of this experience was ambiguous, or changeable, and finally unreliable. Did he touch the woman at the brothel, or only the piano? Was it (as in the *Faustus*) only a later obsessive drive to revisit the woman that led the man to her a second time, in another city, with (or without?) fatal medical consequences? By annexing the episode in the first place, Visconti annexes a doubt, attaching the dynamic of his story to a source that has low initial reliability and a later fictional haze thrown over it.

The film encapsulates this brothel scene, and the effect is enigmatic. But unless we can penetrate the haze, we must ask, does this past event matter at all to the present Venetian narrative? Surely, *this* Aschenbach shows no signs of tertiary syphilis! Finally, of course, we never do know of what Visconti's Aschenbach dies, except that in the world of appearances (as of medical diagnosis) he dies of a broken heart. Not only is source equivocal, so also are whatever consequences may be said to flow from any such equivocal source. The Nietzschean myth of derivation analyzes source and consequence as if the latter might have a paradoxical priority over the former.

The classic modern examples of the power of the equivocal source are to be found as originating moments or episodes in the psychoanalytic case-study. In effect, by interpolating the brothel episode, Visconti seems to be tracing part of a case-study.

Precisely here, however, our sense of artistic style pulls us in the opposite direction. Visconti suggests depth-analysis more than once in this film, and this encapsulated episode has to exist "deeply," but, we might say, it explodes at the surface of a present remembering. And that effect fits. Stylistically Visconti prefers an aesthetic of unforgiving surfaces—ruthless, staring, visual attention. The question then arises: in what surface fashion can the artist probe the depths of his subject? Perhaps film shows depth to be the great illusion. My own feeling is that Visconti follows the Nietzschean plan of trying to render always whatever is exactly right in front of us, as it appears immediately and uncensored, even when screened by the waking dreams of consciousness, but certainly in the domain of perception. The film is hypersensitive, yet outrageously outspoken. Since romantic depths are never thus outspoken, we shall look for depth in another quarter—certainly not in the staring, glancing, peering visual acuity of the camera technique that gives this film its Nietzschean sensibility.

Let us return then to the *Faustus* interpolation. It is surely significant in a general way that the film begins by focusing on one aspect of that narrative material, by literally, silently, tacitly spelling its word. Aschenbach is carried to Venice on a steamer whose name stands out in bold letters, as it docks, the ESMERALDA. Later, following Mann's text, the prostitute he visits is likewise called "Esmeralda," though now we hear rather than see the name. The madam calls out "Esmeralda" in heavy, gutteral German; the young woman must stop her piano-playing, to see the Professor, whom she apparently already knows.

A sharp observer might register the double use of the name, but not know the exact source in Mann, where the name is introduced in yet another context as *Hetaira Esmeralda*. This scientific name labels the butterfly whose symbolic attributes recur throughout *Doctor Faustus* with the force of a Wagnerian leitmotif. As *Hetaira*, the species-name stands for "the concubine," the companion in forbidden pleasure. With its first mention the name starts a metonymic chain that carries through to the very end of the book, and similarly to the end of the film, giving us one mode of originating source: the giving of a name to some effect in the world.

As leitmotif it introduces a set of ideas. "Hetaira had on her wings only a dark spot of violet and rose; one could see nothing else of her, and when she flew she was like a petal blown by the wind."[3] What could seem more magically innocent, we say, than this wind-borne spot of violet and rose? But what more dangerous, in the event? At first the child Adrian responds to such creatures with what Mann calls "infectious mirth," thus linking contagion to the idea and fact of uncontrollable laughter—the Zarathustran theme. It is only a short, ironic step to the ominous experience of Adrian Leverkühn, now a young man, who writes to his friend Zeitblom as follows, with characteristic defensive archaism: in the brothel he had seen "your nymphs and daughters of the wilderness, ribaudes, laced muttons all, six or seven, morphos, clear-wings, esmeraldas, etc." He tells Zeitblom that having struck a chord or two on the piano (chords relating to some "brightening semitone" which then preoccupied him), he met the young woman who, perhaps not then, but perhaps later, would infect him. "A brown wench puts herself nigh me, in a little Spanish jacket, with a big gam, snub nose, almond eyes, an Esmeralda, she brushed my cheek with her arm." (Almost all these details Visconti used.) Horrified, Leverkühn rushed from her, flinging himself "back through the lust-hell," out into the street.

Zeitblom, whose narrative is veined like a systemic disease, takes immediate and hardly restrained pedantic delight in the musical import of this scene and its precursor scenes. He notes that from the name *Hetaira Esmeralda* the composer was to extract a musical anagram, the notes B (German: H), E, A, E, E Flat. Leverkühn labels this anagram or series of notes "a word, a key word, stamped on everything in the song." This "word" is a *determining* source. Wherever it appears, it controls the musical composition so that "there would no longer be a free note." The series includes a half-hidden tritone, the interval A–E Flat, which medieval music always called *diabolus in musica*, because of its forbidden, ambiguating effect for harmony. Yet the series controls musical development; "there would no longer be a free note."

Mann, with hundreds of discursive pages available to him, weaves an immense and everstronger web from his three-termed idea— Esmeralda the spotted butterfly, Esmeralda the brown wench, Esmeralda the truncated tone-row, the "key-word." These evolve into a motivic subsystem, which Zeitblom finally labels for convenience "the Hetaira Esmeralda figure." This figure recurs wherever Leverkühn's music is most tragic and most Faustian. Its serial principle also generalizes to become the method of Leverkühn's whole musical output, one way or another. Its harmonically ambiguous idea underlies what in the film Aschenbach's friend Alfred (his Nietzschean *daimon*) calls a "science of ambiguities." Fixed series implies its opposite, ambiguity, and hence the idea of series gets tied here to a randomized modern notion of fate.

Other associations are at work. Esmeralda is the emerald, the sea-green stone of oceanic depths, contrasting with the strings of orient pearl worn by the mother, who in effect is a Dionysian priestess—Venice, Queen of the Sea, *Serenissima*, who wears the pearls "that were his eyes."

More powerful is the Viscontian structure of bodily gestures, of pose. Esmeralda is seen in two poses. First, reclining as odalisque, her posture exactly doubles that of a photograph we do not see in the film, that of the great dancer Kchessinska as she starred in and created Petipa's version of the once famous ballet, *Esmeralda*. But when Visconti's Aschenbach leaves her, abruptly, she sits open-thighed on the edge of her bed. Now her pose shockingly doubles another photograph, which we *have* already seen, that of the composer's little daughter. Aschenbach had stooped to kiss the photo of his scowling, open-thighed little girl, before descending in full evening dress to eat dinner on his first night at the Grand Hotel des Bains, on the Lido.

Such image-play, such pictorial juxtapositions gradually develop into a symbolic optics. On one level, image is called upon to substitute for the heavy verbal texture of the novella and the *Faustus*.

There seems to be a limit, within this optics, to the degree to which image can reach for the depths normal in the overtoning of language. Image focuses; it frames; it disconnects; and when film sets image in apparent motion, it tends to produce fragments of a life experienced by the viewer as the severed pieces of a broken continuity. Despite Visconti's languorous slow panning shots and almost possessed introspective use of the zoom lens, visual discontinuities shove their way into the foreground, especially with his sudden flashbacks. Something else is required to reconnect, to produce the illusion of cause and effect—the illusion of the wholeness of a flow of events. This must be an illusion, because flow is a process, not a closed productive form with a beginning, middle, and end. Illusion or not, continuity is the assumption of a life that "means something," but a film like this gives us the question, rather than the answer to the question: what breaks the flow of life? The meaning of death is an everpresent question Visconti courts, virtually seduces out of its hiding place.

The strongest resistance to broken flow comes from Visconti's musical use of the Hetaira Esmeralda figure. Now, in a normal sense, music exercises its continuative power. Not only is the assemblage of musical materials a kind of musical ethnography, from high to low musical culture, but, remarkably, all the major items in the score are based on various transformations of the rising (or inverted) intervals of the Fourth—hence B to E, E to A—or are based on the stressed semitone, E to E Flat (there in its falling, flatted form). The rising, *brightening* semitone Zeitblom mentioned appears within the play of Fourths, as the leading tone, which always generates an expectation of a furthering closure. The brightening semitone suspends the listener for a time, an effect that here comes across most powerfully in the central musical piece, the Adagietto from Mahler's Fifth Symphony.

The derivation from the Hetaira Esmeralda figure holds for all the major items Visconti uses: the Adagietto—the Merry Widow waltz (another piece identified with Mahler)—the great slow movement from the Third Symphony, the contralto solo based on Nietzsche's Second Dance Song ("O Man, beware!")—the Mountebank's laughing song which assaults the guests reposing casually after dinner on the hotel terrace—the Mussorgsky lullaby that gives the film its penultimate elegiac close, before the final return to the Adagietto one last time, as the film ends. Visually, sonically, the film ends in pure wave-motion, as it had begun (only in minute stages do we realize at the outset that the film-titles are being shown, by a zoom lens, coming at us over a slowly undulating background of darkened, gently rocking waves of the Adriatic Sea).

Hetaira Esmeralda equally configures the one piece I take to be the *ironic* and *dramatic* center of this universe of sounds. The piece directly links Tadzio and Esmeralda, hence links Aschenbach to them and to his own daughter. It is the archetypal salon piece, *Für Elise*, which begins with and obsessively repeats a slow trill on E, E Flat (though Beethoven wrote these notes, E, D Sharp, for the key of A Minor). *Für Elise* follows the trill with a figured series of rising Fourths, again a structure demanded by the originating musical series, Adrian's "single word."

As a mere pose had linked Esmeralda and Aschenbach's daughter, *Für Elise* links Tadzio and Esmeralda by a mere musical gesture, whose physical performance Visconti emphasizes in the brothel scene, as she practices her piece. This "much loved" composition is an emblem not only in, but of, music as cultural destiny. The piece prompts us to ask: what then is music, if it can be thus imperishable, commanding, infectious, determining, even contaminating, as clearly is the case with Beethoven's apparently trivial bagatelle? (When he was praised for his *Moonlight Sonata,* he dealt with that parallel case by stating a marked preference for his Op. 78 sonata in F Sharp. But the magic of certain melodies in their magic harmonic guise is too much for a discriminating taste to contravene; the *Moonlight* persists as magic.) Is music then an irresistible sonic atmosphere? or the Dionysian pulse of dancing blood? or a sensuous double of mathematics? a Pythagorean emblem of cosmic order? What, indeed, is the nature of its magic? For, among the arts, it appears to have the most strictly controlled logical form. We often say that music expresses emotion, that flux of nonreferential feeling-tones. Perhaps it reveals the structure of the unconscious, and its changes mimic the changes of a hidden self, metamorphosing like the *Liebestod* motifs of Strauss's late string work, the *Metamorphosen.* It appears impossible (perhaps it is analytically undesirable) to *picture* the operations of music in the mind. For, no visual "shot" can express musical tones in motion. The picture would have to be of a special kind.

If we relate our broad question of sound/vision relations to the Venetian aspect of this *Liebestod,* we do, however, open out into a possible answer. *We* should not forget that this death occurs *in* Venice, that is, as an aspect of being contained by Venice. The city completely environs. Let's suppose that one key to the question of musical world is to be found, for Visconti, in *Ecce Homo,* where Nietzsche says: "When I seek another word (*ein andres Wort*) for music, I never find any other word than Venice." This is the romantic vision of Venice, which Offenbach caught perfectly in *The Tales of Hoffman,* with its celebrated barcarolle: undulant Venice.

"I never find any other word than Venice"—music and this one place so rich in food for every sense mutually implicate each other. This city is configured as an extension in sensed time, through musical structure and experience. Nietzsche, Mann, and Visconti were at one in believing that Venice "aspires to the condition of music." Venice is in constant musical motion, so to speak.

Film presents edited pictures of things moving. Although picture disconnects, Eisenstein and other filmmakers have shown us that a moving-picture defies this disconnection. Montage also aspires to the condition of music, which means that, as with music proper, filmic montage-ruptures actually enable the phrasing of a complex flow of images or scenes which would, as still shots, be perfectly closed off from each other. The whole art of film appears to be the search for devices for reestablishing flow on the visual plane. To a great extent this is a matter of illusionistic montage.

Music, by contrast, simply produces the stimulus to an experience of continuous presence. Music then enters film as the most powerful means of connecting distinct visual elements. Recall that if music is a true "world," it is so because it fills the space of a universe. Like an ideal city, such music defines a propagation of space, as space is filled with significant tonal interactions. Film enjoys special powers for defining this propagation of significant space, since the filmmaker can choose to show, or to hide, the actual source of his musical (or other sonic) materials. In *Death in Venice* we begin to learn this choice. We actually see the salon trio perform Franz Lehar's melodies in the lounge of the Grand Hotel; we actually see the mountebanks performing outdoors, in the evening; we actually see the Russian woman sing the Mussorgsky lullaby; and in the most controlled showing of a sound-source, we actually see and are at certain moments prevented from seeing Esmeralda playing *Für Elise* on the piano, as we have just seen Tadzio play this same piece on a quite different piano, a grand, at the Hotel. Aschenbach stares at both performances.

The directorial choice can equally go the other way. Usually in film we do not see the sound-source. Here, two major pieces, both by Mahler, have no visually apparent source. Hitchcock once quipped of some "unreal" background music he wanted (for *Lifeboat*), "it has to come from somewhere." He was right. The most powerful film music simply "comes from somewhere." Such music is present as source, without apparent source, and hence becomes a model of source itself. It simply begins, continues, and ceases to sound. It has no palpable origin, and, oddly enough, thereby gains a greater power than any music whose performing source we are allowed to perceive on the screen.

Visconti performs one twist on this ideal or perfect invisibility— he shows us Aschenbach at the beach writing out the great Nietzschean Dance Song (from the Third Symphony). We see the composer putting notes on paper. At first we do not know what music he is writing. But then, from somewhere unknown, from some unknown orchestra and soloist, but also (simultaneously) from the composer's pen, comes the extraordinary sound of that contralto solo.

Music then begins to bind, to ease, to lift the broken pieces of image and event into a flow the seen world can never possess.

The Nietzschean gift to Mann and then to Visconti is the gift of this idea of music—an art that wells up without origin, out of "an emerald happiness," as Nietzsche described his dithyrambic ecstacy. Musical sound invisibly permeates and structures and stirs and disturbs space by temporal and rhythmic and tonal force. Here too we discover the problem of reliable source, for with regard to music it remains impossible to separate Nietzsche's own sense of this art from that deep life-crisis, his intellectual "marriage" and "divorce" from Wagner and Wagner's music. To what degree is Nietzsche the child of *Tristan*? Better than anyone he was latterly able to describe the loss, in Wagner, of classical form; and to describe the way in which, one might say, Wagner had poisoned Western music. With Wagner music no longer maintains its distance from the listener, who can then no longer *listen*. And listening is the spiritual requirement for a true music. The Wagnerians do not listen to music; they merely react to it. Instead, Nietzsche's philosophy always implies that song calls for its listener, and the art of song tries to define the place or space of a spiritual responsiveness, which is to say, it forms "the soul that loves itself the most, in which all things have their current and counter-current and ebb and flow."

In this sense music provides the medium for the soul's desire to experience metaphysical distance. In Venice, Nietzsche had experienced this distance, specifically as a musical awareness, a musical response. Visconti, by allowing the Nietzschean dimensions of Mann's "musicology" to unfold as *Death in Venice* unrolls before our eyes, allows a similar distance to find its ideal space. "Soul" and "spirit" name this process. There is an old understanding of the soul as a butterfly, Psyche. Here Psyche is again a butterfly, *Hetaira Esmeralda*, and the force of her name has the force of a single, originating word. Her single word crosses over to another single word, the name of an actual city, Venice, where once the philosopher found himself standing on a bridge, "in the brown night."

> From afar there came a song:
> a golden drop, it swelled

across the trembling surface.
Gondolas, lights, music—
drunken it swam out into the gloom . . .
My soul, a stringed instrument,
touched by invisible hands
sang to itself in reply a gondola song,
and trembled with gaudy happiness.
—Was anyone listening?[4]

Scarcely a note in this song is unfamiliar: the words belong to High Romanticism. But Nietzsche attaches the theme of longing for a metaphysical response to the physics of actual musical experience, and thus he hardens and strengthens the logic of his nostalgia. The hands of the instrument-soul are "invisible hands." Always the theme of the invisible.

It remained for a later author, Italo Calvino, to elaborate this Venetian theme to its most precise form, the idea of the "invisible city." Throughout *Invisible Cities*, Marco Polo and Kublai Khan weave a dialogue of interpretation, as they try to share the question: where has Polo "come from" and "where is he going?" It turns out that he comes from a city which he can never describe, even fabulously, because it must remain (as Marco Polo says to the Khan) an "implicit city." Venice is a fictive, logical entity, of which one could never say for sure whether it is subject or predicate, premise or consequence.

Hence Kublai Khan craves each fabled account to begin again with an ever more complete description of Venice, Polo's "source." But this would lead to infinity: "You should then begin each tale of your travels from the departure, describing Venice as it is, all of it, not omitting anything you remember of it."

"Memory's images, once they are fixed in words, are erased," Polo says. "Perhaps I am afraid of losing Venice all at once, if I speak of it. Or perhaps, speaking of other cities, I have already lost it, little by little."[5]

Their dialogue ends there. We turn the page. There follows, for the first time in the book, a fabulous description of the actual Venice, the fifth of the Trading Cities. The description begins: "In Esmeralda, city of water, a network of canals and a network of streets span and intersect each other . . . the ways that open to each passerby are never two, but many, and they increase further for those who alternate a stretch by boat with one on dry land." Esmeralda can be mapped only in the air, by drawing an impossible tracery along the "routes of the swallows . . . dominating from every point of their airy paths all the points of the city." This airy topography reduces Venice to its ideal state, as an empty logical space. Venice finally exists only *nell'aria* and "touched by invisible hands," like the poet's instrument-soul.

Only in the air is the soul free. I have wished to claim a special place for music in the thought of Visconti and his progenitors. I have said that the actual aesthetic invisibility of music—which Visconti over and over examines, asking, what if we see its source? what if we do not see its source?—eventually by means of a good contamination succeeds in binding the disconnected images of memory and perception. These are the images which, as pieces of thought utterly divided from each other, would kill us. Divided, lacking any link, they point only to raw materiality. Divided, they stand between us and our own souls. They obscure; they prevent us from seeing; they are opposed to what Nietzsche meant, when he began *Ecce Homo* with the phrase, "On this perfect day . . ."

Normally, Bertrand Russell claims, immediate memory and perception are paradigms of the self-evident. But in Visconti, as in Nietzsche's song at the bridge, the invisible and sourceless music of the gondolier and the responding soul is an even sharper self-evidence. This music does not have to be *there* to be, evidently, itself. It is the fundamental model, then, of context—it is perfectly all around. It defines the soul's invisible horizon. But this music models context in a secondary sense as well: it permeates and is all through. It touches every object and body in any filled space where it resonates. If there is anything real in any scene where it permeates, music freely touches those real things, which belong to the experienced nearby world of a human life, the life of some listener. Music embraces nearly, and from afar.

To combine this "all through" with this "all around" in one passing moment or extending passage of time is to achieve, in a final Nietzschean and Viscontian sense, the Dionysian. "The more complete phenomenon is always the beginning." In Visconti's film, music is this more complete phenomenon—the complete soundtrack.

The claim of such completeness has about it a touch of the grandiose, or perhaps of the illusory. Even so, the force of musical example is manifestly powerful in this film. Nor does it surprise us, given Visconti's lifelong involvement with music. What does surprise is the way in which the musical components of the film are used to activate the viewer's thought. Usually "movie music" is intended to establish or sustain a mood. Here music actively cooperates with all other allusive elements of the film, to engage us in a vigorous reading of philosophic implications. By centrally evoking Nietzsche through Mahler's Third Symphony, Visconti manages an extension of the script of the film in breadth and depth, and this extension in turn suggests that thought is not to be confined to a verbally writable or speakable medium. Instead thought is here conceived as a manifold, a multiplicity of layered or combined symbolic strata. The result is what Alfred in the film calls a "science of ambiguities," which is his definition of the Schoenbergian revolution in compositional practice. This science of ambiguities is more or less what philosophy itself has had to become, as thought approaches the absurdities of life in the twentieth century. In that philosophy has been forced to take the "linguistic turn," whether in a Wittgensteinian or an opposed Heideggerian fashion, philosophy has also been forced to accept the prime fact about language, namely its ambiguity. Despite all precautions language in its natural state remains an equivocal medium of thought, and since it is also the most flexible and responsive medium of thought, it forces upon the intellect something close to an obligation to accept the ambiguous. It may be that this ambiguity of natural language merely shows us what the world is—not a perspicuously clear object which somehow we fail to observe correctly, but rather a tangled web of phenomena, which can never be shorn of its ambiguous ragged margins. These unraveling edges are a central fact of a life. As the clerk at the Cook's Tourist Agency says to a dazed Aschenbach: "What would Venice be, without tourists?" It is clear that while the man from Cook's is pointing out the cultural phenomenon known as tourism, he is also at that moment describing the outbreak and spread of a cholera epidemic. Tourism is a plague, but inevitably it too is ambiguous. What indeed would our whole world be, without tourists? We live, the film seems to be saying, in a situation of desperate and finally unappeasable quest, the search for a different meaning behind the staring Venetian facade, the search for the significance of death in Venice.

12. The Image of Lost Direction

The labyrinth—Frye's *Anatomy* calls it "the image of lost direction"—appears in literature as just that, an image. Generally it suggests an inextricable tangle. The image has such power that, while it often merely conveys an impression of pleasant or unpleasant intricacy, it also may inform narrative structure at large. *Tristram Shandy*, for example, is not only about a labyrinthine situation (life in the Shandy family); its story too is told through endless mazy digressions, quirky slithers of narrative sequence, which Sterne happily called "the sunshine." Many other works, ancient and modern, share in the rhythms of labyrinthine movement. Frye properly considers the labyrinth an archetypal rather than casual image. Yet owing perhaps to its inherent complexity and its many metaphoric transformations into other mazy shapes (is the fog in *Bleak House* a labyrinth?), "the image of lost direction" has only recently begun to receive the attention it deserves.

Frye's ringing epithet occurs in a discussion of demonic imagery; the idea is already present in *Fearful Symmetry*; *The Critical Path* attacks its problematic directly. The essay "Towards Defining an Age of Sensibility" observes the oracular discontinuities preferred in such periods, when narrative and lyric forms come apart, under pressure from a now familiar type of anxiety whose mark is that "pity and fear become states of mind without objects."[1] Perhaps because such flux is typical of Gothic fictions where terror is a stock in trade, the modern reader will readily assent to a negative, demonic reading of the image. Yet even in the much larger perspective of the *Anatomy*, Frye is able to locate the labyrinth on the downside of mythic vision. Its converse tends to be some apocalyptic heaven, temple, Eden, resolving cadence, home. With twentieth-century literature the labyrinth almost always has negative or at least unsettling associations.

The main advantage of analyzing the labyrinth is that this is a directional image, as Frye observed. The image geometrizes some problems of state of mind. The *Odyssey* has a number of such images, and indeed the whole poem may be conceived as a vastly extended labyrinth, but the iconography of the labyrinth proper can focus on a precise range of shapes of the *space of passage*, to clarify the ways in which we can feel lost, or found. The archetype raises the question: what is a sense of direction in any case?

Frye's account draws for us the traditional crux of lost and found. "Here too are the sinister counterparts of geometrical images: the sinister cross, and the sinister circle, the wheel of fate or fortune . . . Corresponding to the apocalyptic way or straight road, the highway in the desert for God prophesied by Isaiah, we have in this world the labyrinth or maze, the image of lost direction, often with a monster at its heart like the Minotaur" (*Anatomy of Criticism*, 150).

Losing the "straight road" can occur for various reasons, but common to all is a psychological component. The presumption is that the road does exist, but one has lost sight of it. The loss of direction is a lost *sense* of direction. The reader is asked to share in this mental experience, with all its attendant anxiety. We are not misled when sometimes the experience is vaguely pleasant or titillating, as when in the Renaissance and the seventeenth and eighteenth centuries, landscape becomes a high art and the maze becomes an adjunct to the formal garden.[2] The literature describing this art, or using its associations for metaphoric purposes, tends always to emphasize the wandering, meandering, errant aspect of passage through the labyrinth. This wandering is subject to a mental bafflement. One does not pass through a mazy scene unless one thinks one's way through it. The thinking of the labyrinth is the problem of the labyrinth. It is not so much a trial of strength as a kind of perceptual skill. The meandering passage promotes always a thinking into one's state of mind. To a degree the labyrinth leaves its traveler with nothing much but state of mind. As Marvell says, in his poem of the countermaze, "The Garden,"

> Meanwhile the Mind, from pleasure less,
> Withdraws into its happiness . . .
> Annihilating all that's made
> To a green thought in a green shade.

If then, with delight or pain, the experience of the labyrinth is that of thought attempting to experience itself, some *object* or *aim* or some two *points* defining a straight line will have ceased to provide orientation. Yet orientation is always a resource of cosmic dimensions. What could these objects, aims, and points possibly be?

The poets have suggested an answer, which at first seems no answer at all. They compare the labyrinth to life itself. Marvell's contemporary, Bishop Henry King, says: "Life is a crooked Labyrinth, and wee / Are dayly lost in that Obliquity."[3] Michael Drayton, an intermediary between Spenser and those poets, asks: "for what liker to a Labyrinth, than the Maze of Life?"[4] Spenser initiates the action of his immense epic by introducing his essential hero, the Redcrosse Knight, into the Wood of Error, which the poet calls a "labyrinth," in order that we shall see the whole career of the hero as a doubtful traverse of "so many paths, so many turnings seene." This Wood conforms to Frye's account of the labyrinth: at its heart resides the monster of Error itself, a terrifying, self-consuming dragoness of convoluted, deformed thoughts. Before he can proceed, the hero must kill the monster—the monstrous source of error. He manages this, but not before we realize that his life will be devoted to deciphering monstrous error wherever he meets it. He finds that error persists, unavoidable in life, if not elsewhere. The epic rhythm of continuity of *The Faerie Queene*, as of the *Odyssey*, is lifelike, because each poem mirrors the eternal recurrence of directions lost and found, found and lost.

That life is a labyrinth might seem an unduly empty notion, however obvious or natural. Yet even such a precise poet as Dante sees the archetype this way. His *Commedia* begins in a maze: "In the middle way of this life, / I found myself [lost] in a dark wood." Literally Dante says, "of *our* life," of the life of man in general. In the midst of "living," he says, we find we are lost—that, in terms of his poem of the discovery of direction, is what being "in the midst of things" really means. By definition, being in the middle implies that there are too many optional possible paths, so many indeed that the sense of reachable goal is baffled by excessive freedom. A goal that can be reached by too many paths seems to vanish, to be replaced by the mere activity of pathfinding. Discovery and curiosity become ends in themselves; the means becomes the end.

Viewed in a certain light, a definition of human life, as lifetime, would have to include at least some reference to the idea that a life that is lived is primarily a process and therefore that for living to be really living the means *must* become the end. Thus far it seems a reasonable archetypal connection to say that human life is a labyrinth. But when we shall have to reckon with all the negative aspects of the maze that Frye identified in the *Anatomy* and that poets have so persistently recognized, especially in the modern era. Modern mazes are relentlessly frightening. This being so, we need to get a clearer notion, in regard to the labyrinth, of the distinction between ends and means.

Again the archetype and the ideas of "lost direction" will come to our aid. The traditional account does suggest some useful limits to the troublesome openness of the life/labyrinth equation.

So far as the labyrinth has a *mythos* attached to it, Western literature returns to the story of Theseus, Ariadne, Daedalus, Minos, and the Minotaur—the story of the Cretan Labyrinth. Theseus' adventure is clearly a heroic initiation into his destiny as protector of a people. He volunteers to kill the Minotaur, and he succeeds. Whereas, however, many a dragon-slaying encounter could form part of the hero's initiation into manhood, this particular story enhances what Victor Turner would call the "processual" aspects of the achievement.[5] Theseus is "separated" from his folk, he "passes through" a set of thresholds in the initiatory midphase of the labyrinthine hunt for the Minotaur, and he is rejoined with the folk at the end (the *aggrégation*, as it is called in van Gennep's classic terminology). On such a plan Mircea Eliade would say that all labyrinth-passages are myths of initiation ritual.[6] If such accounts hold up, then it would appear that the life/labyrinth metaphor is based on the idea that all of life is a series of initiations. Every intelligible goal or direction will be defined by the particular initiation appropriate to the hero at a given time of life. Life becomes an experience, unfolding in time, of secondary labyrinths. A sense of "the next thing," the experience of the next labyrinth in some due course, will bring order to the larger pattern of existence. So life is organized in primitive societies, as well as advanced societies, though in the latter the profusion of apparent choices makes it often virtually impossible to discern what ought to come next. The only large-scale error would be to believe that there are no labyrinths, no Minotaurs, for then there would never be any beginnings, any possibilities, in a ritual sense, of initiation into any significant actions.

The denial that the labyrinth exists has a curious result: everything becomes labyrinthine. The processual flow of life cannot, in fact, be stopped, as life goes on; it can only be subdivided, more or less fluently, with more or less discipline. The Cretan Labyrinth provides the original literary model for such subdivisions. Theseus enters and leaves a walled enclosure. As a result, the situation changes for the doomed Athenian youths and maidens—they are saved from death—and, more important to our story, the situation changes for Theseus himself. He is now certifiably a hero, a "culture-bringer." Some have argued that the Minotaur is not just a monstrous engine of tyranny but rather the hero's dark shadow, his own evil self, which he kills to liberate his own heroic virtue. Before any further great exploits may be achieved, this initial enlightenment must occur, so that the hero may possess "vision" to perceive the natural sequentiality of his heroic career. For him the idea of the labyrinthine terror can no longer cloud *all* of life's unfolding. Theseus can now always subdivide the maze.

The reader of modern literature may well at this point begin to wonder if this Cretan model is not too neat and optimistic, with its guaranteed escape system. Spenser's Blatant Beast, his Minotaur in one of its shapes, is the typical modern case: the beast cannot be imprisoned, nor can we avoid him. Shakespeare and La Fontaine create the inverse myth from the Cretan, in their poems of Adonis;[7] there the monster kills the hero. Gothic and Oriental romance,[8] "Graveyard," and much Romantic poetry evoke this threat. The labyrinth maps political life for Central and South America.

Negativity increases until in our century Kafka invented virtually boundless, cosmic, bureaucratic mazes; size and boundary are always dubious in Kafka. Borges, a somewhat more cheerful author, because more elegiac, stretches the allusiveness of his labyrinths until he has constructed a universal text larger than our known physical universe.[9] Calvino's invisible cities so proliferate in number, size, and kind that finally they exist only as dots on the pages of an infinite atlas.[10] As Frye observes in a review entitled "The Nightmare Life in Death," Beckett employs "a shaggy-dog type of deliberately misleading humor, expressing itself in a maddeningly prolix pseudologic . . . The most trivial actions of Watt, most of which are very similar to those we perform ourselves every day, are exhaustively catalogued in an elaborate pretense of obsessive realism, and we can see how such "realism" in fiction, pushed to so logical a conclusion, soon gives the effect of living in a kind of casual and unpunishing hell."[11] The modern attempt to break out of this bland inferno through the "freedom" of drugs leads equally to a frightening prolixity, the endless "hide and seek" chronicled by Henri Michaux' *Cannabis Indica.*[12] A classic title would be Lowry's *Under the Volcano,* whose hero, the Consul, sees himself "balancing, teetering over the awful unbridgeable void."[13] The classic shape of the modern story of obsession is a journey to the end of the night, perfect in the sense that night is the very form of the boundless. It is as if the modern form of hell is labyrinthine, the humor is absurdist, every exit a blind alley. Our literature has tended to discover most of its most hellish pains in the workings of social systems organized on plans of "maddeningly prolix pseudologic."

How this modern twist of fate relates to the ancient image of lost direction is the business of the historian. If worlds have changed to such a degree over the millennia, the critic faces two related tasks. He can reconsider the archetypes and myths, as given in their earlier forms; and he can notice what appear to be epochal changes of sensibility, as the virtually unchanged archetypes bend to accommodate the pressure of historical impact.

Here it is possible to note only a few dimensions of the critical problem. It will help, first of all, to distinguish three main uses of the term "labyrinth," following the work of Hermann Kern, who in turn follows, among other guides, the prior work of William Henry Matthews and Paolo Santarcangeli. Kern's monumental *Labirinti* describes the "forms and interpretations of 5000 years of the presence of an archetype."[14]

Kern begins by observing that in current usage the term "labyrinth" has three main meanings: (1) as metaphor for any inextricably difficult situation where the very structure of the difficulty cannot be discerned; (2) as any intricate system of paths [*intrico de vie*], usually in the form of buildings or gardens, presenting the traveler with a choice among many alternative routes, yet always leading him down blind alleys (this second sense has enormous range: it is used by Herodotus in referring to the necropoli of the ancient Egyptians, and by German horticulturalists and landscapers in referring to the ornamental *Irrgarten*), and finally, (3) as labyrinth in the proper sense of the word, that is, as shown in the design of the "Cretan labyrinth," which appears on the face of ancient coins.

There are no blind alleys in the pure Cretan design; thus it differs sharply from the *intrico* (no. 2). The form of movement within is, however, tortuous in one sense: from a single point of entrance the traveler twists and turns between "walls" round and round, but also back and forth. The Cretan traverse does *not* offer any choices of path, but direction in it does keep changing, whether the overall design is circular, rectangular, or polygonal. The Cretan traverse takes the traveler from an outside to a middle area, and then, without any possibility of getting lost as long as he progresses, into a center. Similarly, by retracing his steps he has only one way back out to the edge.

In this labyrinth the traveler has only two choices, and neither has anything to do with choosing a correct path into another correct path (and so on). He can choose only to keep moving or to stop, moving inwards or outwards; and he can choose to stop at the centre, stay there forever, and refuse to come back out from that central point. In effect these two choices reduce to one choice: he must decide whether or not to keep moving. The Cretan labyrinth gives him absolutely no choice of direction.

Unlike the metaphoric sense, and the intricate structural sense, this third, proper sense of the term labyrinth as given in Kern is extremely puzzling to contemplate. Because such a maze forces the traveler to follow the one sole correct path to the center, and back out, he cannot "get lost" here. The question at once arises: why then does Theseus need Ariadne's thread? The immediate answer is one given in ancient lore, namely that the Cretan labyrinth of the coins is not the one Theseus entered. Instead, he entered a vast, intricate structure akin to the Palace at Knossos—an *intrico*. But then the "correct" coin-design would seem an absurdly simple-minded equivalent of the scene of Theseus' adventure, and would have to refer us to some other conception. Perhaps the true Cretan maze symbolized an astrological theory of planetary movement; Kern believes the design has, among other meanings, a calendrical significance.[15] Comparative research indicates that the Cretan model could well be the choreographic plan of a ritual dance, going back to the "dance of the cranes" on the Island of Delos.[16] Such a use would be related to the "Troy Town" games of Northern Europe, to the stone labyrinths found near Scandinavian fishing villages, to the labyrinthine rock carvings of the American Southwest Indians.[17] How such a radical choreographic design could travel almost round the whole world is puzzling, but one thing is certain: the pure Cretan labyrinth of the coins is, in terms of essential complexity, the very opposite of the *intrico*. One could get lost in the Egyptian necropolis or the Palace of Minos or in any such "megastructure," simply because there were too many corridors, stairs, illusionistic recesses, and blind turns. But to "find oneself lost" in a labyrinth of iron determinism, like the Cretan, is to suffer a quite different sort of disorientation. The Cretan model is therefore, I believe, the more important case, since it is truly enigmatic. The fact that, on the surface at least, it is impossible to "get lost" in the Cretan maze makes that maze a very peculiar device for its stated mythic purpose.

If it were not the case that the Cretan maze is associated with dance movements following its form—that is, its structure has an objective choreographic function—we might wish to argue that the ancient coins and other designs strictly following their layout were merely emblems for a much more complex kind of structure, of Kern's Type 2. But the Cretan design passes down the centuries as an intact geometrical shape, as if its significance depended upon its seven "rings," with their permutations to larger numbers, with varied angular shapings (for example, rectangular shapes or polygons) yet never losing the one cardinal property of preventing the traveler from straying from the single possible path to the center. This one severe limit placed upon the design seems to be its essential attribute. Oddly, as we have said, it is a limit that should in principle make it absurd to speak of getting lost in such a labyrinth.

There seems to be no way to explain the paradox except to account for it in psychological terms. Something happens in the

Cretan maze that so disturbs the traveler's mind that he is, in some deeper sense, "lost."

The story of Theseus, told and retold, gives us some clues. From these a line of speculation may proceed. Theseus must move in large arcs of a circle, each arc tighter than the one before it. Before each arc can form a full circle, it swings back (Kern says, with "pendular" motion)[18] to shift the traveler to the smaller arc. What often looks to the casual glance like a spiral is not one, for there the radius of arc being traveled would be *continuously* diminished. In the Cretan maze we have two kinds of movement, the one circular or constricting (like rectangular mazes), the other a backswing or reversal of direction. The backswing is a diametrically reversing movement. A first speculation might then be that in the Cretan maze Theseus suffers a vertiginous loss of clarity as to what "forward" means; to go "forward," he must keep reversing his direction, that is, he must go backward. The tighter the arcs as he approaches the centre, the more frequent will be this enforced "undoing" of the idea of forward motion. We might label this process "the peril of reversing convolutions." Whereas a spiral maintains continuous forwardness, the Cretan maze enforces a discontinuous forwardness at best, and if the pendular reversals have indeed a psychological effect, this forwardness will seem to Theseus always more and more *questionable*.

The mounting centripetal tension of this back-and-forth movement leads no doubt to questions that only a psychologist could begin to answer. The effect appears, however, to be that of a certain type of vertigo.

A second line of psychological speculation would equally take off from the basic elements of the old story. Of these perhaps the most intriguing is Ariadne's thread. Everything said so far would suggest that her "silken string," as Hawthorne calls it,[19] would serve no orienting purpose during the hero's passage to the centre of the maze. It would clearly serve such a purpose if he were doomed to enter and traverse a vast, reticulated structure of merging, angling corridors, stairs, tunnels, and so on, that is, a true *intrico*. Such, following the tradition given in Plutarch, is Hawthorne's version of the maze: "Theseus had not taken five steps before he lost sight of Ariadne; and in five more his head was growing dizzy. But still he went on, now creeping through a low arch, now ascending a flight of steps, now in one crooked passage and now in another, with here a door opening before him, and there one banging behind, until it really seemed as if the walls spun round, and whirled him round along with them."

Hawthorne adds a delicate touch to the story, to indicate a basic implication of the silken cord. She holds the other end of the cord in her hand at all times, so that "every little while" Theseus is made aware of her presence outside the maze; he is "conscious of a gentle twitch at the silken cord." Hawthorne's narrator expatiates on the emotions attached to the word—"Oh, indeed, I can assure you, there was a vast deal of human sympathy running along that slender thread of silk." Human sympathy is perhaps a critical motif in the Theseus story; certainly for Hawthorne that is so. Yet the twitching tug at the cord indicates something more basic even than the bonds of sympathy. In effect the cord becomes an extrusion of Ariadne's hand and implies that, with it in hand, the hero suffers no discontinuity with the outside of the maze. He never, in effect, leaves the outside. Radically reducing the image of the cord to the idea of continuity in space (despite distance), Hawthorne's version suggests that the *intrico* is designed to produce discontinuity, quantal gaps in the hero's perception of his own movements and direction. It is as if, without the silken thread of Ariadne, the hero would suffer from a breaking, a splintering, a rupturing of *continuous* awareness. We may not be able to say what such a flow of consciousness would consist in. But we can assert that the *intrico* disturbs it to the point of vertigo, or rather, Theseus is saved from succumbing to dizziness by the artifice of the cord of continuity.

At once, without elaborating much, it becomes clearer how the Cretan story is tied to Dionysian myth.[20] The Dionysian whirl is not solely that produced by the "peril of reversing convolutions," nor solely that produced by reticulated, Daedalian numerosity of choice-points (though these contribute powerfully). The Dionysian whirl is part of a ritual of discontinuous change of spirit; of conversions of soul so complete that they amount to rebirth. Ariadne in this scheme, as scholars observe, is an earth goddess whose subsequent fate is to go through a sacred marriage with Dionysus. The god of discontinuous conversion marries the goddess of continuous flow. This myth stands apart and around the heroic story of Theseus, giving that story a hieratic ritual framework and "meaning" in a larger cosmic scheme of things.

Yet our interest here cannot be in that larger schema, however tempting its Nietzschean resonance. The cord is a human artifice permitting the defeat of discontinuity. Without it, there would be an unbridgeable chasm between the inside and the outside of the maze; it bridges that gap. The problem of the labyrinth is to bridge such gaps. The result of not bridging them is "lost direction." The cord works because it restates the hero's problem. He no longer needs a sense of direction; all he needs is continuity with the outside, with Ariadne's hand. By definition, anyway, a sense of direction is what the labyrinth forces one to lose. There may be direction in the original Daedalian map of the maze, but there is none in the lived experience of the maze.

In "Ariadne's Thread: Repetition and the Narrative Line," J. Hillis Miller describes a paradox of the thread, according to which "that thread maps the whole labyrinth, rather than providing a single track to its center and back out. The thread is the labyrinth, and at the same time it is the repetition of the labyrinth."[21] Miller means by this paradox the fact that the thread "threads" a space marked out by the "walls" of the maze, which, following Ruskin's insight, are conceived as "spectral," not real walls. Ruskin says, *"Had* the walls been real, instead of ghostly, there would have been no difficulty whatever in getting either out or in, for you could go no other way. But if the walls were spectral and yet the transgression of them made your final entrance or return impossible, Ariadne's clue was needful indeed" (*Fors Clavigera*, XXIII).

The experience of the labyrinth, ghostly and spectral in its channeling, requires, on Miller's view, a full acceptance of endless doublings and "repetitions" within that scene of trial. As with the discernment of a "line of narrative" in a novel, here one must somehow read through multiple reduplications of an originally clear design, or map. What one reads for is continuity. But we ask, what is this continuity? How, given the increased complexity of maze-forms, does continuity increasingly evanesce?

The literature and art of the labyrinth (of virtually any type) indicates that a sense of direction implies a continuous linkage with the past. The "faculty" that fails to work in the maze is memory.

Proverbially, those who cannot remember the errors of the past are doomed to repeat them. The maze induces this forgetting. The story of Theseus makes much of forgetting, and not just the forgotten "way out." On two critical occasions after his escape from the labyrinth, Theseus forgets: he forgets Ariadne on the island of Naxos—he just leaves her there, forgotten; and he forgets to hoist the white sail to signal victory to his father, Aegeus. This act of forgetting drives Aegeus mad with despair; he does not wait to witness the disembarcation from the returning ship, and dives to his death in the sea which is thence named for him, the Aegean. Two forgettings, one of the Mother Goddess, Ariadne, the other of the actual father. A detour into the psychoanalytic history of the hero's destiny would clarify these mental separations from the parent; such separations (though not always through a process of mental repression) would seem necessary for the heroic career to proceed.

One might say that Theseus first experiences his own forgetting in the labyrinth, but because Ariadne gives him the clue, he is, without needing to know how, saved from knowing that experience in full. He begins his true heroic progress by a saving oblivion; after the escape, it is a question whether he does have this oblivion drawn to his attention. On the other hand, the "lost direction" of his labyrinthine oblivion was superseded by a "found direction," discovered on a higher level, that of pure continuity with the past, with the place *outside* the maze. The maze, it would seem, has an excessive presentness; it is a scene of too many instants, too much linear complexity.

This last is a critical factor in the imagery of the Cretan maze. In its pure form it is a flat layout, a plane figure, in which all choices of change of direction are made in a two-dimensional space. Daedalus, the inventor of the maze, knows about this inherent property of his invention. Thus, when imprisoned there by Minos, he adds a knowing third dimension, and flies out. What he gets, by adding the third dimension, is perspective *on*, to replace direction *in*. With every added dimension of perception of the maze, there will be an increase of power over the system of perilous convolutions. These perspectival distancings are mechanisms for achieving what direction alone must always lack, namely orientation. When a fourth dimension of time is added to the thinking of the maze, the traveler is able to know where he entered, what directional changes he has made by following the thread, what is the orientation of these changes, and what is the amount of the total sum of movements. This is precisely the kind of information required by any ocean voyager, if he is to travel toward any destination across the vast, undifferentiated plain of the sea. With such information in hand, the pilot knows where he is, a knowledge of present position entirely dependent upon a continuous link with the past.

It may be that the labyrinth, as image, goes thus quite beyond the phenomenal impression it makes, which is that of "lost direction." It suggests lost origin, lost direction, lost plan, lost orientation, lost position, in fact almost total loss of all controlling awarenesses of the complete manifold of any presentness. If one possessed the present completely, one would possess a summing mechanism in full and perfect operation, and that mechanism would be total memory. For the present in theory is a summation of an infinite past.

At the outer edge of the mythology of the maze there will always be found an insistent theme of the gaining and losing of a more or less complete remembrance.

A number of modern writers have leaned hard upon this theme. Borges imagines a highly "literary" cosmos, in which present narratives are composed of quotations, including quotations of literary styles, as when he imitates the inner cadences of some favorite author (Chesterton, Browne, Beckford, the Arabian Nights). Calvino always studies the reduplication of signs, motifs, narrative doublings, no matter what the scene of his fictions. With such authors the encounter with the Minotaur is endlessly varied in outward circumstances, but common to all such encounters is a projected yearning for an increase of dimensions of perspective, as the key to the loss of memory (and the regaining of the meaning of the memorious).

Modern authors, at least since Cervantes, Montaigne, Swift, and Sterne, agree that the original model (and "the point") of the labyrinth is the process of thinking itself, when that process is subjected to any deeply disorienting stress. Hawthorne is quite clear on this matter. His narrator, like his hero, treads "boldly into the inscrutable labyrinth. How this labyrinth was built is more than I can tell you. But so cunningly contrived a mizmaze was never seen in the world, before nor since. There can be nothing else so intricate, unless it were the brain of a man like Daedalus, who planned it, or the heart of any ordinary man; which last, to be sure, is ten times as great a mystery as the labyrinth of Crete."

Hawthorne chose his words carefully. In theory a perfectly designed automaton could thread the process of even a Daedalian brain. But the human heart is a metaphor for an essentially undecidable yearning. And this spiritual "machine," the heart, is the only guide in the valley of human, ordinary indecision. To allude to the heart is to allude to a dimension of perspective even beyond the summing dimensionality of perfect memoriousness. To allude to this sixth sense is to allude to the domain of spirit, an area beyond technology. To enter upon any discussion of such an area would be to mystify criticism, and we may draw back.

The struggle of recent critical theory has been unusually painful, perhaps because there exists a climate in which it is embarrassing to speak openly of the domain of spirit. Yet, what else has Harold Bloom been talking about, if not *spiritual* "crossings?"[22] What else has given Frye's work its continuing force, if not its connection with that vast, intersecting verbal system of Strange Loops, the Bible? What else gave Milton's poetry its sublime signifying tension, if not the collision (the leap?) between Classical and Christian myth? Similar discontinuous leaps of level, similar Gödelian/Escherian undecidables occur throughout the Romantic tradition, which plays a naturally precursive role in the drama of our critical thought. Our critics have been variously seeking to prevent the illusion that the entrance into the centre of the pan-textual maze is an infinite regress. Instead, as Hofstadter has shown, there may be natural perspectives available to the hero in the maze, of "what is, and is not." Hofstadter sketches the idea of the Strange Loop as a phenomenon where "by moving upwards (or downwards) through the levels of some hierarchical system, we *unexpectedly* find ourselves right back where we started."[23] A system of Strange Loops is called a "tangled hierarchy." That is the perfect definition of a maze, whether of the pure Cretan type or the extended *intrico* type. It would appear, then, that a return to Frye's "image of lost direction" will prove particularly fruitful in times like our own, where hierarchies appear nothing if not tangled. The exit into light is sure to be unexpected.

13. *Style and the Extreme Situation*

Literary style lives and breathes exactly in that space, that interval, where the text meets the reader. The first thing we encounter, with any text, is its style. Style names the front, the arming, of the text. Yet not every individual style affronts the reader to make its point. Some styles are deliberately neutral or easy and perspicuous. Only those that concern me here, Patagonian word games as I call them, styles in extremis, affront by their strangeness.

A critical concern with such matters is not new. Longinus theorized about rhetorical excess in his treatise *On the Sublime.* The ancient rhetorician Demetrius said: "Metaphor is dangerous." Poetry threatens sense, science, and logic. Plato's visionary manias, including the poet's, partake of a similar danger and risk. If we isolate the most powerfully idiosyncratic styles, the oddest of odd mixtures, we again find ourselves on hazardous ground. What follows is a sidelong inquiry into these hazards and their darker purpose.

Style, a planetary term, wanders about like a monad: sometimes it refers to artistic technique; sometimes to manner, manners, and mannerisms; sometimes to these functions seen diachronically, sometimes to their synchronic description; sometimes to an innate or mastered skill of performance; sometimes to flair and sensibility; sometimes to rhetorical effects (the deictics of "point" and "statement," as with interior decoration or the color of a Maserati); sometimes to notions of harmony, control, elegance, economy, taste, and what in American slang is called "class"—John O'Hara said that *Across the River and into the Trees* had "real class." Finally, style is loosely used to indicate structural principles—we find this with writings on architecture—though more properly it should point to the architectonics of the work, as Sir Philip Sidney stated long ago.

Reflection on the wide variety of common uses of the term suggests that we should not seek to entrap the word *style*. We should work simply in the field of its wandering, as with any other planetary term. We must accept the openness of the field. Middleton Murry once observed that "a discussion of the word Style, if it were pursued with only a fraction of the rigour of a scientific investigation, would inevitably cover the whole of literary aesthetics and the theory of criticism."

A similar ballooning occurs when style becomes the object of specific analytic study. Some years ago, reviewing Nils Erik Enkvist's *Linguistic Stylistics*, Samuel R. Levin observed this field diffusion:

> Stylistics is a large and sprawling field. Marks have been left upon it by rhetoricians, dialectologists, literary critics, factor analysts, aestheticians, linguists, information theorists, textual critics, statisticians, psychologists, and computer technicians—to give a partial list. Stylistics evokes such a wealth and diversity of responses because it offers a variety of purchase points for its consideration and discussion. . . . From this complexity in the empirical state of affairs [there is a text, this text was written by someone under certain conditions of time, place, and circumstance and is read by another under different conditions of time, place, and circumstance (the foregoing being obviously simplified)], there arise both the manifold definitions of style (and hence also of stylistics) and their typical failure to represent [style] to everyone's satisfaction.[1]

Fundamentally, Levin is reminding us of the eternal war between subjective response and objectively determinable features of text and context. I believe we invoke style in order to play between these two domains (as Levin too believes), and so long as we recognize that there is no magic way to escape this maze except to stay active within it, we shall not suffer too much anxiety.

In ordinary social situations this anxiety is more or less painful—one does what one can, to achieve a modicum of stylistic individuality and harmony. If a lady and gentleman arrive at a formal occasion wearing egregiously informal costumes, they do threaten the assembly; but the degree of threat implied by the egregious is always proportional to the tightness of the group, and groups have complex ways of rejecting and assimilating a wide range of eccentricities, a wide range of humors. Any group that can openly admit the threat of "difference from the group norm" will always feel less anxious. Interesting cases among writers who transgress a social norm occur when there is a strong professional unity of correct style, as when Erich Segal, a classical scholar, wrote *Love Story,* or—a more interesting case—when William Gass, a philosopher, dazzles and dances in the ballroom of the personal essay.

In the following pages there will not, however, be much in the way of social analysis, though such an inquiry would naturally flow from certain notions that arise. For present purposes I keep my notion of style rather loose. Let us say it refers, in what follows, to the rhythmic articulation of a surface; it links with structure only insofar as it faces or bodies forth that structure. But in any case style is not structure; rhythmic, it always implies movement, motion, vibration, vibrance—the segmentation and continuity of flow. Nor is it mechanical; machines, however complex their motions, have no style in a significant sense. Machines eject style from process. As Schleiermacher saw, the problem of style must include the less effable problem of manner. *Manner* names an almost hidden aspect (a paradox, therefore) of what is going on close to the immediate surface of the work of art. A subsurface ripple. Just under the surface, so to speak, the manner of a work talks back and forth to the inner and the outer membranes.

To be told that manner, if not style, shows itself "just beneath the surface" of the artwork may strike the reader as mystical. I have no desire to be mysterious. All I have in mind is that one can objectively extract from any text the features of syntax, lexis, and so on, and this extraction occurs precisely at the surface of the work. But as Levin's review of Enkvist maintained, the responses of readers so vary and complicate their own processing of surface features that "something" stylistic occurs that cannot be deduced merely from an assembly of the extracted features. We today may not yet be in any position to account exactly for that something, but we are aware it occurs. My impression of Schleiermacher's hermeneutic project is that he gives what I am calling a "just beneath the surface" function to the interpreter's play of mind, a play corresponding to a similar play that partly generated the text to be read. A later aphorism, dated Friday, 23 March 1810, virtually says that the reader must look inside the author's mind: "(1) Combining the objective and the subjective so that the interpreter can put himself 'inside' the author. (2) On understanding the author better than he understands himself . . ."[2] Schleiermacher sees that writing occurs in a mental context, a context where the "mental" role of words is not clearly definable but where we should never neglect our uncertainty as to what authors are thinking of when choosing their words, because surely they think of something besides or beyond those mere words and the choices to be made among available words.

The process I have just called "thinking" is the unclear part of the poetic or hermeneutic labor, and I cannot clarify of what it consists. But the marvellous articulation of the poem, the speech, the play, the novel, the essay, and the like—this working of words involves feelings in the activity Hart Crane used to call "poetic logic." And logic suggests thought, albeit thought conditioned by emotional climate. Thus Schleiermacher observes,

> The coherence of the leading ideas [of the work] is recognized along with the author's peculiar view of the subject matter of the work. The coherence of the secondary representations is to be recognized from the relationship between the author's ability to use ideas and the subject matter of the work—with the interest he had in one thing or another, especially during the preparation of the work, and therefore with the entire relation of his personality to the work. Consequently, it is especially important to trace, in addition to the actual train of thought, the sequence of the leading and secondary ideas as they are interwoven.[3]

What follows in Schleiermacher's draft is a sketchy outline of questions that arise when we ask, in effect, how an author finds a style or manner of expression that indicates "leading thoughts." The philosopher distinguishes a wide range of authorial situations and verbal capacities that enable—but may also interfere with—this task. The complexity of the artist's task (and the interpreter's) lies in the understanding of an ever-shifting interplay between leading thoughts and the means of "secondary representations"—it is the mental interplay, not the linguistic elements as such, that needs to be considered.

On this basis we are justified in speculating about the subsurface activity of the verbal artifact, as if indeed we might try to understand authors better than they understood themselves. We never shall, of course, but we may act as if we could. The task, we admit, is impossible. Yet we undertake it, in part for the sake of interpreting any specific work, but also—and this is necessary too—that we may begin to see how a theory of any type of work may be produced. In this case theory will lift the notion of style to a higher level of generality than is required for its use in connection with the specific work. To grasp style technically, to extract stylistic features, we need only record what is in a work, linguistically, and how it is set forth as narrative, drama, argument, and so on. But to grasp a particular style of a particular work as belonging to the larger domain where style is a basic purpose of making texts (or speeches) in general, we shall have to think about authors' mental, emotional, and spiritual states as they undertake the practice of art. In terms of those odd touches of manner that so interested Schleiermacher, we shall have to shift from idiosyncrasies of style to styles of idiosyncrasy.

Style and idiosyncrasy have long been associated terms. The *idiosynkrasis* (the "odd, peculiar, or strange mixture") rests on a deeper sense of the term, the mix of *ta idia* ("things that are one's own; one's private affair"). Tradition woos us with the idea that style may be understood in terms of that which marks it, namely the personal idiosyncrasy of the author's literary manner. But do we understand much about oddness itself, about the conditions and nature of excess that is marked or signaled as the expression of some overpowering privacy? Idiosyncrasy itself is the obscure aspect of the problem of style. We need, as Mary Ann Caws has suggested, to examine styles of idiosyncrasy before we can be sure we are ready to speak of the idiosyncrasies of style. The two phrases are not quite symmetrically reversible. Idiosyncrasies of literary style occur and persist in any author's work for reasons that go beyond the mere literarity of that work, reasons that involve "extreme situations." In my own shorthand I call these situations Patagonian, and their writing I call Patagonian word games—after the early and modern explorers of that "uttermost part of the earth." Patagonia, the metaphorical Patagonia, names a state of mind and feeling virtually entrapped in the regions of deep paradox.

To introduce some notions of this entrapment (and escape?) I have chosen to discuss two apparently different authors, whose works are strange, with a strangeness that tests the larger implications of the problem of style.

My first case is the last known letter written by the English poet John Clare. We presume that a Dr. Edwin Wing addressed the letter for him. We know that Clare wrote the letter, in his own hand, with his own pen, and signed it. The letter went to James Hipkins, an "unknown inquirer from the outside world," as certain editors call him, about whom we know nothing except that this letter was indeed sent to him. At the time of transmission, 8 March 1860, John Clare was an inmate of Saint Andrew's Asylum, Northampton. He had been in that asylum, by this date, for some twenty years.

Clare was doubtless crazy, lucid at intervals. He thought he had two wives—the first was nonexistent; he suffered from other wilder hallucinations. His madness was tragic. To James Hipkins he wrote as follows:

March 8th, 1860

Dear Sir

I am in a Madhouse & quite forget your Name or who you are You must excuse me for I have nothing to communicate or tell of & why I am shut up I don't know I have nothing to say so I conclude

Yours respectfully
John Clare[4]

Odd this certainly is—also, is it not humorous? It would make a fitting document for the final pages of *Jokes and the Unconscious* or Freud's late essay "Humor."

We can begin by asking where, in the letter, any stylistic oddity resides. Surely, on the plane of genre, where the writer has somehow twisted the form chosen, the genre "personal letter." Frame analysis gives the following:

Date

Opening salutation (Dear Sir)

the text proper
transition element (so I conclude)

closing salutation (Yours respectfully)
signature (John Clare)

***Style and the Extreme Situation* 249**

Genre normalizes. The older manner of personal correspondence was generally more formal than our own, but a more or less formal salutation tends to frame any letter—a "letter" is what is thus framed.

In this case the closing "Yours respectfully" rings peculiarly odd—an empty shell of decorum, proper to communicating with a friendly stranger and yet here eccentric to the main text. Body and limbs are somehow not working together as they should. At least, frame and text interact in a weird, slightly spastic fashion, as if Clare (without expressly intending it) were asking James Hipkins (and now us) to consider what indeed respect and regard amount to, when directed to a correspondent from "the uttermost part of the earth." Normal retroactivity, re-specting and re-garding, are all rendered baseless.

Having claimed that Clare (witting or not—it hardly matters) has achieved an oddness in relation to generic frame, the standard letter form, we could equally wish to argue that he is not so very deviant after all—and on quite ordinary grounds. The personal letter permits a loose and infinitely open and variable shaping of its matter. Of all genres it is, with the private diary, capable of greatest unselfconsciousness about the writer's own thought connections, feelings, language, and unbuttoned self.

Byron, for example, says whatever he pleases in his letters. He moves freely at lightning speed from one item to another. His spirit, what Schleiermacher understood as the entire relation of personality to work, is such that the oddest mixtures cohere. Passion and brilliant verbal adolescence override any pedantic need for reasons and explanations; Byron just lets things happen. John Clare, who hallucinated at times that he was Lord Byron, had always gone his lordship one better in the matter of epistolary form and style: he typically punctuates with dashes; he omits the period at the close of every paragraph of his letters, which is not so surprising as at first it appears—there are scarcely any periods at all in his correspondence, early or late. Clare, like Byron, knew this to be part of a style. To Chauncy Townshend, he had written in 1820 that "Letter writing is a thing I give no brush of correction or study too—tis just set down as things come to my 'tongue's end'." Clare had never constructed or composed his letters. He allowed the tumble of streaming thought to take its own way. Point and punctuation were not for him.

Their absence or mystification constitutes a style, however. The chosen frame of "personal letter" permits this choice.

Analogously, throughout the vast territories of literature forms abound, to enable the framing of different idiosyncrasies of style. The drama directly controls voice and distributes voices among different characters; so, more narrowly, the voices resound in the dramatic monologue and its introspective precursor, the Shakespearean soliloquy; so also the personal essay; so the novel; so also the lyric, especially in its modern deformities—one could extend the list of permissive forms far and wide.

The opposite applies in technical writing, which tends to rinse out the oddness of the author's own private mannerisms. Is oddness then the enemy of the technical, where standardized, repeatable, numberable language is the final goal? The current of such discourse does seem to drift away from or against the current of individual differences, at least in normal science. Only when science reaches out to the edges of its unknown does its language begin to acquire a more poetic—that is, idiosyncratic—flavor. The real language of science—mathematics—becomes no less idiosyncratic as the data to be explained become more and more extreme, as they approach the status of "naked singularities."

All this is only to say that much concerning idiosyncratic styles can be done by analysis of frames and norms and by deviance from them.

As a goal or purpose or hidden agenda, however, idiosyncratic style (occurring for my purposes in nontechnical imaginative literature) is rather a kind of self-expression, interesting in and for itself.

Starting from norm and deviation, we get idiosyncrasies of style. But starting from the manner itself, we get into the problem of styles of idiosyncrasy. This second field overarches the first and forces us to speculate more freely about the normality and oddness of oddness.

In this light one notices that John Clare's letter presents a paradoxical conniption of oddness. At first hearing or first reading, the note to Hipkins is a shock. But to what, exactly, in our expectations is it a shock? The question arises as to what makes for a normal communication emanating from an insane asylum. Let me quote the letter again.

March 8th 1860

Dear Sir

I am in a Madhouse & quite forget your Name or who you are You must excuse me for I have nothing to communicate or tell you of & why I am shut up I don't know I have nothing to say so I conclude

Yours respectfully
John Clare

This time, the letter appears perfectly sane. Clare states that communication itself is puzzling to him, which is surely the most analytically intelligent sort of reflection. What, he asks, should he talk about, given that in "prison," as he elsewhere called the asylum, there is no "about." That is why the letter appears to come from beyond the grave. It is *outre tombe*. In higher style it might have been penned by a resident of the inferno, or Dante's limbo. The effect is ghostly. The dangerous linguistic site, as Foucault would call the asylum, is a first-order Patagonian locus; the asylum defeats communication, and the extreme situation is actual and objective. It could be located: Saint Andrew's Asylum, Northampton (in the Midlands), in the year 1860, on the eighth day of March.

The question that counts, however, is just how Clare relates to this objectivity of site. If we decide that Clare (an author who, like Hölderlin, wrote some of his most powerful poems while certifiably "mad") remains painfully clearheaded and perspicuous about his extremity, then we shall have discovered a paradox of writing in the extreme situation. The more perspicuous and incisive Clare's vision of his state, the more lucidly he expresses his own insanity. If he were not mad, he would make small talk. It is true, he may only have lost his short-term memory, so far as anything this letter alone can tell us. Yet we suspect a madness of some kind— the madness of an undue or misplaced or displaced perspicuity. (This condition, we are told, characterizes certain forms of schizophrenia—the splitting allows moments of clarity to alternate with moments of darkness.) Perhaps only the rhythm of repetition in this letter provides the clue. My method has been to trust the text completely, and I am left with the impression that whatever is most illuminated about Clare's letter is what feels like madness.

There is a factor of naming and lost naming, which in due course I want to bring into my speculations. For the moment it suffices to point out the local, situational aspect of Clare's oddness—the Patagonian aspect of things here. A double-binding linguistic event (the mutual antagonism of frame and textual body) makes it impossible for us to decide where lie the edges between inside and outside Clare's word space, his "asylum." The letter shows its author searching for that boundary, which he cannot find, because he is on it. "Give me a place to stand, and I will move the world." The arrested liminality is complete. It can only generate more of the same. Utter oddness comes to be absolute sameness.

Postmodernist criticism tends to discover such documents and then to erect virtually metaphysical capriccios around their inscrutable self-contradictions. We do better to recall that Clare is objectively anchored in fact, when he writes, "I am in a Madhouse." This clearly stated avowal is the base for all the subsequent disorientation. It would have been less disturbing to us, had Clare written, "They claim this is a madhouse . . . I know better; but they will not let me out, because I am indeed mixed up, and a nuisance." No, not so. He says, "I am in a Madhouse," and goes on to make some brief remarks about how it all works in a madhouse. For these reasons we are drawn to emphasize the letter genre, which is the vestigial frame of Clare's sanity, that structure still persisting from a world outside the asylum. Only on a higher level of interpretation, when we raise the whole question of this letter's meaning to a higher perspective, do we discover that there is no way of knowing whether in Gödelian terms the letter is inconsistent or incomplete. In the realm of language it appears that a system can oscillate forever between the two states of lack. Sometimes Clare's letter seems complete but inconsistent; sometimes consistent, but incomplete. Gödel's proof could now be renamed "Clare's Final Madhouse Theorem." Gödel's proof applies to any situation extreme enough to raise questions about man's actual relations to the more intransigent paradoxes of self-reflexivity. As with Bruce Chatwin's journey "in Patagonia," we can ask if Clare's mental and physical state prevents any resolution of the endless Gödelian debate.

What needs to be hammered home is that with any valid case of extremely odd mixture, of deep idiosyncrasy, we cannot tell where to look for the origin of the oddness. Shall we look in mind (the "inner"), or in situation (the "outer")? The two are confounded. Absolute oddness melts and merges the solid ground of difference. Stylistic suicide is the next and final step, and I follow classical stylistic wisdom in this regard: classical stylists have always said that any pervasive and exaggerated trait of style will undermine its initially delightful or animating effect; it will kill the effect it was intended to produce. With Clare, of course, the problem of style has gone right out of orbit. We can still speak of a problem of style correctly, in this case, only because of the almost studied perfection of the way Clare uses genre frame and his own easy epistolary rhythms to effect his escape from earth's gravitation. It is as if he had waited many years to be able to write this perfect "letter from an asylum." The letter is a supreme fiction. It defies augury. It is a tale of cock and bull. It goes nowhere.

Transition to a Description of the Opposite Case of Odd Mixtures

Antinomies are boring, infinitely replaceable by one another, but they are useful and apparently irresistible. A structuralist could make up a list of binary oppositions to cover Clare's letter, and it would generate arguments about the writer and his writing. Instead of a grid of binaries I shall now resort to a single one that seems applicable to the problem of writing in general: either the author's mind is too full of words or too empty. By words I mean words that the author can use. Shakespeare uses about thirty thousand words in his canon, Racine about two thousand. The one is perhaps too full of words, the other too empty of words. Instead of saying, then, that authors are either inside their lexica or outside them, I shall say that they are either filled or emptied by them. (There might be a useful analogy to be drawn from the art of cuisine.) Relatively, this is only to say that full/empty is only the extreme situation of the classical stylist's principle of a natural economy of literary means—that is, the "nothing too much" of ancient Greek wisdom.

Clare's case suggests a dictionary bled white. Earlier he had loved earth, its creatures, its pools, streams, bushes, thorns, and rinds—he tells us in one prose piece how the bark of trees in spring "kindles" into a new birth every year. Clare the naturalist, whether in poem or prose, achieves a miraculous passivity for years, standing empty before nature, letting it fill him, letting it instigate a play of his mind—the naming game. He bows before nature. Ashbery's prose poem, "For John Clare," salutes the clarity of this homage: "Kind of empty in the way it sees everything, the earth gets to its feet and salutes the sky."[5] Earth-Clare is also empty in the way he sees everything. He looks and bows to the sky, as to his own reflection in a mirror, and knows his own emptiness.

In Peter Neumeyer's *Homage to John Clare*, itself a Patagonian work, there is a footnote on emptiness and the poet in his madness:

During the asylum years there was a period of time during which Clare would capitalize the initial letters of words,—later he would write in a code omitting all vowels. In 1860 [the year of our letter]—very late in his life, when much of his reason had deserted him—he attributed his inability to write to the fact that "they have cut off my head, and picked out all the letters of the alphabet—all the vowels and consonants—and brought them out through my ears; and they want me to write poetry! I can't do it."[6]

That is what I mean by emptiness, and if you must go to a schizophrenic to find it in extremis, of course that is where and how far you must go.

You go to art movements like minimalism, or to the greater emptiness of Beckett, to a work like Beckett's *Sans*, which reduces the story of Job to a series of twenty-four revolving paragraphs that turn round and round on slight additions and subtractions made on the ground of its first paragraph:

Ruins true refuge long last towards which so many false time out of mind. All sides endlessness earth sky as one no sound no stir. Grey face two pale blue little body heart beating only upright. Blacked out fallen open four walls over backwards true refuge issueless.[7]

My sense is that while all the phrasal units recur in some form or other, the generative phrase is "only upright," that is, a deprivation not preventing a sense of deprivation. One is held, in short, without.

The other side of the coin is the case of excessive fullness, a fullness that might result from any number of *engloutissements*.

The case I choose is the fullness of a certain kind of charm: the charm of idle curiosity. The example is John Aubrey (1626–1697), the celebrated, slightly mad antiquarian biographer of Elizabethan and seventeenth-century men and women. Anthony Wood, rival and contemporary, called Aubrey "roving and maggoty-headed." His mind, from his youngest years, was a kind of informational sluice. Friends expected him to fall and break his neck, running downstairs to catch one last anecdote from a departing guest. Despite a lifelong serious interest in mathematics and science, he instinctively chose to chronicle the uncountable odd bits of gossip that alone could show that X or Y actually lived and breathed. Aubrey could accept the most dubious evidence. He gathered stories as if he intended to live forever, and the *Brief Lives* treats over 425 individuals. Why so many lives? one wonders, until one recalls that Aubrey mourned the loss or transformation of a whole world, the England as it existed before the Civil War. Science and scientific learning fascinated him, but the pervasive tone of his *Lives* is nostalgic royalism, with its belief that the ancient magic of "the land" was the chief support of permanent worth.

Aubrey never published the *Lives*. Each biography is in principle incompletable, hence consistent at least with its open-ended mode of production. The manuscripts agglomerated while to the main pages of a given life were added the later marginalia, the "one more story" that would confer actuality, for certain, on its subject. There could never be too many stories, no matter how tangential or even absurd they might look to a more analytic biographer. For Aubrey was collecting materials sufficient to furnish an old curiosity shop. The abiding mood is one of almost overpowering affection for his subjects. Like Herodotus, on his humbler plane, he is the curator of legend.

Thus, of Dr. Ralph Kettel, the president of Trinity College, Oxford (1563–1643), he writes:

> He dyed a year after I came to the Colledge, and he was then a good deal above 80, and he had a fresh ruddy complexion. He was a tall well-growne man. His gowne & surplice & hood being on, he had a terrible gigantique aspect with his sharp grey eyes . . . One of the Fellowes (in Dr. Francis Potter's time) was wont to say that Dr. Kettel's braine was like a Hasty-Pudding, where there was Memorie, Judgmente and Phancy all just so jumbled together. If you had to doe with him, taking him for a Foole, you would have found in him great subtlety and reach; *e contra*, if you treated him as a Wise man you should have mistaken him for a Foole . . . He was irreconcileable to long haire; called them hairy Scalpes, and as for Periwigges (which were

then very rarely worn) he beleeved them to be Scalpes of men cutte off after they were hang'd, and so tanned and dressed for use. When he observed the Scholars haire longer than ordinary (especially if they were Scholars of the House) he would bring a paire of Cizers in his Muffe (which he commonly wore) and woe be to them that sate on the outside of the Table. I remember he cutt Mr. Radford's haire with the knife that chipps the bread on the Buttery Hatch, and then he sang (this is in the old play of *Gammer Gurton's Needle*):

> And was not Grim the Collier finely trimm'd?
> Tonedi, Tonedi.

Mr. Lydell, said he, how do you decline tondeo? Tondeo, tondes, Tonedi?

He was constantly at Lectures and Exercises in the Hall, to observe them, and brought along with him his Howerglasse; and one time, being offended with the Boyes, he threatened them that if they did not doe their exercise better, he would bring an Howerglasse two hours long.

Aubrey recalls, too, that during the Civil War a Parliament soldier broke in, while Kettel lectured on rhetoric, and smashed his hourglass.

Aubrey loves an eccentric. One movement of his thought is away from the center of normal behavior. His own life, reported in Oliver Lawson Dick's Aubreyan introduction to the 1949 edition of *Brief Lives*, never went right and smooth until he had lost his considerable fortune—a series of incurable erotic and monetary bafflements preceded Aubrey's later complete enslavement by antiquarian obsession. So he tends to notice how obsessions may rule human lives. Of William Outram he notes only that he was "a tall spare leane pale consumptive man; wasted himself much, I presume, by frequent preaching." Aubrey, as Dick says, had such a reductive and epithetic skill "that he could conjure a living being out of a mere *list* of facts," thus: "Mrs. Abigail Slope, borne at Broad Chalke, near Salisbury, A.D. 1648. Pride; lechery; ungratefull to her father; married; runne distracted; recovered." And another such list:

Richard Stokes, M.D. His father was Fellow of Eaton College. He was bred there and at King's College. Scholar to Mr. W. Oughtred for Mathematiques (Algebra). He made himself mad with it, but became sober again, but I feare like a crackt-glasse. Became a Romancatholique: maried unhappily at Liege, dog and catt, etc. Became a Sott. Dyed at Newgate, Prisoner for debt 1681.

The sequence "runne distracted–recovered" fascinates Aubrey. Equally fascinating to him are body language and those windows to the soul, the eyes, of which he has the portraitist's keen awareness—for instance, James Bovey, Esquire: "a dark hazell eye"; Venetia Digby: "Her face, a short ovall; dark browne eie-browe about which much sweetnesse, as also the opening of the eie-lids"; Sir Walter Raleigh: "He had a most remarkable aspect, an exceedingly high forehead, long-faced and sour eie-lidded, a kind of pigge-eie." The eyes of his friend Thomas Hobbes elicited an unusually lengthy description:

> He had a good eie, and that of a hazell colour, which was full of Life and Spirit, even to the last. When he was earnest in discourse, there shone (as it were) a bright live-coale within it. He had two kinds of looks: when he laugh't, was witty and in a merry humour, one could scarce see his Eies; by and by, when he was serious and positive, he open'd his eies round (i.e. his eie-lids.) He had midling eies, not very big, nor very little.

That such physical details are not trivial in Aubrey's work is to be seen in the recurrence of the eye motif. To the following picture of the poet John Denham, the motif gives a culminating focus:

> Sir John Denham was unpolished with the smallpox; otherwise a fine complexion. He was of the tallest, but a little incurvetting at his shoulders, nor very robust. His haire was but thin and flaxen, with a moist curle. His gate was slow, and was rather a Stalking (he had long legges). His Eie was a kind of light goose-grey, not big, but it had a strange Piercingnesse, not as to shining and glory, but (like a Momus) when he conversed with you he look't into your very Thoughts.

Quoting Aubrey for a systematic recurrence will give a skewed impression of his method. His method is to pursue the curious fact. Thus of Denham he further tells us that the poet suffered a seizure of ecstatic madness, during which he went to visit the king "and told him he was the Holy Ghost." "Runne distracted–recovered" applies here too (Denham recovered), but the charm of the curious detail was to persist beyond recovery: "His 2nd Lady had no child: was poysoned by the hands of the Countess of Rochester, with Chocolate."

Poisoned with chocolate! "How these curiosities would be quite forgott, did not such idle fellowes as I am putt them downe." "I have nothing to say so I conclude, Yours respectfully. . . ." Too full of words, too empty of words, the two worlds of the ground of oddness.

Yet to leave the matter here is to materialize the problem of style unduly. Something underlies this excessive emptiness and fullness, some kind of epistemic rule is governing the vacuity and the plethora. Otherwise there would be no resultant manner in Clare or Aubrey. What can we say of the problem of searching for such a rule? We can certainly see that style and manner are not mere matters of an itemized lexical numerosity; otherwise Aubrey would be plethoric merely as the Hammacher Schlemmer catalog is plethoric, the latter being odd and itemized enough to represent the word bank of any plethoric odd mixture of stylistic elements, in short, style as gadget list:

The World's Only Travel Steam Iron—La Valtromplina Nut and Bean Roaster—The Electronic Wine Guide—The English Heated Towel Stand—The Electric Shoe-Buffing Wand—The Rotating Electronic Chef—The Blomberg Solarium—The Osake Electric Massage/Stereo Chair—The Self-Adjusting Wide-Mouth Toaster—The Infrared Yard Sentry—The Wellington Boot Jack—The Best-Designed Travel Iron— The Sculler's Ergometer—Le Petit Electric Mincer—Electrically Heated Socks—Talking Clock—The Sonic 2000 Rodent Eliminator— The World's Best Corkscrew—The Nantucket Steamer—The Classic Syphon—Genuine Ostrich Plume Telescoping Duster—Squirrel-Proof Bird Feeder—The Talking Scale—The Double Wedge Electric Log Splitter—Solid Brass Spyglass—The Hammacher Schlemmer Winter Supplement—The Suburban Consumer—The Narcissism of Small Differences—The Anxiety of Influence—The Deconstruction—The Selfconsuming Artifact—The Fizzle—The Blanchot Folie Du Jour— The Misfits—The Original Maldoror Song Book—The Professional's Costume Stilts—The Hammacher Schlemmer Winter Supplement— The Definite Article—The Indefinite Article—The Alchemist—The Shifter—The End.

One can make a bad poem out of any list, or a good one. As by the same token, one can make good or bad poetry, develop a strong or feeble style, out of any truly reductive sequence of ideas such as we found in John Clare's letter. The pile of stuff or the reductive formula needs its appropriate manner, even when this pile or reduction is strange. Choice of topic is only the opening move. Here we must reach out toward a further speculation.

> But as the wind the waters stir
> The mirrors change and flye   (Clare, "A Song")
>
> The sea whispers me   (Whitman, *Song of Myself*)

The list of greatest poems, plays, novels, discourses, and so on does not easily come to include works written with highly idiosyncratic style. What is most valuable to us lies more in the middle range. No one denies that *Finnegans Wake* is amazing. Yet there is a human scale of values according to which a handful of Shakespeare sonnets is worth more than the whole *Wake*. If, however, it became possible for average intelligent readers to read the *Wake* without struggle, then the *Wake* might even surpass Shakespeare.

The value of the most eccentric works falls on another scale, yet it is not easy to say exactly what that scale measures. It seems to measure a literary activity akin to the production of the sublime, hence a Patagonian word game. One aspect of the sublime is its self-reflexive encounter with the means of its own coming into being. The characteristic trait of sublime works is the way they affront us with their medium. An Alpine poem will thrust on us rock words, cataract words, ice words, mass words, and so on. Such language is never drawn from the lexicon of ordinary speech, because that vocabulary would stop or deflate the elemental connection between the special (odd) words and their idea (in the poem). Or, to put it another way, ordinary language returns vision to the field of history and the irreversible passage of time, that field where we all live.

The superordinate category is the rhetoric of extreme situations, the sublime being only one such modality, the picturesque another, dada and *humour noir* another, Calvino's "cosmicomic" style another, and so on. What all strong idiosyncrasies of style have in common is a peculiar, undue thoughtfulness. Serious odd mixture is intended to show forth the almost verbal activity lying "just beneath the surface" of the work. The style, instead of being natural or transparent, is designedly opaque, but in a special sense: the aim is to produce a language that, instead of communicating something, reveals its own elemental laws and rhythms. Thus Clare's letter in effect draws on the logic of the liar's paradox (Epimenides the Cretan announces, "All Cretans are liars"). Aubrey's *Brief Lives*, it could be shown, draws on the logic of various paradoxes of infinity. Anthony Wood perceived the latter clearly. When Aubrey asked Wood, "Is my English style well enough?" the testy Oxonian replied, " 'Tis well. You should never ask these questions, but do them out of hand. *You have time enough*" (ci). Wood, an intelligent if bitter man, saw that Aubrey wrote in such fashion that for him there would always be time enough, since his whole method made the passage of time an issue in the work and in its coming into being. Only by doing too much could Aubrey know what would be enough. Which is another way of saying that an Aubrey is always testing something more fundamental than the materials (in his case, antiquarian data) at hand. Rather, he is testing the possibility of even doing antiquarian collection and narrative, testing a deeper logic.

The idiosyncratic author embeds the logical issue right in the utterance of this text, just beneath the surface, and thus leads the reader to notice always how the text is being uttered, to notice a certain opacity of the text. That is what strikes the reader of Whitman's and Poe's verses. Every odd stylistic mixture has a way of saying, like a child, "Look at me!" With Whitman, for example, one has to master the oddness until one can read through its opacity of participles, anaphoras, tone clusters, and so on and only then discover that on a certain plane of philosophic discourse Whitman is as clear as a bell. Hart Crane is a lesser Whitman, in this regard, but he was quite right to claim that he worked according to a "poetic logic" that only his baroque extravagance of diction could veil and reveal. A fortiori these remarks apply to Mallarmé and to Rimbaud.

Although he does not explain exactly how this works, as I too have failed to explain exactly how it works, Edward Sapir tried to describe what is really going on at the outer reaches of idiosyncrasy. In the final chapter of his *Language*, Sapir draws a contrast between scientific and imaginative literature or discourse: "There is really no mystery in the distinction . . . A scientific truth is impersonal, in its essence it is untinctured by the particular linguistic medium in which it finds expression. It can as readily deliver its message in Chinese as in English."[8] Sapir, who here regards thought as "nothing but language denuded of its outward garb," is of course thinking about a properly verbal scientific expression. He knew what Galileo had taught, that in the stricter sense numbers and mathematics constitute the natural language of science. "The proper medium of scientific expression is therefore a generalized language that may be defined as a symbolic algebra of which all known languages are translations. One can adequately translate scientific literature because the original scientific expression is itself a translation. Literary expression is personal and concrete, but this does not mean that its significance is altogether bound up with the accidental qualities of the medium" (223–224). The poet's Vichian use of myth would bear out this last statement, as would the Borgesian view of basic metaphors (for him the labyrinth is one). Sapir continues:

> A truly deep symbolism, for instance, does not depend on the verbal associations of a particular language but rests securely on an intuitive basis that underlies all linguistic expression. The artist's "intuition," to use Croce's term, is immediately fashioned out of a generalized human experience—thought and feeling—of which his own individual experience is a highly personalized selection. The thought relations in this deeper level have no specific linguistic vesture; the rhythms are free, *not bound, in the first instance,* to the traditional rhythms of the artist's language. (224; emphasis mine)

"In the first instance" seems to mean at some level of "thought relations" where a style evolves. Sapir wants to contrast two kinds of author, two styles, the normal and the odd. Two Sapirian instances of the normal, Shakespeare and Heine, achieve transparency and a kind of natural manner. They seem to have "known subconsciously to fit or trim the deeper intuition to the provincial accents of their daily speech. In them there is no effect of strain." Oddness, by contrast, does show strain.

> Certain artists whose spirit moves largely in the non-linguistic (better, in the generalized linguistic) layer even find a certain difficulty in getting themselves expressed in the rigidly set terms of their accepted idiom. One feels that they are unconsciously striving for a generalized art language, a literary algebra, that is related to the sum of all known languages as a perfect mathematical symbolism is related to all the roundabout reports of mathematical relations that normal speech is capable of conveying. Their art expression is frequently strained, it

sounds at times like a translation from an unknown original—which, indeed, is precisely what it is.

These artists—Whitmans and Brownings—impress us rather by the greatness of their spirit than the felicity of their art. Their relative failure is of the greatest diagnostic value as an index of the pervasive presence in literature of a larger, more intuitive linguistic medium than any particular language. (224)

With the classic artist of a natural economy of style the opposite is true, while there is little sign of struggle to reach back and down to Sapir's deeper level. With Heine, he observes, "one is under the illusion that the universe speaks German" (225). The linguistic material, the opacity of the poet's medium, "disappears," to use Sapir's word. Whereas with the artist of the odd mixture this sense of linguistic material increasingly pushes to the foreground.

There is then method in the madness of the odd manner. It is, on Sapir's view of Whitman and Browning, virtually a research project into theoretical linguistics—Chomsky *avant la lettre.* Our conclusion must then be that the idiosyncratic style provides the testing ground of that "literary algebra" which subtends any style, of any kind, including the classic style. Only by going to the verge of meaning can one discover the norms of meaning; only if someone twists and distends and extrudes and dilates the primary materials of discourse can it be seen where the normal styles are naturally at work and how these styles articulate the surfaces and subsurfaces of texts.

Taking a larger view of idiosyncrasy, I find it relates closely to the prophetic, which in turn always implicates the writer and reader, speaker and listener, in a consideration of thresholds—and, one might add, in the balancing of the too much and the too little, not as quantities but as qualities. Late in this century we have no comfortable terms with which to describe these relations. Pater, who thought deeply about such matters, wrote in his essay "On Style" that mind and soul need to be distinguished.

Hard to ascertain philosophically, the distinction is real enough practically, for they often interfere, are sometimes in conflict, with each other. Blake, in the last century, is an instance of preponderating soul, embarrassed, at a loss, in an era of proponderating mind. As a quality of style at all events, soul is a fact, in certain writers—the way they have of absorbing language, of attracting it into the peculiar spirit they are of, with a subtlety which makes the actual result seem like some inexplicable inspiration. By mind, the literary artist reaches us, through static and objective indications of design in his work, legible to all. By soul, he reaches us, somewhat capriciously perhaps, one and not another, through vagrant sympathy and a kind of immediate contact.[9]

We might instance others along with Blake. Our present critical activities have enabled us to decode authors like Blake—Frye's great career began in just such fashion, with a desire to decode a prophetic canon. What might be called high deconstruction is a prophetic mode of reading. We have come to appreciate those authors in whom there are grounds for such reading. Prophecy is the search for veiled, not buried, meaning, and it requires what Sapir called a "generalized linguistic," an underlying and yet not entirely lost order of language—perhaps only the memory of a lost harmony.

I should not leave my reader with the idea that authors like Clare and Aubrey, Whitman and Browning, were mad semioticians in search of a universal language. Though Gertrude Stein, just about the oddest of all authors who ever published, does often appear to follow that star. What I mean to say, as Stein might and indeed did sometimes say, is that certain authors force the fundamental question as to why and how they can be writing in the first place, as if they doubted their right to exist, as authors. Ben Jonson's aggressive and epochal publication of his *Works* (1616) betrays an intense self-doubt in this regard. Of all works for the theater written by Englishmen *The Alchemist* is, I think, by design lexically the most estrangingly strange; it has to be so, because Jonson in that play—which Coleridge called our most perfect comedy—discovered a deeper algebraic system (alchemy) through which he could explore the question, What indeed are the styles of idiosyncrasy? Whatever be our final answer, we can at least say they will result from some attempt to speak across a wide gap, as John Clare wrote his strange letter to "an unknown inquirer from the outside world."

Critical theory seeks to understand the gap across which the idiosyncratic author speaks. Recent critical parlance identifies various kinds of *aporia*, deep meaningless pits, pits of nonmeaning, various nothings. These appear to be moments in the discourse where the author reaches a final blanked-out area, where the "poetic logic" has led the text to a double bind, to a finally undecidable issue. Often such issues are contained in a single term—let us say, the "whiteness" of the whale in Melville, or the "perfect whiteness of the snow" of "the shrouded human figure," the final vision in *The Narrative of Arthur Gordon Pym*. A more radical example, one of the deepest in our literature, is given by the letter "O" in the play *Othello*. By the time we reach Mallarmé we discover that Sterne's blank page is scarcely framable, anymore, by the containing book or genre. With Mallarmé and the surrealists later, *the frame is blank*. Aporia is no longer the product of a certain line of discursive motion; it is now the process of that motion. In that state of thought and poetics we still in part share a certain terror: of frameless extremism.

The preceding pages have, I think, been speaking to such problems in a slightly less philosophical way than is usual. The kind of threatening gap that Clare and Aubrey illustrate has a look of the childish about it, as if they were children who could not "communicate" with grownups. Learning to speak, the child has either too few or too many words. I have not shown this, but I believe that the child's early and continuing encounters with language provide the model for Patagonian word games. Further research should reveal whether this is true or not.

The analogy between idiosyncrat and child has one final, furthering consequence: both are engaged in a struggle to acquire an adequate metalanguage for their expressive purposes. In this light extreme oddness seems to come from a defect of metalinguistic fluency. Hence the struggle! By contrast, normality in style, as elsewhere, seems to imply a power of drawing easily at all times on multiple systems of linguistic self-regulation, namely on the perspective powers of metalanguage.

14. Stevens and the Influential Gnome

In a review of *Transport to Summer* by Wallace Stevens, R. P. Blackmur wrote, "This is a poetry of repetitions, within the poem and from poem to poem." What is true of this volume of verse is true for Stevens's production in general. More than most poets he makes us aware that poetry, understood to mean poems, commonly repeats where prose departs anew. Prose may exhibit recurrences of phrasal, narrative, or discursive elements, but poetry is the definitive verbal art of intensified recurrence; literally, its verses turn and return. While metrical techniques permit repetitions of form and rhythm, the poet may also repeat favored motifs and images on the thematic plane. A personal rhythm always results: the poet's signature.

Blackmur is not alone in observing the repetitive aspect of Stevens's work. Frank Kermode, Northrop Frye, and Harold Bloom have shared such a view. Kermode thought the repetitions in Stevens egregious. Frye observed the poet's method of avoiding monotony: "We cannot read far in Wallace Stevens' poetry without finding examples of a form that reminds us of the variation in music, in which a theme is presented in a sequence of analogous but different settings." Frye instances "Thirteen Ways of Looking at a Blackbird" where the varied recapitulation of the common blackbird theme "gives more the effect of a chaconne or passacaglia." This musical parallel, which certainly fits a poet in the High Romantic tradition, indicates that repetitions need not always be discernible at first sight. When the poet, like the composer, uses a technique of free variation-form, the persistently repeated elements may not stand out. Yet they are present in the texture of the poem, and they avoid monotony through the magic of variation.

In a commentary on "Domination of Black,"[1] Harold Bloom observes that Stevens "knows fully what it may mean to say that the colors of the fallen leaves are *'repeating* themselves.' Thirty times and more in the next forty years Stevens's poetry would repeat, crucially, some form of the word 'repeat,' until Stevens could write of his Penelope meditating the repetitious but never culminating return of her Ulysses:

> She would talk a little to herself as she combed her hair,
> Repeating his name with its patient syllables,
> Never forgetting him that kept coming constantly so near."

Bloom identifies the onset of the art of repetition with the significant beginning of Stevens's achieved success. This view implies that, for reasons which need to be examined, the Stevensian vision of life required a developed art of recurrence beyond the usual levels of repetition associated with verse as a medium of thought and feeling.

The fact of recurrence is not hard to document in Stevens: archetypally recurrent seasons, quasi-liturgical orders deriving from early religious experience, the nagging of certain metaphysical quandaries, phases of traditional philosophic rehearsal in ethics and aesthetics, recurrences within a lexicon of punning and word-play, certain stamps of metrical order that return with the football of a steady march, the gait of a determined long-distance walker—there are indeed many sides to the Stevensian cycle, and these have received critical attention. Laury Magnus has defined the microstructures of Stevensian iterative syntax in her book *The Track of the Repetend*. The myth of seasonal cycles is perhaps the most powerful of recurrences. Here spring, summer, autumn, winter are as richly, and more systematically, developed in their archetypology than with any of the great Romantics. By allowing force and position to the seasons, Stevens provides a recurrent mythic ground (as in an immense chaconne) for the central and centrally recurrent natural motif—the sun as First Idea.

A similar repetition occurs with the Evening Star, to which Barbara Fisher has drawn particular attention in her book on Stevens,

The Intensest Rendezvous. Vesper is especially critical to our sense of an iterative "nature" in Stevens, since the natural star can transform itself into an artificial candle flame—down from the heavens to earth and the poet's study. Interchanges of celestial and terrestrial permit recurrence as alternation of scale. Like a clock thrown out into space to test the theory of relativity, the intimate domestic candle flame is cast out to become the Evening Star, which then returns as candle flame. Esoteric and exoteric keep changing places. The farthest notion of a divinity, the Sun, becomes the strong man, while the ethereal space of interacting ideas becomes an actual New Haven, or an actual Hartford, in an actual state (or is it "state"?), Connecticut.

Such instances of the mythic structuring of Stevensian space suggest that the poet is always inventing a malleable, flexible, fusible universe, in which mythic or other motifs recur on different scales of magnitude. Shelleyan, even Blakean, in its metamorphic variety of scene, this universe of turning and returning is firmly grounded in High Romantic discourse. Yet this High Romantic mythography is not the most "egregious" of repetitions in Stevens. There is another field of repetition far more powerful even than the poet's Sun or Evening Star. This is the repetition of elements in the language of mind.

A special problem arises when one describes what mind means to Stevens. So fully does the nature of mind preoccupy him that after a certain point in his career (and this occurs perhaps as early as 1921 with "The Snow Man" and certainly from the late 1930s until his death), he seems unable to write poetry without adverting to the theme. His lecture of 1948, "Imagination as Value," indicates the source of the concern for mind. Stevens says: "We live in the mind . . . If we live in the mind, we live with the imagination." One of the *Adagia* announces that "we have to step boldly into man's interior world or not at all." When Stevens asks, what is it to live in the mind with the imagination, the mind appears to be a place and imagination appears to be a demiurgic instrument. The imagination, he later says, "is the power that enables us to perceive the normal in the abnormal, the opposite of chaos in chaos." This ordering view of imagination derives from Romantic theorizing about the nature of poetry, as, for example, in Coleridge's *Biographia Literaria*. For Stevens, as for Coleridge, the imagination is a creative, "esemplastic" power, which shapes images and ideas of the confusion of the world into visionary orders, or "poems." We are not surprised, therefore, to find that Roy Harvey Pearce devoted a chapter to Stevensian imagination in *The Continuity of American Poetry*. Since Stevens closely identifies the poetic with the imaginative, it is further not surprising that he could say: "Poetry is the subject of the poem." To a degree, this statement means narrowly, as Joseph Riddel and others have shown, that here poetry is a Symbolist combination of magic words. From start to finish, Stevens displays a firm belief in the force of verbal magic, although it is more spectacular in his early orotund poetic diction. What is less obvious is that such magic acquires its compelling "nobility" by virtue of a special derivation. It is precisely the language of mental process that is most magical.

For Stevens, the earliest determining precursor of this theurgy is doubtless Shelley. Shelley's "Mont Blanc" records the sublime transaction, which allows language and "a legion of wild thoughts" to merge. The poet says that, in a mental transport, "I seem as in a trance sublime and strange / To muse on my own separate fantasy, / My own, my human mind." With Shelley the power of thought is personified and placed in dramas of mental action. Asia in *Prometheus Unbound* (Act II, Scene 3) hears the roar of the sun-awakened avalanche:

>   . . . whose mass,
> Thrice sifted by the storm, had gathered there
> Flake after flake, in heaven-defying minds
> As thought by thought is piled, till some great truth
> Is loosened, and the nations echo round,
> Shaken to their roots, as do the mountains now.

There is, above all, the Shelleyan antecedent of "The Ode to the West Wind," where the poet establishes a radical connection between thought and the life or death of the green or fallen leaves—the poet's "wild thoughts."

By the time that Stevens writes, the internalization of the Romantic quest, its descent into the mind, has progressed even further. Mind has become, in and for itself, the chief object of the poet's concern. As this concern increases, a complementary change occurs. Stevens comes to believe, almost from the first, that the function of mind is to meditate a powerful contact with reality. Two problems of interpretation thus arise. What, for Stevens, is meant by the term, reality, and what is meant by the term, mind? Frank Doggett expresses the multivalence of reality as follows:

> Reality, in Stevens's use of the word, may be the world supposed to be antecedent in itself or the world created in the specific occurrence of thought, including the thinker himself and his mind forming the thought. Often the term offers the assumption that if the self is the central point of a circle of infinite radius, then reality is the not-self, including all except the abstract subjective center. Sometimes reality is used in the context of the nominalist position—then the word denotes that which is actual and stands as a phenomenal identity, the existent as opposed to the merely fancied. Stevens usually means by reality an undetermined base on which a mind constructs its personal sense of the world. Occasionally he will use the word real as a term of approval, as a substitute for the word true, and, therefore, no more than an expression of confidence.[2]

Quoting this paragraph, Harold Bloom comments that reality is "a word I wish Stevens had renounced, since it takes away more meaning than it tends to give. He was addicted to it in prose; he used some form of it well over a hundred times in his poetry, and it appears in thirteen different sections of 'An Ordinary Evening'." One wonders how the use of such an empty term can fail to undermine the poetic effect. As a term, reality is devoid of all particular reference. Yet insofar as it refers to the general category of the thing, the res, the term may be called promissory, and perhaps this is all it needs to be. The word signals in Stevens a situation which promises for the scene of a given poem that some condition bodes well for an enhanced sense of things as they are. Stevens understands the imaginative promise as an exuberance or abundance, as in the Adagia: "The poet feels abundantly the poetry of everything," such that he "makes silk dresses out of worms," whether or not the thing partakes of beauty or good. Reality calls forth such a promise.

To a many-sided reality corresponds a many-sided mind. Particularly in the latter part of his career, Stevens uses the word mind, or some affiliated word such as thought, in almost every serious poem that he writes. His subject has become mind and its relation to the real. His "Collect of Philosophy" expresses the aim, as well as the substance, of this later poetry by calling it "a poetry of thought," the phrase that provides the title of Doggett's investigations into the parallels between Stevens and the philosophers that he read or resembled.

The word "mind" seems to present a riddle requiring interpretation. Do we or do we not need to know exactly what it means in a given line of verse? The moment we seek a more exact delimitation we find a word of extremely various appearance. Like students of Hans Vaihinger's "philosophy of *as if*," we can see the mind only under variable poetic aspects, the mind *as* this or *as* that. Stevens's "Of Modern Poetry" invokes "the poem of the mind in the act of finding what will suffice." Here the mind is an agency that searches and discovers. Its power is linked with the sound of words "that in the ear, / In the delicatest ear of the mind, repeat, / Exactly, that which it wants to hear . . ." This mind is tuned to choose a language corresponding to its invisible activity, "Sounds passing through sudden rightnesses, wholly / Containing the mind, . . ." In the theater of mind the active principle is like a stage actor, here called "a metaphysician in the dark."

In "Man and Bottle," besides being "the great poem of Winter," mind is the destroyer of illusions, the "romantic tenements of rose and ice." (Stevens seems to be criticizing the mental complacency of Frost's "Fire and Ice.") Driven by "a manner of thinking, a mode / Of destroying, as the mind destroys, / . . . The poem lashes more fiercely than the wind." Antithetically, in "Mrs. Alfred Uruguay," the mind creates "the ultimate elegance: the imagined land." "Poem with Rhythms" shows us that "the mind turns to its own figurations and declares," that is, the mind here is both interpreter and spokesman for its own mode of action. As interpreter, the mind possesses "the powerful mirror of [its] wish and will." Stevens can entertain the possibility that "The law of chaos is the law of ideas" and elsewhere in these "Extracts From Addresses to the Academy of Fine Ideas," he imagines the mind as a vulnerable structure designed for unity: "Or is it the multitude of thoughts, / Like insects in the depths of the mind, that kill / The single thought?" This mind seeks a oneness: it would not be "half mind." It craves fulfillment, as "the mind is the end and must be satisfied." Satiety of thought comes to the "impossible possible philosopher's man, / The man who has had time to think enough." Yet the poet knows that "it can never be satisfied, the mind, never," as we learn from "The

Well Dressed Man with a Beard." In this dissatisfaction there may be a redeeming sustenance. "Examination of the Hero in a Time of War" recalls the possibility "of summer's / Imagination, the golden rescue: / The bread and wine of the mind." If what Stevens calls mind is the central force of a life worth living, then imagination is the fire that ignites this force.

Stevens' central meditation on the most visionary idea, "Notes Toward a Supreme Fiction," inevitably gives a place to the mind's concerted powers: "there is a war between the mind / And sky, between thought and day and night. It is / For that the poet is always in the sun." In the imaginative quest of the "Notes," mind is even conceived as the pulse of life, as "the strong exhilaration / Of what we feel from what we think, of thought / Beating in the heart, as if blood newly came, / An elixir, an excitation, a pure power." Elixir suggests the magic-seeming illuminations wrought by thought. Finally, even when the mind is drawn as maker of the supreme fiction, there remains "the hum of thoughts evaded in the mind, / Hidden from other thoughts." Owing to this hum of distracted wit, the mind always occludes part of a total meaning so that we cannot be absolutely certain of the truth of fiction.

Such a consideration of mind comprises a small and nonsystematic sampling of poems from 1940 to 1942. A systematic survey of the complete canon of Stevens's poetry would probably reveal that well over 80 percent of the poems examined would show a similar use of the language of mind, including a range of associated terms such as thought, feeling, imagination, perception, memory, and the like. Further, thought is often behaviorally represented: one says of a thinking man that he is known by "this leaning on his bed, / This leaning on his elbows on his bed, / Staring, at midnight at the pillow that is black / In the catastrophic room" ("The Men That Are Falling"). The sum total of direct mentioning, indirect rendering, or oblique allusion to the process of thinking is quite staggering. The mind and its process are literally everywhere in Stevens, the motif most frequently repeated throughout the canon.

The question at once arises: are these repetitions an obsession? If they were, it would not be hard to show, and experience would verify, that as an obsessive writer, Stevens is thus necessarily an allegorist. Yet the experience of Stevens's readers testifies to a strong belief that he does not write allegory. He is far from the maker of simple analogies, such as the Bunyan of *Pilgrim's Progress*. Rather, as his lecture "Effects of Analogy" intimates, Stevens himself deliberately uses metaphor, along with analogical figures, in a free, loose, inventively various and flexible style, which prevents allegory. It is this freedom of combination which departs from reality as the "base" of poetic vision. It is the freedom employed by the great masters of color and composition in the visual arts, on which Stevens lectured under the title "The Relations Between Poetry and Painting." As noted in the *Adagia:* "To a large extent, the problems of poets are the problems of painters, and poets must often turn to the literature of painting for a discussion of their own problems." The emphasis arising from such a relationship always falls on the discipline and freedom allowed to the act of composition. For example, "The Anecdote of the Jar" becomes immediately comprehensive if one imagines a painter placing, that is, adding, a jar to a painting of a landscape in Tennessee. The placement of a jar makes the composition cohere into a unity.

"In the long run," Stevens once wrote, "the truth does not matter." While for him this statement is meant to be enigmatic, it leaves open an alternative, the idea that order or composition do matter. The nature of art, its technical crafts, the imagination, and the perceptual powers with their relation to what Stevens called reality are such that the strong poet will compose sufficient poems of encounter between the individual and his world. If these encounters are not obsessive, it follows that they dispose of a liberating parley that allows intercourse between mind and "things as they are." Like Wittgenstein with his forms of life, Stevens would invent language-games of mind to play through "the life that is lived in the scene that it composes."[3]

The critic's aim may be to ask how, in a general sense, Stevens motivates the demand for composition. We have already seen that he can use a thought-sign, like "mind," with seemingly endless variety, suggesting that he uses this mentalistic repertoire precisely in order to achieve "the extension of the mind beyond the range of the mind, the projection of reality beyond reality, the determination to cover the ground, whatever it may be, the determination not to be confined, the recapture of excitement and intensity of interest, the enlargement of the spirit at every time, in every way."[4] Stevens the poet enjoyed a virtuoso's command of language and of what he called "imaginative objects."

The poet identifies the articulation of his thoughts with a freedom of diction reaching far beyond the usual.

> The deepening need for words to express our thoughts and feelings which, we are sure, are all the truth that we shall ever experience, having no illusions, makes us listen to words when we hear them, loving them and feeling them, makes us search the sound of them, for a finality, a perfection, an unalterable vibration, which it is only within the power of the acutest poet to give them. Those of us who may have been thinking of the path of poetry, those who understand that words are thoughts and not only our own thoughts but the thoughts of men and women ignorant of what it is that they are thinking, must be conscious of this: that, above everything else, poetry is words; and that words, above everything else, are, in poetry, sounds.[5]

In this essay Stevens makes an explicit connection between the sounding word and thought; among his fundamental notions of language is that "a poet's words are of things that do not exist without the words." He is clearly the post-Mallarméan writer, and among his contemporaries Hart Crane, at least, would have endorsed the privilege accorded to the sound of words.

To the armory of resonant words, Stevens's lecture "The Figure of the Youth as Virile Poet" summons that other power, "the acute intelligence of the imagination," which enlists memory and perception. The same lecture speaks of a belief in "imaginative objects" that Stevens held throughout his life. These objects, to be distinguished from what he called "poetic ideas," are largely made up of remembered perceptions so sharply present to the eye of the mind that they seem, however processed by and in the mind, to be objects. "Much of the world of fact is the equivalent of the world of the imagination, because it looks like it." Stevens's examples include "a rock that sparkles, a blue sea that lashes, and hemlocks in which the sun can merely fumble"—all these being the familiar imaginative objects to be seen and experienced in Maine, their "region." Poetry then is a transaction between such objects and specially chosen, memorably sounding words.

The motivation of such poetic perceptions might be sought on a personal level through the help of letters and biography, as Frank

Doggett has done in his second book on Stevens, *The Making of the Poem* (1980). Yet we can also ask: what motivates the poems in themselves? We can always conjecture the source of meaning *in* a poem, as the chosen poetic form discloses an inscribed poetic intention. Following this latter line of inquiry, we may ask: how would we characterize Stevens's poetry as a whole? Scholarly accounts have seen in him a mythmaker of the self, an epistemological jester, a singer of Emersonian insights and warnings, a son of the Romantics or of Walt Whitman, a poet of the Platonic eros, a poet-philosopher, a philosopher-poet, a deconstructor of blanks in the established language—whatever the scholar's mind has conjured and defended. Various imaginings of Stevens will be part of the curriculum. To supplement established views, one might say then that the Stevens of the mind is a seeker, a quester.

It is not entirely fanciful to suggest that Stevens is chivalric in his quest, or often a *jongleur*, with a touch of the dandy. Such manners make his quest all the more remarkable. He intervenes where old beliefs in a knowable God have faded. In 1940 he wrote:

> The major poetic idea in the world is and always has been the idea of God. One of the visible movements of the modern imagination is the movement away from the idea of God. The poetry that created the idea of God will either adapt it to our different intelligence, or create a substitute for it, or make it unnecessary . . . The knowledge of poetry is a part of philosophy, and a part of science; the import of poetry is the import of the spirit. The figures of the essential poets should be spiritual figures.[6]

Perhaps the import of such a pronouncement may be reduced to a single line from "The Final Soliloquy of the Interior Paramour": "We say God and the imagination are one . . ."

In formal terms and in the context of the post-Romantic, the demonized imagination seeks to produce a poetry which will bring order out of a chaos of impressions. Such chaos is at the same time retained as part of, and in the course of, its reduction to order. Romantic and Symbolist poetry is for this reason always turbulent: chaos is marginally retained even as it is being dispersed.

The seeking aspect of Stevens, amidst the turbulence, comes through as a driving desire to repeat and recapitulate. It is as if he writes one poem and then another on the same theme, and in the second poem clarifies and enhances the quest of the first poem. Placed in sequence, such loops or linkages begin to suggest that the poet always seeks a more perfect ordering of mind, its aspects, and its constructions. Always the mind is set into the poem as a force working toward a more perfected, if varied, order of description, in Stevens's sense of the thing in itself or, at times, the plain sense of things.

As we have said, what is remarkable about his quest, his "blessed rage for order," is that Stevens evades the trap of obsession, redundancy, and final boredom. His variations are freshly venturous, so that his abstract terms continue to evoke wonder and puzzlement. Descriptions of mind remain lively, inventive, and moving. The poetry establishes an almost ritual place for itself in an idealized vision of the hours. "Wine and music are not good until afternoon. But poetry is like prayer in that it is most effective in solitude and in the times of solitude as, for example, in the earliest morning" (*Adagia*).

Identifying poetry in certain aspects with prayer, Stevens indicates a cyclical philosophy by which his poetry fits naturally into a harmony of the daily, monthly, seasonally solar cycle. There is an element of ritual in such a practice. It promises a more personal view of Stevens's quest. On many occasions he speaks of the absence of God and of our need to allow the imagination to find a substitute fiction that will suffice. This quest for the supreme fiction is *based* on a continuous encounter and negotiation with the plain sense of things. Stevens thus speaks to the man or woman in whom the mind has guided belief away from traditional images or ideas of the divine. Stevens's quest will touch their hearts and will perhaps satisfy their minds, as he enraptures their senses. Like Keats in the "Ode to Psyche," Stevens will lead the enlightened children of doubt into untrodden regions of the mind. For them the quest of an intellectually grounded imaginative faith will be almost a life-giving necessity. To such persons he seems to have dedicated his work.

In terms of the iconography of thought, it remains necessary to describe the chief innovation in poetic technique by which the quest of fictive music is furthered, as Stevens's poetic career moves toward its close. His style, in general, becomes increasingly austere, or perhaps one should say more obviously ascetic—in this development he resembles Yeats. Technically, his late poems achieve complete ease in a more deliberate, spare style, a style that is not so much an innovation as the perfection of an ideal toward which his poetry had always been leaning. Almost parenthetically, we might surmise that the Romantic impulse, or perhaps the Whitmanian impulse, to accumulate "fragments" of imagery will find its satisfaction in the enlarged version of "An Ordinary Evening in New Haven." Such fragments, as Philippe Lacoue-Labarthe and Jean-Luc Nancy have shown in *The Literary Absolute,* accompany the deep Romantic commitment to visions of the whole, of the world-system. In this Romantic tradition Stevens would seem to be a rebel against the fragmentary—his poems appear fully and completely formed. Yet he never abandons the quest for the extravagant excursion into a further region of mind, and hence *insets* the fragmentary within the forms of longer poems. In *Wallace Stevens: The Making of the Poem,* Frank Doggett points out the effects of predicate nominatives and appositions on the later style. One of these effects is that the style resembles improvisation, which will easily bear a fragmentary tone. Appositive phrases, as in Whitman, together make a web of ensemble parts that are close to the fragments in Romantic theory. All in all, it is by no means obvious that Stevens purges his work of fragmentary traces. The technical mastery of an austere yet rich manner gives the late Stevens its compelling aesthetic force. More critically, in light of the fictive quest, it allows a place for terms like mind, thought, and particular, on a high plane of meditation. He is finally free to make full use of mentalistic terms to figure forth a complex iconography.

The presentation of mind appears by a process of gnomic abstraction—abstraction from the plane of the real by means of gnomic sentences, phrases, or words. As his career proceeds, Stevens would appear to cultivate the gnomic more frequently and more deliberately. Even in his early work, however, there are examples. The whole of "The Anecdote of the Jar" is gnomic, both its opening and closing lines display a compositionally enigmatic relation between general and particular:

> I placed a jar in Tennessee,
> And round it was, upon a hill . . .
>
> It did not give of bird or bush,
> Like nothing else in Tennessee.

There is a sharp and entirely gnomic discontinuity between the particularity of the jar in *its* space and the generality of a Tennessee without borders. Another famous early example is "The Snow Man":

> One must have a mind of winter
> To regard the frost and the boughs
> Of the pine-trees;

A gnomic reading of these and the ensuing lines depends upon a sense that in them the poem has reached a rock-bottom level of perception: winter as known, and its appearances, are not the consequence of natural forces but of "a mind of winter." The poet's imagination comes to share this mind of winter. As the poem builds its image of the mind of winter, it centers upon the figure of the snow man and his blankness:

> For the listener, who listens in the snow,
> And, nothing himself, beholds
> Nothing that is not there and the nothing that is.

The final lines show a marked increase in the gnomic, which is required in order to express a final question: what equivalence is there between a statue made of snow (a snowman in the ordinary sense) and a human, when this human thinks coldly, with blank eyes? The poem makes the ontological point that we may need to speak and think about the existence of "nothing," but only in the depth of such a wintry scene can we come to understand, to identify with, the numbness of a mind congealed by a long duration of cold. The poem thus plays upon an aphoristic difference between "nothing" and "the nothing." A third early example might be "Valley Candle":

> My candle burned alone in an immense valley.
> Beams of the huge night converged upon it,
> Until the wind blew.
> Then beams of the huge night
> Converged upon its image,
> Until the wind blew.

Like the jar in Tennessee, the candle is placed in a scene which is "immense." The poem hinges upon this discontinuity of scale. The implication might seem to be that the wind extinguishes the candle, both actual and image, but even this implication is uncertain. The gnomicity of the poem, however, resides in the teasing mixture of scales. There is no reason why a candle should not burn somewhere in a valley, but the sharpness of the juxtaposed elements, candle and valley, shocks the reader into a gnomic frame of mind. The reader is forced to think about the thinking process which leads to such incongruity. Similarly one asks: by what mental process does the darkness of night possess "beams," whence the reversal, from beams of light to beams of night? Effects of the gnomic occur because the particularity of details in the poem is almost instantly replaced by implications of extreme, if somewhat mysterious, generality.

"Thirteen Ways of Looking at a Blackbird" remains one of the poet's great successes. The poem is in part Imagist, but its force comes largely from its overall composition into thirteen gnomic observations. Number four is pure gnomic:

> A man and a woman
> Are one.
> A man and a woman and a blackbird
> Are one.

Number twelve mixes image and folkloric precept:

> The river is moving.
> The blackbird must be flying.

Everywhere the stanzas hint at general principles, which underlie "an indecipherable cause." We see how early in his career Stevens became the master of the cryptic apothegm.

These early examples point to the strangeness of gnomic utterance. It makes jarring connections between general and particular, between the small scale and the large scale, and between these connections and an unspecified power called mind or thought. Further, the gnomic seems to rest on an ambiguous coexistence of the typical iterative experience with a quite opposed atypical, once-in-a-lifetime experience. Yet so far we have no clear idea about the poetic status of gnomic elements—gnomes, as they are sometimes called—in Stevens's poetry as a whole.

There is a personal note of some pertinence to this question.

A. Walton Litz observes that "few writers of any time or place can have given so much concentrated attention to the gnomic saying, both as private ritual and public utterance."[7] Into his first *Adagia* notebook Stevens copied the words, "from Goethe proverbs poured incessantly." Stevens too acquired an extensive library of sayings— "there are more than thirty collections of aphorisms, proverbs, or pithy journal entries." The authors range from Pascal and La Rochefoucauld to Baudelaire, Henry James, Proust, Rilke, Georges Braque. The poet even acquired Francis Quarles's *Divine Fancies Digested into Epigramms, Meditations, and Observations* (London, 1641). Besides these collected volumes, of course, there are the two notebooks called *Adagia* and a third notebook containing "poetic exercises of 1948." Samuel French Morse's edition of the *Opus Posthumous* includes most, but not all, of the entries in the three notebooks. Stevens had mixed feelings about the practical use of such materials. In his journal for April 27, 1906, he wrote: "There are no end of gnomes that *might* influence people—but do not. When you first feel the truth of, say, an epigram, you feel like making it a rule of conduct. But this one is displaced by that, and thus things go on in their accustomed way." All this evidence suggests that Stevens consulted and collected memorable sayings in much the same manner as did the Elizabethans, with their strong sense of the proverbial and their willingness to use dictionaries.

Some advantages to the poet are obvious: the sententious affirms even when negating; it is well formed, *formosam;* it sounds to have authority; if laconic, it can be forcefully mysterious; if at all pointed, it will be memorable. This last quality is supremely important to a poet like Stevens, who wants to develop "inescapable" rhythms.

Another aspect of the gnomic is the tantalizing way it permits well-rounded statements, or phrases, to be inset into the continuous flow of a poem, as discontinuous inlays. Stevens's appositives are often of this type. As a result of these gnomic interruptions (including even nonsense syllables), the poem suggests always the fragmentary aspect of reality while retaining a vision overall of larger coherences. This antithetical effect of the "Romantic fragment" harks back to the most obscure of gnomic writers, Heraclitus, who insisted at once that all is one, and that phenomenal existence was a scene of strife and polar opposition. Yet poetry has formal powers of containing such discords and discontinuities within the bounds of an imagined unity, the poem.

Like Heraclitus, gnomics hint at, but do not fully expose or explain, contradictory aspects of reality. If "the way up and the way down are the same," we do not learn in what respect this is or is not a tautology, or exactly how we are to understand "the same." If, as Plato reports, Heraclitus said you cannot step twice into the same river, it is still, on the face of it, not clear whether the philosopher has perceived a contradiction or not. The gnome, in short, hovers conceptually on the edge of asserting a contradiction or deep paradox. But owing to its surface appeal, its aesthetic, the gnome leaves the reader with an impression of a wise, *knowing* vision of perspectival contradictions, which result from adopting a slightly skewed viewing position. Such sentences are useful when writing in a field of scientific or other natural uncertainties. Such was the case with early Ionian science. Such is the case for the poet, Stevens, but not quite in a scientific sense. Even here Stevens is in touch with the ancient Greek protoscientific motivations of the gnomic. After attempting two other conclusions (of a poetical kind) for his "Collect of Philosophy," Stevens used a description of Max Planck's ultimate doubts concerning a rigidly deterministic, theoretical position. Stevens takes comfort in the physicist's belief in "the provisional and changing creation of the power of the imagination." Even Planck, when confronted with quantum mechanics, must loosen the hold of strict determinism. The physicist's flexibility is a model for Stevens's own attitude regarding the existence, or even the naming, of God. Throughout his life, and not just toward its end, Stevens was deeply troubled by the need for dealing with the ineffable notion of a supreme being. When he was able finally to conceive of God as the supreme "poetic idea," this conception required a special language, or approach to language, which I would associate with the gnomic.

That gnomics and their conceptual uncanniness might serve to express the quest for a supreme fiction is indicated by the poet's association of this quest with irrational dimensions of discourse. Gnomics contend with the irrational, in a certain sense. In his lecture on "The Irrational Element in Poetry," Stevens grants that "it is probably the purpose of each of us to write poetry in order to find the good which, in the Platonic sense, is synonymous with God."

The good, in this Platonic sense, Stevens links with the harmonious and orderly, categories to which the gnomic utterance makes tentative, approximating approaches.

The aim of a verbalization of an idea of God, if only as the Platonic good, is more than most ordinary or poetic language can directly compass. Yet Stevens says repeatedly that he is concerned about an idea, about finding some equivalent idea, of God. He is explicit that belief feasts upon fiction, and the supreme feast will be the feast upon a fiction divine in origin. He makes poems upon many subjects, but none of greater motive force than the question of an order which at least partly satisfies the yearning for God. One might say, therefore, that he needs in general a language and language-games that will allow him to approach the ineffable highest poetic idea.

The quest of the ineffable is made yet stranger when Stevens wants to pursue it through an encounter with "the real," with "reality." Such a pursuit (leaving aside what philosophers might say of it) would seem paradoxical: what is real is known to the pragmatist as the thing that can be instrumentally described or indicated, whereas here the real is the "portal" to something that cannot be rendered exactly. It is by virtue of this paradoxical quest that the poet approaches what I am calling a gnomic style. There is a temptation to wish upon Stevens a knowledge of Heidegger, which he did not possess, in order to explain the affinity between the Heidegger/Hölderlin notion of "dwelling" to Stevens's renderings of man "inhabiting" various mythic regions. Yet the proper link is not to the modern German philosopher and the Romantic poet (despite Stevens's curiosity about them). Rather the link is with the gnomic tradition that was richly and sumptuously represented in Stevens's own library—the books of *pensées*, maxims, aphorisms, sayings.

From one point of view, those books betoken the excessive refinement of fine bindings and *belles lettres*. But for Stevens the collection clearly has passionate importance, and the later poetry expecially reveals this passion. "Ordinary Evening" begins: "The eye's plain version is a thing apart, / The vulgate of experience," and this sententious gnome catapults the poem into an almost baroque exploration of plain reality, ending enigmatically "a shade that traverses / A dust, a force that traverses a shade." Gnomic abstraction colors all such Stevensian language. "His statement is complete because it contains / His utmost statement." "The rock is the habitation of the whole." These are examples of what may be called the classic version of the gnomic, which takes the form *X is Y*—"the rock is the habitation of the whole." Or, "The common man is the common hero." Or, "The major abstraction is the idea of man." Or, "The poem is the cry of its occasion, / Part of the res itself and not about it." We have seen, however, that gnomic thinking may be expressed or represented in less obviously copular propositional forms, such as "a shade that traverses / A dust, a force that traverses a shade." Or, "The leaves cry." Or, perhaps, "He could not bend against its propelling force."

The occurrence of gnomic elements, especially in the *X is Y* form, is so frequent in the later Stevens that they provide, in effect, the fundamental base of his mature style. While gnomicity was present in the early poems, quite undeveloped, now the style has matured to admit a seemingly inexhaustible fund of finely tuned gnomic forms and variants. They announce, call forth, convoke the imagery and symbolic action of each poem. Yet they do not convert the poem to flat statement, because they themselves have the force of conceptual metaphor; they are, to quote the title of one of the poems, a "Thinking of a Relation Between the Images of Metaphors." The austerity of late Stevens has much to do with this lively treatment of abstract relations, as if he had discovered a way of following the tracks and traces of thought itself.

Perhaps the most mysterious and haunting of Stevens's gnomic utterances is one of his last, "Of Mere Being."

> The palm at the end of the mind,
> Beyond the last thought, rises
> In the bronze decor,
>
> A gold-feathered bird
> Sings in the palm, without human meaning,
> Without human feeling, a foreign song.
>
> You know then that it is not the reason
> That makes us happy or unhappy.
> The bird sings. Its feathers shine.
>
> The palm stands on the edge of space.
> The wind moves slowly in the branches.
> The bird's fire-fangled feathers dangle down.

Certain properties of the gnomic are immediately evident. There is the proposition "that it is not the reason / That makes us happy or unhappy." This could be a merely sententious adage, but other elements combine to be in themselves enigmatic ("permanently enigmatic," as Stevens once said) and to project their enigma onto the central gnomic proposition. The poem establishes an iconography of thought, which is at once obscure and sharply realized. As in a surrealist painting, the palm tree stands in a region called "mind." A question arises: what is the relation between this particular, a palm, and this generality, the mind? Particular and general no longer have a simple super- and subordinating class relationship. One index to the strangeness of this order is the disproportion of scale, which places the palm "beyond the last thought," at the final border of mental space. We have already seen this sort of disproportion in "Valley Candle," where the single candle "burned alone in an immense valley." The question of scale occurs naturally with sentences in a Heraclitan or Parmenidean tradition. Such sentences always refer, if indirectly, to a universal order, which is only partially perceived or understood. As Stevens writes in another late poem, "July Mountain": "We live in a constellation / Of patches and of pitches, . . . / Thinkers without final thoughts / In an always incipient cosmos . . ."

"Of Mere Being" then prompts the reader to ask, is not the palm itself "the last thought," and then to ask, what kind of thought this might be? The poem can only suggest an answer, for there is nothing certain about even the most sharply drawn picture, or icon, of thought. There is only a cosmic decor, which is associated with what Stevens elsewhere called "a radiant and productive atmosphere." In this atmosphere idea becomes artifact, and the gold-feathered bird sings a song, an unknown foreign song, of its own absolute specificity, that of a bird, which is conceived in its own terms, as a bird in itself. Such a vision, which is almost hallucinated, no longer requires the pathos of a human frame of reference; neither human meaning nor human feeling are germane in this extreme perception of reality. The song, the bronze decor, the bird are projected away from the mind and feeling of a human category or type, becoming part of a world that cosmically exists outside of us, outlasting us. The gnomic expression of such ideas is slightly uncanny, as if the epiphanic vision of the bird and the palm had occurred some other time, once or perhaps many times before, and was now returning, like the recovered memory of a lost sensation of the truth. What makes us happy or unhappy is the recognition, the re-cognition of the phenomenon. Thus the surface of the gnomic utterance may appear to be impersonal, but it has a vital center which allows the poem to gain access to the deeper meaning of the manifest repetition so easily observed throughout the canon. Stevens's poem manages to stimulate in the reader a peculiar awareness of "mere being," so that the final four lines reduce an experience of mind to its fundamental form. This form is given by language and *its* forms. In these last four lines, five separate thoughts are given in five separate sentences. The most gnomic section of this poem is the simplest, namely the sequence of these five sentences. These sentences are, as it were, written in such a way as to baffle interpretation. They are stripped of cues to analysis. As Wittgenstein says, "Look on the language-game as the *primary* thing. And look on the feelings, etc., as you look on a way of regarding the language-game, as interpretation."[8] One might say then that the last four lines block interpretation. Yet this is not entirely true, since the final line is heavily marked as a product of the poet's imagination. Not only is the line made "musical" by the alliterations, but there is also the coinage "fire-fangled." On both counts the poem is signed, as having been made by a master craftsman who can fearlessly employ the most extreme devices of his art. These devices, and indeed the whole poem, are generated from the gnomic regard for the order of being that makes us happy or unhappy. As Stevens always maintained, such experience of what he called reality is not to be reached by the powers of reason alone.

The example of one poem, "Of Mere Being," will serve to represent the gnomic processes that are observable in a multitude of cases elsewhere in the canon. The plea for the gnomic in Stevens in fact urges that we read him in a certain way. He asks of us what he asks of nature and himself, that there be a participation in a process of understanding. He is fond of the phrase "part of." For Stevens, it signals an acceptance of our need to discover what, in nature, we can be part of, to what order we can belong. Such a question is the origin of the gnomic utterance.

In American verse before Stevens, the question marks the poetry of Whitman, who used the word *thoughts* as a title for poems. Even more obviously it marks Emily Dickinson, who is gnomic throughout her poetry. In Stevens's own time, the gnomic characterizes one of his favorite poets, Marianne Moore. That gnomic style transforms prose into the suggestion of an intellectual poetry is apparent in the work of the four strongest New England prose writers—Hawthorne, Melville, Emerson, Thoreau. To all four individual styles, a gnomic coloration adds the peculiar mystery of a complex "wisdom literature," producing an oblique transformation of the proverbial in these writers. Among modern authors, the prose style of Hemingway, like that of Stephen Crane, but in an even more pronounced form, moves in wave-like sequences of gnomic narrative. The presence of the gnomic throughout the American tradition is quite stunning and would be even more so were we to add ironic authors such as Poe, Twain, Nathaniel West, Henry James (think of his ending *Washington Square* with the darkly ironic phrase, "as it were"). It may well be that the use of gnomics is the central core of what has been most effectively powerful in American poetry and prose. They establish a rhythm, mainly cyclical, and they turn the poetry toward an iconography of thought. As we have seen, when such utterances comment crisply on some aspect of nature, it is precisely an *aspect, as processed by mind,* that is at issue. Only by inspecting our thoughts of "the real" do we come to possess any clear notion (or question) about what might be considered the real. Only then can we grasp what Wittgenstein called "the dawning of an aspect." There is a need to accept what Stevens called "the pure good of theory." Where Stevens rises above his commentators, including me, is in the way he attaches such questions of mind and world to a vision of actually surviving in this world. To this end, Stevens uses gnomic abstractions to call forth, to figure forth, to let loose the forces of thought.

We may then ask, what ground does the thinking, the gnomic poet trust? The clarity of gnomic elements seems always to have a devious sheen, like the bright nighttime reflections from rain-soaked asphalt streets. Hence, as the poet wrote in his journal, "There are no end of gnomes that *might* influence people—but do not." Stevens may be wanting to have it both ways—trusting the gnomic wisdom, doubting the gnomic allure. If so, the greater burden will fall upon the particular images and metaphors and fables that compose the body of each poem. What cannot fail to amaze his reader is that, in the midst of almost incessant repetition (much of it explicitly gnomic in an *X is Y* form), little of Stevens causes immediate and lasting boredom. Like a great painter, he appears to have mastered the art of continuous subtle variation in tone. He enables the reader to think one poem after another, almost as a ritual exercise. In that sense, and because he is questing always the form of the supreme fiction, Stevens is to be understood as a poet of spiritual searching. His coldness, which he knew so much about, is almost irrelevant; to complain of it would be like objecting to the silence of a Zen master. It is therefore all the more important to insist, wherever possible, on the glint of broad American humor in Stevens's poems. Humor, the kindly form of wit, redeems the colder, the aloof calculations from their more shivery effects. Stevens is rare in that his flexible exercise of mind makes that entity resemble a body, his mind almost is a body, his mind feels with sensations of pain to pleasure, his mind is the "vital boundary." Like other embodiments, it is subject to the humor of comic deflations. This iconography of embodied thought comes at us humanly scaled. Intellectual, intellective, gnomic, this poetry is capable of touch—the morality of the poem, as Stevens said, lies in its practice of "the right sensations."

Notes

1. Iconographies of Thought

1. Jean Rhys, *Voyage in the Dark* (New York, 1982), p. 177.
2. See Sharon Cameron, *Thinking in Henry James* (Chicago, 1989). Regretably Cameron's very important study came to my attention too late to be a clarifying influence in the course of my work.
3. Italo Calvino, *Mr. Palomar*, trans. William Weaver (San Diego, 1985).
4. Wittgenstein treated knowledge of colors as an aspect of the problem of private language; most simply, one asks how one person can know or express what another means by the terms "red" or "green." See Ludwig Wittgenstein's *Remarks on Colour*, trans. Linda McAlaister and Margarete Schiattle (Berkeley, 1978).
5. See "The Relation of Habitual Thought and Behavior to Language," in Benjamin L. Whorf, *Language, Thought and Reality*, ed. John B. Carroll (Cambridge, Mass., 1956), and also Carroll's Introduction to this volume, pp. 27–31.
6. Ludwig Wittgenstein, *The Blue and Brown Books*, ed. Rush Rhees (New York, 1960), p. 3.
7. Ludwig Wittgenstein, *Zettel*, ed. G. E. M. Anscombe and G. H. von Wright; trans. G. E. M. Anscombe (Berkeley, 1970), par. 126.
8. Hannah Arendt, *The Life of the Mind: One / Thinking* (New York, 1977), pp. 213, 218.

2. Two Frames in the Iconography of Thinking

1. The Cervantean naturalizing of dialogue and narrative is anticipated by and dependent upon prior developments in Spanish prose romance. More important, however, is the parodic vision of the *Orlando Furioso*. With Ariosto the door between parody and realism opens. Recognizing this, Cervantes is able to shift formal declamation to a mode of novelistic dialogue. One cannot but ask if Milton, in rejecting the epic claims of chivalric romance, is not also rejecting the need for the novel.
2. The *Quixote* predicts Hegel's master/slave dyad. On conversation see Paul Grice, *Studies in the Way of Words* (1989); Dan Sperber and Deirdre Wilson, *Relevance* (1986)—both Cambridge, Mass.
3. José Ortega y Gasset, "Notes on Thinking," in *Concord and Liberty*, trans. Helene Weyl (New York, 1963), p. 75.
4. Edward Said, *The World, the Text, and the Critic* (Cambridge, Mass., 1983), p. 44.
5. Miguel de Unamuno, "The Essence of Quixotism," in *Our Lord Don Quixote: The Life of Don Quixote and Sancho with Related Essays*, trans. Anthony Kerrigan (Princeton, 1967), p. 359.

3. The Distractions of Wit

1. Frank Percy Wilson, *The Plague in Shakespeare's London* (Oxford, 1927).
2. Brian Vickers, *Francis Bacon and Renaissance Prose* (Cambridge, 1968), p. 59.
3. John Donne, *Sermon lxxx*, folio of 1640: "I neglect God and his angels for the noise of a fly, for the rattling of a coach, for the whining of a door; I talk on in the same posture of praying, eyes lifted up, knees bowed down, as though I prayed to God; and if God or his angels should ask me when I thought last of God in that prayer, I cannot tell. A memory of yesterday's pleasures, a fear of tomorrow's dangers, a straw under my knee, a noise in mine ear, a light in mine eye, an anything, a nothing, a fancy, a chimera in my brain troubles me in my prayer. So certainly is there nothing, nothing in spiritual things perfect in this world."
4. Huck Finn gives this example of pure liminality as controlled passage: "It was kind of solemn, drifting down the big, still river, laying on our backs looking up at the stars, and we didn't ever feel like talking out loud, and it warn't often that we talked—only a little kind of a low chuckle. We had mighty good weather as a general thing, and nothing ever happened to us at all—that night, nor the next, nor the next."

4. Standing, Waiting, and Traveling Light

1. T. M. Greene, *The Descent from Heaven* (New Haven, 1963), p. 387.

2. Northrop Frye, *The Return of Eden: Five Essays on Milton's Epics* (Toronto, 1965), chap. I.

3. C. S. Lewis, *A Preface to Paradise Lost* (London: Oxford University Press, 1960), p. 30.

4. See Stanley Fish, *Surprised by Sin: The Reader in Paradise Lost* (New York: St Martin's Press, 1967), pp. 107–130 for discussion of seventeenth-century Cratylism.

5. Encyclopedia Britannica, 15th ed., IX, 568a.

6. Stanley Fish, *Self-Consuming Artifacts: The Experience of Seventeenth-Century Literature* (Berkeley, 1972). See also Fish, "Driving from the Letter: Truth and Indeterminacy in Milton's *Areopagitica*," in *Remembering Milton: Essays on the Texts and Traditions*, ed. Mary Nyquist and Margaret W. Ferguson (New York, 1987), pp. 234–254.

7. See Thomas S. Kuhn, "Mathematical versus Experimental Traditions in the Development of Physical Science," in *Post-Analytic Philosophy*, ed. J. R. Rajchman and Cornel West (New York, 1985), pp. 166–195, especially p. 195 n. 11.

8. Geoffrey Hartman, *The Fate of Reading* (Chicago, 1975), p. 287.

9. Christine Brooke-Rose, "Metaphor in *Paradise Lost*: A Grammatical Analysis," in *Language and Style in Milton*, ed. R. D. Emma and John Shawcross (New York: Frederick Ungar, 1967), p. 271.

5. Allegorical Secrecy, Gnomic Obscurity

1. Paul de Man, *Allegories of Reading: Figural Language in Rousseau, Nietzsche, Rilke, and Proust* (New Haven, 1979), p. 275.

2. Ibid., p. 217.

3. Walter Benjamin, *The Origin of German Tragic Drama*, trans. John Osborne; intro. George Steiner (New York, 1985), p. 166.

4. Sissela Bok, *Secrets: On the Ethics of Concealment and Revelation* (New York, 1984), p. 6.

5. Walter Benjamin, *Central Park*, trans. Lloyd Spencer, in *New German Critique*, 34 (Winter 1985):38.

6. Bok, *Secrets*, p. 138.

7. George Steiner, *On Difficulty and Other Essays* (Oxford, 1980), pp. 18–47.

8. Ibid., pp. 40–41.

9. P. M. S. Hacker, *Insight and Illusion: Wittgenstein on Philosophy and the Metaphysics of Experience* (New York, 1975), pp. 167–168.

10. Jacques Derrida frequently invokes concepts of play. See, for example, *Of Grammatology*, trans. G. C. Spivak (Baltimore, 1976), p. 50. See also his *The Ear of the Other: Otobiography, Transference, Translation*, trans. Peggy Kamuf, ed. C. V. McDonald (New York, 1985), pp. 67–71.

6. The Language-Game of Prophecy

1. Martin Buber, *The Prophetic Faith*, trans. Carlyle Witton-Davies (New York, 1960), p. 8. See various studies by Mieke Bal.
2. Geoffrey Hartman, "Poetics of Prophecy," in *High Romantic Argument*, ed. Lawrence Lipking (Ithaca, 1981), pp. 15–40. This article deals with Wordsworth in relation to the biblical prophetic "voice," particularly in Jeremiah.
3. Louise Schleiner, "Spenser and Sidney on the Vaticinium," *Spenser Studies*, ed. Patrick Cullen and Thomas P. Roche, Jr. (1985), 6:142.
4. Hartman, "Poetics of Prophecy," p. 15.
5. Montaigne, *Essays*, Bk. III, "Of Repentance."
6. Hartman, "Poetics of Prophecy," p. 16.
7. "A Poet amongst Poets: Milton and the Tradition of Prophecy," in *Milton and the Line of Vision*, ed. Joseph Anthony Wittreich, Jr. (Madison, 1975), p. 142. Wittreich deals extensively with the apocalyptic and its relation to *Lycidas*.

7. The Father of Lies

1. Arnaldo Momigliano, "Herodotus in the History of Historiography," in *Studies in Historiography* (New York, 1966) p. 129.
2. Ibid., p. 130. For a more general overview of the problem of historical versus mythical "truth," see Paul Veyne, *Did the Greeks Believe in Their Myths? An Essay on the Constitutive Imagination*, trans. Paula Wissing (Chicago, 1988), chap. 1. Veyne observes the central and troublesome role of legend, as opposed to the "authentic kernel" of originary myth.
3. Philip Wheelwright, *Dictionary of Poetry and Poetics* (Princeton, 1965), p. 538b.
4. Ernst Cassirer, *Language and Myth*, trans. Suzanne Langer (New York, 1946). I quote from the Dover Publications reprint (New York, n.d.), p. 41.
5. *Greek Historical Thought*, ed. and trans. Arnold J. Toynbee (New York, 1962), p. 187.
6. Ibid., p. 188.
7. Ibid., p. 40. See the comparison with Thucydides, drawn in John H. Finley, Jr., *Thucydides* (Ann Arbor, 1963), p. 80ff.
8. Momigliano, "Herodotus," p. 137.
9. Ibid., pp. 137, 140.
10. F. M. Cornford, *Thucydides Mythistoricus* (London, 1907).
11. Gérard Genette, *Figures of Literary Discourse*, trans. Alan Sheridan (New York, 1982), pp. 127–146.

12. Ibid., p. 138.
13. Ibid., p. 139.
14. Hayden White, "The Value of Narrativity in the Representation of Reality," in *On Narrative*, ed. W. J. T. Mitchell (Chicago, 1981), p. 4. See also, by White, "The Fictions of Factual Representation," in *The Literature of Fact* (New York, 1976), ed. with a foreword by Angus Fletcher.
15. White, "The Value of Narrativity," p. 5.
16. Arthur Danto, *Analytical Philosophy of History* (Cambridge, 1965), p. 208.
17. Ludwig Wittgenstein, *Philosophical Investigations*, trans. G. E. M. Anscombe (New York, 1968), p. 224e. Pagination is identical with that of the bilingual second edition (Oxford, 1963).

8. Dipintura

1. Margherita Frankel, "The 'Dipintura' and the Structure of Vico's *New Science* as a Mirror of the World," in *Vico: Past and Present*, ed. Giorgio Tagliacozzo (Atlantic Highlands, N.J.: Humanities Press, 1981), pp. 43–51.
2. Frankel refers ("Dipintura," p. 44ff.) to Paolo Rossi, *Clavis universalis* (Milan, 1960) and "Schede vichiane" in *Rassegna della letteratura italiana* 62/3 (1958): 375–377; Giorgio Tagliacozzo, "Epilogue," in *Giambattista Vico: An International Symposium*, ed. Giorgio Tagliacozzo and Hayden White (Baltimore, 1969; hereinafter GVIS), pp. 599–600; and to Frances A. Yates, *The Art of Memory* (London, 1966). The "art of memory" is perhaps the most fertile Renaissance usage of a speculative, heuristic number symbolism. In addition, Frankel's argument holds that "all the Books and Sections of the *Scienza nuova* are a gradual development of those ideas [contained in the Table], from the utmost compression of the engraving to a maximum expansion in the entire work, following however not a straight unfolding but the widening circles of a spiral. And as the curve of the spiral keeps passing through the same radial lines, through larger distances, so the writing of the *Scienza nuova* passes through the same points already mentioned at earlier stages and increasingly develops and simplifies them" (50).
3. Antonio Corsano, "Vico e la tradizione ermetica," in his *Omaggio a Vico* (Naples, 1968), pp. 13–14.
4. W. J. T. Mitchell, *Iconology: Image, Text, Ideology* (Chicago, 1986), p. 43.
5. The *ingegnoso pittore* (*New Science*, sec. 24) was Domenico Antonio

Vaccaro, the engraver was Antonio Baldi. That Vico had a more or less coherent theory of figurative expression, such as could be applied to analysis of the *Dipintura*, is clear from *New Science*, secs. 404–411, the "Corollaries concerning poetic tropes, monsters and metamorphoses." Kenneth Burke's essay "Four Master Tropes," in his *A Grammar of Motives* (New York, 1945), pp. 503–517, treats the same four tropes that Vico finds to be cardinal: metaphor (perspective), metonymy (reduction), synecdoche (representation), and irony (dialectic). See Michael Mooney, *Vico in the Tradition of Rhetoric* (Princeton, 1984).

6. See Robert Klein, "Etudes sur la perspective à la Renaissance, 1956–1963," in his *La Forme et l'intelligible* (Paris, 1970), pp. 278–293, especially 289ff., on curvilinear shapes and the art of anamorphosis.

7. Quoted by John Shearman, *Mannerism* (Baltimore, 1967), p. 81. My examples come from Shearman; see also Klein, *La forme*, pp. 174–192, "Les sept gouverneurs de l'art selon Lomazzo."

8. A. William Salomone, "Pluralism and Universality in Vico's *Scienza nuova*," in GVIS, pp. 517–541, especially p. 538. Salomone identifies the source of variability as temporal warpings of the otherwise "constant" *space* of the "ideal eternal history."

9. See my study on Spenser, *The Prophetic Moment* (Chicago, 1971), which shows how in an archetypally romantic work, *The Faerie Queene*, the poet creates a series of threshold passages between two spatial forms—the temple and the labyrinth. The need to make a clearer definition of threshold has led to further work in "liminal poetics," the poetics of passage considered phenomenologically and as an aspect of ritual structure, following A. van Gennep's processual theory, first set forth in his *The Rites of Passage* (Chicago, 1960), a theory developed in new contexts by Victor Turner in several books and monographs.

10. On the Vichian search for a "precategorial encyclopedia of all the disciplines," to be found in the darkness of the original *forest*, see Enzo Paci, "Vico, Structuralism, and the Phenomenological Encyclopedia of the Sciences," in GVIS, pp. 497–515. See also Enzo Paci's *Ingens Sylva* (Milan, 1949).

11. John Pope-Hennessey, *The Portrait in the Renaissance* (New York, 1966), p. 126.

12. Bacon's chief effort in *The Advancement of Learning* and elsewhere is to dispel "errors" of thought such as come from fantasy and superstition. He shares in the mythography of his time, assuring King James, "Thus have I made as it were a small Globe of the Intellectual World, as truly and faithfully as I could discover." He is continuously aware,

as was Vico, of what he calls "the labour of man." It should be noted that Bacon's discussion of the role of Metaphysic (*Advancement*, Bk. II), as handling formal and final causes, leads apparently to the idea of mind which Vico told the "ingenious painter" to depict: "Thus have we now dealt with two of the three beams of man's knowledge; that is *Radius Directus*, which is referred to nature, *Radius Refractus* which is referred to God, and cannot report truly because of the inequality of the medium. There resteth *Radius Reflexus* whereby Man beholdeth and contemplateth himself." Bacon, *Essays, etc.* (London, 1900), p. 273.

13. E. G. Boring, *A History of Experimental Psychology* (New York, 1950), p. 166.

14. In favor of a Vico-Shaftesbury connection, Max H. Fisch (introduction to *The Autobiography of Giambattista Vico* [Ithaca, 1944], pp. 81–82) gains support from Fausto Nicolini (*Bibliographia Vichiana* [Naples, 1947], pp. 174–175). Without clear positive proofs of Shaftesbury's notes and manuscripts being directly shown to Vico, René Wellek will not be persuaded of a mutual influence. On the other hand, Shaftesbury's letters of the Naples period seem to indicate that he would not have been unavailable to Vico and his friends. And the circumstantial evidence seems to indicate that Vico had pondered the questions raised in Shaftesbury's essay on "The Choice of Hercules," an essay that would serve as the best of possible introductions to the Vichian plan for the *Dipintura*.

15. See Erwin Panofsky, Raymond Klibansky, and Fritz Saxl, *Saturn and Melancholy*, "The New Meaning of Melancholia I" (London, 1964), pp. 317–373, particularly p. 327ff., on the significance of geometrical symbols: thus the compass of Melancholia is taken to symbolize "the unifying intellectual purpose" that governs all the particular arts and devices of measurement—whose culminating intellectual aim is in some sense the development of the theory of perspective.

16. With all their differences, the *New Science* and the *Muqaddimah* display remarkable historicist similarities, owing surely to their common goal, which is to provide a type of universal historiographical sketch of a certain set of "nations." Ibn Khaldun appears often ultramodern by comparison, particularly in the depth and range of his sociological inquiry. Yet he begins his Introduction with words that Vico might have spoken: "The inner meaning of history [as opposed to annalistic compilations of dates, names, events, etc.] involves speculation and an attempt to get at the truth, subtle explanation of the causes and origins of existing things, and deep knowledge of the how and why of events. History, therefore, is firmly rooted in philosophy. It deserves to be

counted a branch of [philosophy]." Quoted from the translation by Franz Rosenthal of Ibn Khaldun, *The Muqaddimah: An Introduction to History* (Princeton, 1967), I, 6.

17. Mitchell, *Iconology*, p. 158.

9. Threshold, Sequence, and Personification in Coleridge

1. Thomas De Quincey, *Recollections of the Lakes and the Lake Poets*, ed. David Wright (Harmondsworth, 1970), pp. 43–44.

2. Geoffrey H. Hartman, "Reflections on Romanticism in France," *Studies in Romanticism*, 9 (Fall 1970), 4: 245.

3. Angus Fletcher, *The Prophetic Moment: An Essay on Spenser* (Chicago, 1971), pp. 11–56.

4. Lawrence Gowing, *Turner: Imagination and Reality* (New York, 1966), p. 13, quotes Hazlitt: "We here allude particularly to Turner, the ablest landscape-painter now living, whose pictures are, however, too much abstractions of aerial perspective, and representations not properly of the objects of nature as of the medium through which they were seen. They are the triumph of the knowledge of the artist and the power of the pencil over the barrenness of the subject. They are pictures of the elements of air, earth and water. The artist delights to go back to the first chaos of the world, or to that state of things, when the waters were separated from the dry land, and light from darkness, but as yet no living thing nor tree bearing fruit was seen on the face of the earth. All is without form and void. Someone said of his landscapes that they were *pictures of nothing and very like*" (Hazlitt's italics). Gowing tells a parallel anecdote: "After Mr. Lenox of New York had received a picture which heralded the later style, Turner met C. R. Leslie who had bought it for him:

'Well, and how does he like the picture?'

'He thinks it indistinct.'

'You should tell him that indistinctness is my forte.' "

Hazlitt and Turner assert the need to de-create, to undo, to unmake elemental nature, when the artist wishes to rediscover pure medium.

5. G. J. Whitrow, *The Natural Philosophy of Time* (New York, 1961), p. 3.

6. In his profoundly Coleridgean *The Doors of Perception* (Harmondsworth: Penguin), Aldous Huxley draws an analogue between the "living hieroglyphics" of flowing drapery and the "implicit philosophy" of the Coleridgean "knowledge of the intrinsic significance of every existent": in Watteau's painting there is "a silken wilderness of countless tiny pleats and wrinkles, with an incessant modulation—inner uncertainty

rendered with the perfect assurance of a master hand—of tone into tone, of one indeterminate colour into another" (p. 28).

7. Walter Pater, *Appreciations: With an Essay on Style* (London, 1944), p. 65.
8. Geoffrey H. Hartman, *Beyond Formalism* (New Haven, 1971), p. 334. See also Hartman, "History-Writing as Answerable Style," *New Literary History*, 2 (1970), 1: 73–83.
9. Walter Jackson Bate, *Coleridge* (New York, 1970), p. 176.
10. Henry Nelson Coleridge, in the *Quarterly Review* (1934), quoted from the anthology *Coleridge*, ed. J. de G. Jackson (London, 1971), p. 627.
11. Frank Manuel, *The Eighteenth Century Confronts the Gods* (Cambridge, Mass., 1959), and Hartman, *Beyond Formalism*.
12. Michel Foucault, *Madness and Civilization* (New York, 1973), p. 176.
13. Johan Huizinga, *Homo Ludens* (Boston, 1950), pp. 136–145. A similar view underlies much of the commentary by Edgar Wind in his *Pagan Mysteries in the Renaissance* and the encyclopedic treatise of D. C. Allen, *Mysteriously Meant: The Rediscovery of Pagan Symbolism and Allegorical Interpretation in the Renaissance* (Baltimore, 1970).
14. Hartman, *Beyond Formalism*, p. 335.
15. See Paul De Man, *Blindness and Insight: Essays on the Rhetoric of Contemporary Criticism* (New York, 1971).
16. In connection with ideas of threshold and personification, I have been helped particularly by three essays: Heinrich Ott's "Hermeneutics and Personhood" and Owen Barfield's "Imagination and Inspiration," collected in S. R. Hopper and D. L. Miller, *Interpretation: The Poetry of Meaning* (New York, 1967); and Hartman, "History-Writing as Answerable Style." For the related problem of what he calls "stationing," see James Bunn, "Keats's *Ode to Psyche* and the Transformation of Mental Landscape," *ELH*, 37 (1970), 4: 581–594.

11. Music and the Code of the Ineffable

1. Friedrich Nietzsche, *The Will to Power*, trans. Walter Kaufmann and R. J. Hollingdale (New York, 1967), sec. 809.
2. Ibid.
3. Thomas Mann, *Doctor Faustus: The Life of the German Composer Adrian Leverkühn as Told to a Friend*, trans. H. T. Lowe-Porter (New York, 1948).
4. Friedrich Nietzsche, *Ecce Homo*, trans. R. J. Hollingdale (Harmondsworth: Penguin, 1979), pp. 62–63.
5. Italo Calvino, *Invisible Cities*, trans. William Weaver (New York, 1974), p. 87.

12. The Image of Lost Direction

1. Northrop Frye, *Anatomy of Criticism* (Princeton, 1957), p. 150; Frye, *Fearful Symmetry* (Princeton, 1947), pp. 221, 369–370, 380. *The Critical Path* (Bloomington, 1971) begins with an account of the way Frye experienced the Dantesque labyrinth of *Inferno*, canto 1: "About twenty-five years ago, when still in middle life, I lost my way in the dark wood of Blake's prophecies, and looked around for some path that would get out of there . . . The critical path I wanted was a theory of criticism which would, first, account for the major phenomena of literary experience, and, second, would lead to some view of the place of literature in civilization as a whole" (13). The same desire to get a perspective *on* literature, while remaining in touch *within* it, is apparent in such essays as "Towards Defining an Age of Sensibility," reprinted in his *Fables of Identity: Studies in Poetic Mythology* (New York, 1963), pp. 130–137.
2. In this essay I deliberately understate the difference between "maze" and "labyrinth." The latter is a term from building, or architecture. The former has a stronger etymological overtone of *psychological* sense, since it derives from Middle English *masen*, to confuse, puzzle; the word is akin to the Norwegian, *masa-st*, to fall into a slumber, to lose one's senses and begin to dream (Skeat). Thus Marvell says, "How vainly men themselves amaze."
3. Henry King, "The Labyrinth," in *Poems* (Oxford, 1965), p. 173.
4. Michael Drayton, *Works* (Oxford, 1961), II, 138.
5. Victor Turner, *The Ritual Process* (Chicago, 1969); *Dreams, Fields and Metaphors* (Ithaca, 1974); Arnold van Gennep, *The Rites of Passage*, trans. M. B. Vizedom and G. L. Chaffee (Chicago, 1960).
6. Mircea Eliade, *Patterns in Comparative Religion* (New York, 1963), p. 381. See my discussion of these comments in *The Prophetic Moment* (Chicago, 1971), pp. 33–34.
7. The boar in *Adonis* is "a tyrant of the forests," an "enormous and cruel monster, who sullies [i.e., contaminates] the fountains [natural springs?]" (*monstre énorme et cruel, qui souille les fontaines*). Like a bandit, he lives in a tangled, inaccessible fortress. La Fontaine identifies the boar with contagion: in the depths of the forest there is a poisonous pool of stagnant water, where the monster drinks in the vapors it exhales. See the French text in the *Oeuvres diverses*, ed. Pierre Claran (Paris, 1948). Paul Valéry's famous essay "Concerning *Adonis*," in *The Art of Poetry*, trans. Denise Folliot (New York, 1958), does not probe the implications of the labyrinthine monster, but observes that

"Adonis, about to become intelligent, hastens to order a hunt. Death rather than reflection."

8. William Beckford's Gothic/Oriental romance, *Vathek*, ends at the Hall of Subterranean Fire. The story weaves its way there through a series of high camp episodes, whose formal dependence on coincidental happenings makes the story as a whole mazy. Beckford's later account of the book suggests, to use his own word, that it was a visionary account of an actual house party of his youth, a party occurring in the "labyrinth" of his father's home. In Gothic and Oriental romances it appears that the idea of the labyrinth gives the author the plan of the narrative form as a whole. Cf. Charles Robert Maturin's *Melmoth the Wanderer*, where the whole narrative consists of nested sub-narratives, deliberately coiling in upon themselves, so that the form of the book projects the disorientation of the hero and narrator.

9. In Kafka psychological terror frequently is the result of a deformity, a metamorphosis, or even a slight physical defect of the body. There is always an assault on the integrity of the body-image. This discomfort over the body then expands obsessively to the point where there is no "world" in which the body will be at home. Gregor Samsa's insect-body has many terrors, but perhaps the most acute is that it is too large; as insect, he cannot fit through the door in his house (end of Part 1, *Metamorphosis*). The house becomes an inappropriate universe—for an insect. Space is always, in Kafka, on the verge of becoming too large or too small for any given body in it. Thus in the final chapter of *Amerika*, Karl's quest takes him to a scene of ingrown cosmic expansion, "the nature theater of Oklahoma": "only now [as he journeys West] did Karl understand how huge America was." The obsession with cosmic expansion is characteristic of all major labyrinth-authors, Borges as much as Kafka: for instance, Borges's *Lottery in Babylon*, where the Company grows like a cancer, until its location, Babylon, expands to universal dimensions; the final speculation of its Babylonian interpreters is that the Lottery "is nothing else than an infinite game of chance." This story is reprinted in *Labyrinths*, ed. D. A. Yates and J. E. Irby (New York, 1964).

10. Italo Calvino, *Invisible Cities*, trans. Warren Weaver (New York, 1964). This "bestiary" of labyrinthine structures and phenomena returns over and over to the question: how can one tell whether a limit (as produced by city walls, gates, etc.) is a benign or malign constraint? Thence, in Calvino, arises the further, continuous speculation: how can one tell the difference between an "inside" and an "outside"? This latter is the basic formal question to be asked about the process whereby, in

labyrinth-literature, temples transform into labyrinths, and vice versa. Of his city, Penthesilea, Calvino's Marco Polo asks: "Outside Penthesilea does an outside exist? Or, no matter how far you go from the city, will you only pass from one limbo to another, never managing to leave it?" The indeterminacy of space is paralleled by indeterminacies of time. Thus, of Berenice, the final invisible city, Marco Polo says: "all the future Berenices are already present in this instant, wrapped one within the other, confined, crammed, inextricable" (avvolte l'una dentro l'altra, strette pigiate indistricabile). The ultimate indeterminacy of limit upon space and time is provided by the dialogues, interpolated, between the Great Khan and Polo; even these are unable to decide what semiotic system would capably mark, designate the placement and extent of each city, relative to every other. To a degree they exist only in the mind, invisibly, and share in the final lack of edge which characterizes thought (as distinct from action).

11. Northrop Frye, "The Nightmare Life in Death," in On Culture and Literature: A Collection of Review Essays, ed. R. D. Denham (Chicago, 1978), p. 222.

12. Henri Michaux, Cannabis Indica, in Light through Darkness, trans. Haakon Chevalier (New York, 1963), pp. 61–128. See also Michaux, Miserable Miracle, trans. Louise Varèse (San Francisco, 1972). Virtually all the literature of drug experience, from Coleridge and De Quincey to the Americans writing in the fifties and sixties, not to mention Aldous Huxley, explores an artificially induced vision of the dialectic of temple and labyrinth.

13. The phrase is embedded in a Hermetic passage: "Or do you find me between Mercy and Understanding, between Chesed and Binah (but still at Chesed)—my equilibrium, and equilibrium is all, precarious—balancing, teetering over the awful unbridgeable void, the all-but-untraceable path of God's lightning back to God? As if I ever were in Chesed! More like the Qliphoth" (Under the Volcano [New York, 1947], p. 39). Douglas Day, Malcolm Lowry: A Biography (New York, 1973), p. 344, glosses the Cabbalistic terms as follows: Chesed is Mercy; Binah is Understanding; Qliphoth is the realm of husks and demons. Day's fine biography goes far to rescue Lowry from the misfortune of becoming an underground cult hero.

14. Hermann Kern, Labirinti, trans. Libero Sosio (Milan, 1981). Kern includes an extensive bibliography of the subject. Labirinti was written for exhibitions in Munich and Milan, the latter held, with a symposium, in June 1981. For this symposium I presented a paper entitled "Definitions of Threshold for a Theory of Labyrinths," in Beauty and Critique, ed. Richard Milazzo (New York, 1982).

15. Kern, *Labirinti*, pp. 27–30. See also Kern, *Kalenderbauten: Frühe astronomische Grossgeräte aus Indien, Mexico und Peru* (Munich, 1976).
16. See Hubert Damisch, "La Danse de Thesée," *Tel Quel*, 26 (Summer 1966): 60–68. For Damisch the labyrinth is "the metaphor, or figure" of an aboriginal recess, the aboriginal "cave" of unformed matter. He notes that even Daedalus does not provide a plan of the labyrinth for Ariadne, since "l'auteur lui-même ignorait le plan." Here lost direction is involved with the loss of design; the labyrinth is "the image of the lost map."
17. Kern, *Labirinti*, pp. 393–397.
18. Ibid., p. 13. The Italian reads "questo movimento pendolare."
19. Nathaniel Hawthorne, "The Minotaur," in *A Wonder Book, Tanglewood Tales, and A Grandfather's Chair* (Boston, 1883), p. 238.
20. On the obscure question of the role of Ariadne as Dionysian goddess/heroic maiden, see Giorgio Colli, *La nascita della filosofia* (Milan, 1980), chap. 2, "La signora del labirinto."
21. *Critical Inquiry*, Autumn 1976, p. 70.
22. In Harold Bloom's studies of poetic anxiety, the critic attempts to analyze, and to analogize, the many ways in which the poetic act, at its most powerful, involves cata-strophic turnings against some figure of overpowering authority, be it the earlier pre-text, or image of the earlier poetic master, or some earlier phase within the poet's own work or experience. All poetry on this account appears to be "revisionist." The great value of Bloom's work is its emphasis on a psychoanalytic perspective, however gnostified, mystified, cabbalized that perspective may be. A significant comment, relating to the labyrinth, would be from *Agon: Towards a Theory of Revisionism* (New York, 1982), 110: "Freud's revised account of anxiety is precisely at one with the poetic Sublime, for anxiety is finally seen as a technique [i.e., a defence] for mastering anteriority by *remembering* rather than *repeating* the past" (Bloom's italics).
23. Douglas R. Hofstadter, *Gödel, Escher, Bach: An Eternal Golden Braid* (New York, 1979), p. 10. Hofstadter points out that the concept of "level" is among the most elusive, as it is among the commonest we employ to indicate sub-routines in a larger program of problem-solving. A typical case would be: what is happening when a melody is replayed, in a fugue or sonata, in a different key? What are the "levels" of modulation doing? This question leads, for instance, to the essential theoretical studies of Heinrich Schenker, among modern musicologists; it has much to do with the way certain pieces need to be played—perhaps the most obvious being the extended instrumental works of Schubert. Hofstadter's cases are chiefly drawn from Bach, one being the "Little

Harmonic Labyrinth." In general, each loop in a program may or may not work at a different "level" within the whole structure. The strangeness of loops results from the fact that while each level may, on one view, mark a separable stratum, the strata are not always experienced as distinct from each other, on some other view. Hofstadter gives the example from Escher, *Drawing Hands*, where each of two hands draws the other hand emerging from a plane which, as plane, exists only by virtue of being drawn by one hand or other. The two hands and their products are distinctly separate—but which of the two draws *the* plane which establishes a base for the whole image? The question is undecidable. On the surface, a strangeness results, since it follows that each hand is both plane and three-dimensional at once. Hofstadter resolves the paradox by showing that there is a third hand at work, Escher's own actual hand. That hand remains "invisible" and yet provides us with the "higher" way out of the tangled hierarchy. Generally this resort to an invisible source of perspective on the tangle will be found at every moment when a labyrinth is suddenly transformed into a temple-like structure, a place of clarified vision. The trick is to increase the number of dimensions in which the puzzle is seen. Thus in my essay "Definitions of Threshold for a Theory of Labyrinths," I attempt to show that all complex labyrinths require a capability of "reading" threshold-passages (choice-points of shift from one loop to another) in at least *five* dimensions, the last of which assumes the virtual undecidability of knowing if one is making a progressive move toward exit. Topologically, I believe, decision-making in the maze always comes down to a question: what at a given moment is the edge between inside and outside? In literature we seek a parallel type of decision: what at a given moment is the "sense" of symbolic terms, what is included and excluded, for without making these cuts we cannot proceed in our reading. To proceed means to let some puzzle of meaning merely continue in a state of continuous looping. The looping is not a repetition; it is a "remembering." And an odd, strange kind of remembering, since the reader now allows a specific "memory" within the text of its web of allusions to other texts to be "forgotten," bypassed as the whole program moves forward. Any system with an inadequate number of dimensions of decision-making, cut-making, will not be able to forget steps previously passed through (as an event remembered is passed through), but will attempt to repeat and repeat that passage, never jumping up or down within the system. The reader will behave as a viewer of Drawing Hands would behave, fixating on the drawn hands, instead of asking: but which hand is doing the drawing? The ingenious aspect of Escher's print, as Hofstadter points out, is that the third hand,

Escher's own, is a mental as well as physical fact for a complete response to the picture. Final cuts are then "invisible," as thought is.

13. Style and the Extreme Situation

1. Samuel R. Levin, *Foundations of Language*, 12 (1975), 467.
2. Friedrich Schleiermacher, *Aphorisms*, in *Hermeneutics: the Handwritten MSS.*, ed. Heinz Kimmerle, trans. James Duke and Jack Forstman (Missoula: Scholars Press, 1977), p. 64.
3. Ibid., p. 155.
4. John Clare, *Letters*, ed. Mark Storey (Oxford, 1985), p. 683. Storey notes that a James Hipkins, of 2 Smith Square, Westminster, had written to Dr. Edwin Wing [of the Northampton Asylum] about Clare. Dr. Wing replied: "In reply to yours of the 6th inst respecting John Clare I beg to inform you he is still living and in good bodily health though very feeble in mind and still the subject of many mental delusions. I endeavoured to induce him to write a few lines to you and to make an effort at poetical composition but I could not get anything from him but the few words I enclose."
5. John Ashbery, *The Double Dream of Spring* (New York, 1976), p. 35.
6. Peter Neumeyer, *Homage to John Clare* (Salt Lake City, 1980), p. 21.
7. Beckett's French text of *Sans* was published in Paris, 1969; his own English translation was published in 1970.
8. Edward Sapir, *Language* (New York, 1921; reprinted Harvest Books), p. 223ff.
9. Walter Pater, *Appreciations: With an Essay on Style* (London, 1944), p. 22.

14. Stevens and the Influential Gnome

1. Harold Bloom, *Wallace Stevens: The Poems of Our Climate* (Ithaca, 1976), p. 376.
2. Frank Doggett, *Stevens' Poetry of Thought* (Baltimore, 1966), quoted in Bloom, *Wallace Stevens*, p. 307.
3. Wallace Stevens, *The Necessary Angel: Essays on Reality and the Imagination* (New York, 1951), p. 25.
4. Ibid., p. 171. On Stevens's notion of "the poetry of thought," which should be "the supreme poetry," see "A Collect of Philosophy," in *Opus Posthumous*, ed. S. F. Morse (New York, 1957), pp. 187–188.
5. Stevens, *The Necessary Angel*, p. 32.
6. Quoted in Milton J. Bates, *Wallace Stevens: A Mythology of Self* (Berkeley, 1985), p. 212.

7. A. Walton Litz, "Particles of Order: The Unpublished Adagia," in *Wallace Stevens: A Celebration*, ed. Frank Doggett and Robert Buttel (Princeton, 1980), pp. 57–77.

8. Ludwig Wittgenstein, *Philosophical Investigations*, trans. G. E. M. Anscombe (New York, 1968), sec. 656.

Index